SOVIET LITERARY THEORY AND PRACTICE DURING THE FIRST FIVE-YEAR PLAN, 1928-32

Soviet
Literary Theory and Practice
during the
First Five-Year Plan
1928-32

HARRIET BORLAND

GREENWOOD PRESS, PUBLISHERS
NEW YORK

Copyright © 1950 by Harriet Borland

Reprinted by permission of Harriet Borland

First Greenwood Reprinting, 1969

Library of Congress Catalogue Card Number 69-13833

SBN 8371-1075-0

PRINTED IN UNITED STATES OF AMERICA

To
C. B. B. and B. M. B.
in appreciation of
their help and encouragement

ACKNOWLEDGMENTS

IT WAS THE "maximal" requirements set by Professor Ernest J. Simmons, of Columbia University, which are responsible for this study; and I am greatly indebted to him, both for this stimulus and for his guidance. I wish also to thank Rose Raskin and Louise Luke for their interest in, and assistance with, many *slozhnyie* problems.

My appreciation is expressed to the staff members of Columbia University's Russian Institute and Department of Slavic Languages for various helpful suggestions while this work was in progress.

Grateful acknowledgment is made to the following publishers and authors for their kindness in granting permission to quote material from copyrighted books and articles: George Allen & Unwin, Ltd., for H. R. Westwood, ed., *Tendencies of the Modern Novel*; William Henry Chamberlin, for *Russia's Iron Age* and *Soviet Russia*; Crown Publishers, for George Reavey and Marc Slonim, *Soviet Literature*; Dial Press, Inc., for Leonid Leonov, *Soviet River*; Louis Fischer, for *Machines and Men in Russia*; Harcourt, Brace and Company, Inc., for Leonid Leonov, *Skutarevsky*; Henry Holt and Company, Inc., for Ilya Ehrenburg, *Out of Chaos*; Houghton Mifflin Company, for Eugene Lyons, ed., *Six Soviet Plays*; Inter Nation Literary Agency, for Leopold Averbakh, ed., *Belomor*; International Publishers Company, for Alexander Avdeyenko, *I Love*, for Maxim Gorky, *On Guard for the Soviet Union*, for V. Ilyenkov, *Driving Axle*, for Karl Marx and Friedrich Engels, *Literature and Art*, for H. G. Scott, ed., *Problems of Soviet Literature*, for Joseph Stalin, *Selected Writings*, and for Leon Trotsky, *Literature and Revolution*; Alfred A. Knopf, Inc., for Max Eastman, *Artists in Uniform*, for Eugene Lyons, *Modern Moscow*,

viii ACKNOWLEDGMENTS

and for Mikhail Sholokhov, *Seeds of Tomorrow;* Lawrence & Wishart, Ltd., for Ben Blake, ed., *Four Soviet Plays;* Martin Lawrence, Ltd., for Fyodor Panfyorov, *Bruski;* Literary Masterworks. Inc., for Benjamin Goriely, *Les Poètes dans la révolution russe;* Mercure de France, for John Charpentier, *Napoléon et les hommes de lettres de son temps;* New Directions, for *New Directions in Prose and Poetry 1941;* New York *Herald Tribune,* for Louis Fischer, "A Revolution in Revolutionary History"; New York *Times,* for Drew Middleton, "Soviet Arts Trace Political Patter"; New York *Times* and Stuart Chase, for his "How Russia Charts Her Economic Course"; Pilot Press, Ltd., for Herbert Marshall, ed., *Mayakovsky and His Poetry;* Putnam & Company, Ltd., for Fyodor Panfyorov, *And Then the Harvest;* Rinehart & Company, Inc., for Valentin Katayev, *Time, Forward!,* for Ilya Ilf and Evgeni Petrov, *The Little Golden Calf,* and for Boris Pilnyak, *The Volga Falls to the Caspian Sea;* Routledge and Kegan Paul, Ltd., for Gleb Struve, *25 Years of Soviet Russian Literature (1918–1943); Science & Society,* for Alexei Tolstoy, "Trends in Soviet Literature"; University of California Press, for Alexander Kaun, *Soviet Poets and Poetry;* and Vanguard Press, Inc., for Joseph Freeman, Joshua Kunitz, and Louis Lozowick, *Voices of October.* Full bibliographical material appears in the Bibliography.

H. B.

Washington, D.C.
December 31, 1949

CONTENTS

1. INTRODUCTORY MATERIAL ... 1
   EARLY ATTEMPTS TO REGIMENT LITERATURE ... 1
   DEVELOPMENT OF LITERARY GROUPS AFTER THE OCTOBER
      REVOLUTION ... 3
   IN THE PERIOD OF WAR COMMUNISM, 1918–21 ... 3
   DURING THE PERIOD OF THE NEW ECONOMIC POLICY,
      1921–28 ... 7
   FORMATION OF RAPP ... 15
   SITUATION ON THE EVE OF THE FIRST FIVE-YEAR PLAN ... 18

2. THE LITERARY FIVE-YEAR PLAN ... 20
   THE FIRST FIVE-YEAR PLAN, 1928–32 ... 20
   THE FIVE-YEAR PLAN OF ART AND THE "CULTURAL
      REVOLUTION" ... 22
   ATTITUDES TOWARDS THE FIVE-YEAR PLAN ... 24
   THE "SOCIAL COMMAND" ... 26
   MAYAKOVSKY ... 26
   1929 CONTROVERSY ... 30
   RAPP's THEMATIC REQUIREMENTS ... 33

3. DEMANDS MADE OF THE "SKETCHERS" ... 38
   FINAL OBJECTIVES ... 38
   PROFESSIONAL WRITERS→OBSERVERS→WORKERS ... 40

CONTENTS

CONTACT WITH THE MASSES	40
Readings and Talks to Circles, 41; Observation Trips and Visits, 43; Participation as Member of an Enterprise, 48	
SOCIALIST COMPETITION	53
WORKERS→*Rabkors*→LITERARY *Udarniks*	54
WORKER AND PEASANT CORRESPONDENTS	54
"SHOCK WORKERS OF THE PEN"	56
SKETCH-WRITING	62
COLLECTIVE WRITING	67

4. SOME LITERARY WORKS OF THE FIRST FIVE-YEAR PLAN PERIOD — 75

CONTENTS AND CHARACTERISTICS	75
INDUSTRY	77
THE OLD AND THE NEW	79
TEMPOS	86
WRECKERS	90
HUMAN RECONSTRUCTION	92
SELF-CRITICISM	94
AGRICULTURE	96
COLLECTIVIZATION	98
PROLETARIANIZATION	101
GRAIN COLLECTION	103
INTELLIGENTSIA	107
POETRY	112
QUALITY OF FIRST FIVE-YEAR PLAN LITERATURE	115

5. THE LIQUIDATION OF RAPP — 119

THE CLASS WAR IN LITERATURE	119
DECREE OF APRIL 23, 1932	124

CONTENTS

 First Plenum of the Orgcommittee, October 29–
  November 3, 1932   127
  RAPP'S TWO PERIODS   129
  ADMINISTRATIVE MISTAKES   132
  ERRORS IN CRITICISM   137
  AVERBAKH   147
  PRINCIPAL CAUSES OF RAPP'S DISSOLUTION   153
  The Union of Soviet Writers   158

6. CONCLUSION   161
  Results of the First Five-Year Plan   161
  Literature Which Helped the Plan   162
  Conclusions   167

NOTES   171

RUSSIAN TRANSLITERATION TABLE   228

BIBLIOGRAPHY   229

INDEX   243

The pen is often a more powerful weapon than the rifle. It cannot replace the rifle, but it can mobilize rifles and it can multiply these rifles.

—Karl Radek

I. INTRODUCTORY MATERIAL

Early Attempts to Regiment Literature

IN THE SOVIET UNION during the First Five-Year Plan (1928-32), the most widespread and intensive effort of all times was made to mobilize literature for use as propaganda. There was an attempt to create a literary Five-Year Plan under which the writer became a professional worker with definite duties determined by political, social, and economic considerations.

When Lelevich [1] said that the main purpose of art is to infect the reader with the ideology of the ruling class, he was not startling the country with a new idea. In reading about Catherine the Great, we find that "art for art's sake, to Catherine, is nonsense. When she applies herself to the task of writing comedies and tragedies, she does not for an instant dream of making a work of art: what she does is criticism, satire, and above all, politics. . . . Literature, to her, is merely a branch of her military and repressive powers." [2]

Under the autocracy, however, government regimentation of literature, with the exception of Catherine's own writings, consisted almost entirely of negative censorship. Under the First Five-Year Plan, Glavlit (the supreme board of censorship) saw that no ideas which were out of line with Party policies reached the masses; but more was expected of an author than merely to refrain from openly criticizing the Soviet régime. He was expected to strike a positive note under pain of being branded a class enemy.

It is interesting that Napoleon held very similar views on literature as an instrument of propaganda and that he tried to subjugate it to an entirely military discipline, believing that it had no other aim than to serve and that it did not need liberty. He conceived of literature as official; "it ought to contribute to the formation of citizens of the fatherland and to assure its prestige." [3] To Napoleon a poet was "a man, undoubtedly gifted, who had learned to make verses as a soldier does exercises, and who must obey orders." [4]

There was a well-rooted tradition of the social significance of literature in Russia where writing had long been regarded as a social task. As early as 1840 Belinski had insisted that art must serve society and that literature should have a social purpose. In the 1860's the critic Chernyshevski had claimed that the value of literature is determined by the amount of its utilitarian function.

The point of view of a former chairman of the Fine Arts Department of the Commissariat for Education, Felix Kon, was that "art is for the masses. It must aid in remoulding all economic life. Art organizes thought. And, as it formerly served the priesthood, the feudal classes, and the bourgeoisie, it must serve the proletariat of the Soviet Union." [5] From the very beginning, the Soviet government and the Communist party had intended to subordinate literature to political designs and to the aim of creating a proletarian state; but, because of outside circumstances and of changing political and economic conditions, the line of their literary policy has necessarily been a zigzagging one. Nevertheless, one thing has remained unchanged: "In Soviet Russia politics preside over the destinies of literature." [6]

Lenin had written in 1905 that "the socialist proletariat should promote the principle of *Party literature*, develop this principle, and carry it into actual life in the fullest and most complete form possible." "Down with non-Party writers! Down with supermen-authors!" he exclaimed.

Literature should become a *part* of the general proletarian movement, a cog of one great, unified Social Democratic mechanism, which is set in motion by the conscious advance guard of the entire working class. Literature should become a component part of the organized, planned, unified Social Democratic party work.[7]

Lenin believed that a classless literature would be possible only in a socialist classless society because it is impossible for a writer to live in society and be free from it.

Development of Literary Groups after the October Revolution

IN THE PERIOD OF WAR COMMUNISM, 1918–21

The history of the first fifteen years of Soviet literature is largely the ideological struggle for a proletarian socialist literature. The "Proletcult" (movement for proletarian culture, 1917–23) was formed during Kerensky's Provisional Government and continued in a widespread and more or less haphazard fashion throughout the period of War Communism. It wanted to provide mass education and organized thousands of workers' studios. The principal Proletcult theoretician was A. A. Bogdanov, who had begun to expound the foundations of his theory of proletarian culture in 1910. He held that there are three independent roads to communism: the economic, the political, and the cultural; and he looked upon "culture" as something apart from economics and politics while Lenin considered these three "independent roads" as an organic whole. Lebedev-Polyanski, another Proletcult critic and head of Glavlit, urged that the proletariat establish a cultural dictatorship, as well as an economic and a political one. The Proletcult must stand outside of the state apparatus, its methods of work untouched by government decrees, since proletarian culture could develop only under conditions of complete independence.[8]

Bogdanov believed that the vital principle of bourgeois culture is individualism while that of proletarian class culture is collectivism, "which ought to reflect the world from the point of view of the labour collective." [9] "Art is part of the ideology of a class, an element of its class-consciousness, hence an organized form of class life, a means of uniting and welding together class forces." [10] Art is "capable of organizing not only the opinions of the people but also their knowledge, thoughts, feelings and dispositions. . . . Art . . . has always been more powerful than science as a weapon for the organization of the masses, because the language of living symbols is nearer and more comprehensible to the masses." [11]

The Proletcult took little interest in peasants and intellectuals, but it initiated the question of the place of the proletariat in literature. One of the Proletcult organizations, the All-Russian Union of Workers-Writers, sought to unite all the writers of the laboring class who had a proletarian point of view and "to create a proletarian socialist literature, both artistic and scientific, answering to the ideals of the revolutionary communist proletariat." [12] Proletarian poets formed circles, studios, and similar units—the Leningrad groups bearing such names as "Crimson Pennants," "The Chisel," "Construction," and "Red Star."

Although the creations of the proletarian writers and critics did not, as they had hoped, "revolutionize literature as profoundly as the Bolsheviks had revolutionized the social-political order," [13] many young writers were influenced by the Proletcult and a number of poets, trained in its circles. However, this attempt to create an autonomous art organization was not popular with many government and Party leaders. Lenin had no patience with efforts to manufacture proletarian culture in laboratories or studios. "Art belongs to the people," he said in 1920.[14] It must be comprehensible to the great toiling masses and be loved by them. "It must unite and elevate their feelings, thoughts, and desires. Artists must be born and grow up in the heart of these masses. . . . So that art can come to the people, and the people to art, we must first of all raise the general level of culture." [15] That is, people must first learn to read and write and must study the heritage of the past.

Lenin told the Third Congress of the Komsomol (Young Communist League) that

proletarian culture is not something that has sprung nobody knows whence; it is not an invention of those who call themselves experts in proletarian culture. That is all nonsense. Proletarian culture must be the result of a natural development of the stores of knowledge which mankind has accumulated under the yoke of capitalist society, landlord society, and bureaucratic society.[16]

Lunacharski, Radek, and Bukharin, like Lenin, believed that the Proletcult's effort to build a proletarian culture was premature but that such a culture was not impossible, in time. Trotsky, however, flatly stated that "there is no proletarian culture and . . . there never will be any and in fact there is no reason to regret this. The proletariat acquires power for the purpose of doing away forever with class culture and to make way for human culture." [17] "A cultural and artistic harvest of full value will be, happily! socialist and not 'proletarian,' " [18] he exclaimed. "The dictatorship of the proletariat is not an organization for the production of the culture of a new society, but a revolutionary and military system struggling for it"; [19] and the period of its rule is merely a brief transitional epoch between capitalism and socialism. Trotsky considered such terms as "proletarian literature" and "proletarian culture" to be dangerous because "they erroneously compress the culture of the future into the narrow limits of the present day." [20] The importance of organizations such as the Proletcult cannot be measured, he said, by the speed with which they create a new literature but by the amount by which they help in raising the literary level of the working class. "It is impossible to create a class culture behind the backs of a class." [21]

In 1920 the worker-poets of the Moscow branch of the Proletcult formed a group of their own, the "Smithy," whose story is "the first chapter in the history of proletarian literature in the epoch of the dictatorship of the proletariat." [22] Its members, almost without exception, came to literature from factories and plants. They proclaimed themselves the only group of proletarian writers standing for the revolutionary advance guard of the workers, the Russian Communist party, and declared that "proletarian art is the prism in which the personality of a class is concentrated, a mirror in which the working masses can see themselves." [23]

These early proletarian poets wrote about the Revolution, giving it cosmic dimensions. Carried away by revolutionary enthusiasm and attempting to express in verse their materialistic and collectivist points of view, they produced rather abstract hymns of praise to labor, to the muscles, to iron and steel, and especially to the factory, which they almost deified. In "We" Vladimir Kirillov explained:

We have fallen in love with the might of steam and power of dynamite,
With the song of the siren, the motion of shafts and wheels.
We have become kindred with metal, have merged our souls with machines.[24]

Both the collective urge and the new urge towards industrialization were shown by Alexei Gastev when he wrote: "I stand among workbenches, hammers, furnaces, forges, and among hundreds of comrades." [25] Many of the characteristics which were to reappear during the period of RAPP's (Russian Association of Proletarian Writers) dictatorship are to be seen in these poetic "shock workers of the pen." The Smithy poets claimed to be the only literary group representing the Communist party; they regarded art as a weapon and a tool; they had boundless enthusiasm and the worker's love for the factory and the machine; they were interested mainly in the subject matter of their literary works, which, taken as a whole, showed a distinct monotony and were remarkable chiefly for their bulk. They even tried to write co-operative poetry but had to give it up as a failure.

The early proletarian poets worked out no new forms; it was the Futurist, Vladimir Mayakovsky, who contributed a style to the Revolution, which he accepted immediately and enthusiastically and whose poet he became. He "personified the new generation, its revolutionary materialism and contempt of sentiment, its striving towards collective construction and love of big numbers." [26] Vulgarizing and popularizing futurism, he turned it into a suitable weapon of revolutionary propaganda and launched the slogan, "Futurism at the Service of the Revolution." In his "Decree to the Army of Art" of December 7, 1918, Mayakovsky urged his followers on with these verses:

> He alone is a Communist true
> Who burns the bridge for retreat,
> Stop marching slowly, Futurists,
> Into the future . . . leap! [27]

Ordering them to hurl their song like a bomb, he predicted that

> The streets shall be our brushes,
> Our palettes shall be the squares.
> The thousand-paged Book of Time
> Revolution's songs shall know:
> Into the streets, Futurists,
> Drummers and poets, go! [28]

Mayakovsky was the first writer to identify himself with the class struggle, and he unhesitatingly subordinated his art to politics.

The Futurists were arrogant and aggressive and, although they lacked a concrete program, tried to assume exclusive leadership and control of proletarian literature. As a result, futurism was attacked by Lunacharski for its attempt to speak in the name of the government, although it merely represented one school, as well as for its sweeping rejection of everything connected with the past. The Bolsheviks considered the Futurists an aesthetic school which represented the degeneration of bourgeois art and was therefore incapable of solving the problems of revolutionary art.

The period of War Communism, which in literature was characterized by the monopoly of futurism, the exclusive predominance of poetry, and the unsuccessful attempts at fostering artificially a proletarian literature in the Proletcult studios, ended in 1921.

DURING THE PERIOD OF THE NEW ECONOMIC POLICY, 1921–28

In March of 1921 Lenin inaugurated the NEP, a "strategic retreat," or partial and temporary compromise to suit the realities of the time. Soviet economy had virtually collapsed as a result of the Civil War and of a famine, and it was necessary to increase industrial and agricultural production and to reorganize transport. The state retained "the commanding heights of industry" and monopoly control of foreign trade, but restrictions were removed on private trade and small-scale industry, which led to the recrudescence of kulaks and "nepmen" (small private traders). The Soviet government acted on the assumption that, without a speedy reconstruction of the country's economy, it would be impossible to solve those ideological problems for the sake of which the Revolution had been fought. But the proletarian poets, especially those belonging to the Smithy, were overwhelmed by a feeling of dismay, not realizing that what seemed like the capitulation of the proletariat before a resuscitated bourgeoisie was merely a breathing spell.

In literature, the NEP was a prose period. There was more paper available, and private publishing companies reappeared. The first Soviet literary periodicals, *Krasnaya nov* (Red Virgin Soil) and

Pechat i revolyutsiya (Press and Revolution), began to come out in 1921. Non-proletarian writers were now able to get their works printed, and this unequal competition was one of the causes of the Proletcult's dissolution about 1923.

Trotsky called these non-proletarian writers "fellow-travelers" and defined them as writers "who fail to grasp the Revolution in its entirety, its final Communist aim being alien to them." [29] To the moderate Marxist critic, Vyacheslav Polonski, they were "a bridge thrown across from the old art to the art of tomorrow." [30] They were not an organized group but, rather, talented individualists who, while loyal to the Soviet state, yet wanted to be free to express their personal views. The fellow-travelers had a neutral Right wing and a Left wing which supported the Revolution, but neither wished to be regimented or coerced. The NEP period was their golden age, especially after the "literary Magna Carta" of 1925 was promulgated, disavowing the proletarian organizations' claim to hegemony.

Under the new conditions, Mayakovsky and his Futurists reorganized as LEF (Left Front of Art, 1923-28),[31] boasting, "We are . . . master-executors of a social order." [32] The Revolution and the working class must be served by a documentary art, and artistic literature is to be condemned. "Now there's no time for art," wrote Brik.[33] The writer should become a reporter of facts, whose best expression is the newspaper sketch. "Today's Leo Tolstoy," declared Tretyakov, "is the newspaper." [34] Meanwhile, Mayakovsky in verse was imploring poets to stop writing verse. These same extreme Left tendencies reappeared subsequently in the "Litfront," an opposition group formed within RAPP.

During the second year of the NEP, some of the militant younger members of the Smithy seceded as a protest against the group's softness and, passing through MAPP (Moscow Association of Proletarian Writers),[35] organized their own group, "October." Among the Octobrists, fiercely loyal to the Revolution and the Party, were the poet A. I. Bezymenski, the novelist Yuri Libedinski, and the critic L. L. Averbakh, who became the first editor of the literary journal, *Oktyabr* (October). They repudiated the Smithy as antiproletarian and, following in its footsteps, also claimed to be the *only* group representing the revolutionary proletariat.

The "At-the-Post" group was formed in 1923 by Libedinski, the critics G. Lelevich and S. Rodov, and others,[36] to war more pugnaciously against the Smithy, the fellow-travelers, and especially Voronski, who thought that the Party should be neutral in literature. According to Libedinski,

We said that the Party must without fail rule literature. We said that proletarian literature, which existed as a movement, must be organizationally consolidated. We said that the center of gravity during the whole transition period would be, not as much in the literature of the fellow-travelers, as in proletarian literature.[37]

The first number (June, 1923) of *Na postu* (At the Post) carried an editorial manifesto declaring that "the most inexcusable muddle reigns in our ranks upon all questions of literature," that this state of affairs must come to an end, and that a stand must be taken for a consistent proletarian line in literature. No one would now deny the existence of a proletarian literature which has acquired a definite social significance. The framework of its content must be widened by the addition of proletarian construction to the two fundamental themes of labor and struggle and by making use of the rich material provided by "living, concrete contemporaneity." Content requires a "search for a corresponding *form*, which can only be *synthetical*"; and only an epic approach will permit the creation of "a monumental work adequate to the epoch." The manifesto concludes with the assertions that *Na postu* will stand steadily on guard over a firm and clear Communist ideology in proletarian literature and make a point of bringing to light all ideological doubts, which are "absolutely inadmissible"; that it will stand "*on guard over the organizational structure*" of VAPP (All-Russian Association of Proletarian Writers) and fight for its consolidation; and that

we count it our duty to fight not only against manifest white-guard and finally discredited literary tendencies, but also against those writers' groups which disguise themselves with the false mask of revolution, but which are, in reality, reactionary and counter-revolutionary.

A clear, firm, and severely consistent Communist policy in art and literature will be the leading principle of our review.[38]

The platform of the October group became the ideological platform of the At-the-Postists, and the latter's views before 1925 were formulated in the resolution, based on I. Vardin's report, adopted by the First All-Union (or Pan-Soviet) Conference of Proletarian Writers (which they dominated). It stated that the rule of the proletariat is incompatible with the existence of non-proletarian ideology and, therefore, of non-proletarian literature; that, in a class society, imaginative literature has no right to be neutral and must actively serve the ruling class; that literature is an arena of class war; and that the principle of the hegemony of proletarian literature must be officially recognized.[39]

Vardin had briefly remarked in the first number of Na postu, wrote Polonski,

that "the literature of the past was saturated with the spirit of the exploiting classes." From this, the conclusion was drawn that "first of all, proletarian literature must definitely free itself from the influence of the past in the field of ideology and in the field of form." [40]

Polonski went on to say that "the At-the-Postists showed themselves greater Bogdanovites than Bogdanov himself, who recognized the practical significance of the elements of 'excellence' in bourgeois literature." The fellow-travelers were regarded as especially harmful since they reflected the Revolution in a crooked mirror.[41] Unlike the Proletcult, which wanted to emancipate the proletariat from the Communist party in the field of cultural work, At-the-Post wanted to conquer its literary adversaries with the help of the Party, with all the power of Party influence.

Lelevich gave the basic proposition of the At-the-Post's point of view (also MAPP's and VAPP's) as,

a recognition of the conception that the working class, in the epoch of its dictatorship, could not but create its own class literature, that is, a literature "which organizes the mind and the consciousness of the working class and of the wide toiling masses towards the ultimate tasks of the proletariat—the reconstruction of the world and the creation of a Communist society" (platform of the October group). "Because proletarian literature appears today as the only serious force in the realm of artistic expression, it should be recognized even now that the interests of the ideological front demand the acquisition of dominating proletarian literary influence in the principal literary Party-Soviet organs of the press. Only under this condition is it possible to use profitably for the Revolution the auxiliary forces of the fellow-travelers, just as in the political sphere only the commanding position of the proletarian vanguard, the R.C.P. (b)—permits *smenovekhovstvo* [42] to be used in the interests of the dictatorship of the proletariat" (theses of the First Conference of MAPP).[43]

VAPP had been founded at the All-Russian Congress in 1920,[44] and in April of 1924 its reactionary administration was changed and a new board installed.[45] In 1921 the Union of Peasant Writers had appeared.

When the theses of the October group received organizational sanction and expression in VAPP, a considerable number of young writers did not enter the association because they did not share the views and methods of the journal *Na postu*. Most of them were peasants and proletarians, some were petty-bourgeois, and a significant number were Communists and members of the Komsomol. They needed organizational unity and therefore banded together in the "Pereval" as a protest against the extremes of the At-the-Post group and to defend revolutionary literature against VAPP's "imperialism and mistakes." As Polonski put it: "The theses of the At-the-Postists called forth the anti-theses of the Pereval." This group was almost unique then in declaring that it did not "appropriate to itself the right to hegemony." [46]

The leader of the Pereval was the critic A. K. Voronski,[47] editor of *Krasnaya nov*. He believed that there was no proletarian art in the sense in which bourgeois art existed. "That which is called proletarian art is a former art, having, however, an original and specific object: to be useful, not to the bourgeoisie, but to the proletariat." [48] He considered art as the expression of class interest, but as a "peaceful occupation," and thought that "it is hard to devote oneself to art in a period of wars." [49] In art itself he stressed "direct impressions," [50] the purely observative side. Left critics declared that in such a system of views "the very core of the Marxian conception of literature . . . class activity, is lost," and accused Voronski of "Trotskyism." [51]

Each literary group had an ideological platform, its critical views, its special literary policy, and its own literary journal. In 1923 the periodical *Na postu* opened a vehement campaign (carried on in the name of October and the allied "Young Guard," [52] MAPP, and VAPP) by a direct attack against the fellow-travelers:

The prevailing type of Fellow Traveller is a writer who distorts the Revolution in literature and calumniates it, who is steeped in the spirit of nationalism and mysticism. Fellow Traveller literature is essentially literature directed *against* the proletarian Revolution. A decisive war must be waged against these anti-revolutionary elements.[53]

Such writers as Boris Pilnyak and Ilya Ehrenburg were denounced as counter-revolutionaries, and the necessity of liberating Soviet literature from the influence of the past was proclaimed.

The problems set and not settled, or erroneously settled, by the Proletcult were propounded anew during the 1923–25 fight, and their various solutions split the literary movement. These basic problems were: the proletariat and art; the attitude towards the heritage of past literature, towards the fellow-travelers and towards bourgeois literature, towards formal literary traditions; and, finally, the main problem—the problem of leadership and hegemony of the proletariat in the realm of artistic and cultural creative work in general.

The concept of a distinct and superior proletarian literature, which deserved priority in a workers' state, appeared in successive groups from the Proletcult to RAPP:

The tendency typified by Averbakh in criticism and by Bezimensky in poetry may be regarded as the heritage of the "uncompromising" Proletcult epoch. Both Averbakh and Bezimensky insist upon the creation of a Proletarian Art, based on absolute fulfilment of Marxist ideology, on the development of dialectical materialist methods, on the necessary portrayal of current actuality and on a rationalistic interpretation of heroes and events.[54]

In 1924 Averbakh announced that, since "we have the press, the publishing houses, etc., we can and ought . . . to influence and to a certain degree determine the manifestation of the new literature." [55]

Na postu approved the alliance of the proletarian groups with definitely non-proletarian groups such as the Union of Peasant Writers, LEF, and the Constructivists [56] as a strategic move to win supremacy over the fellow-travelers by organization, since they could not gain it by superior talent. The Smithy, worsted in a bitter contest with October, declined and eventually merged with RAPP. LEF entered into a formal alliance with MAPP, as did the Constructivists. They were united by the common conviction of the need for a *new* art, expressive of the new order.[57]

The policy of the At-the-Post group "threatened to disrupt literary activity by sowing discord and suspicion, by showering flattery and undeserved praise on unripe talent, and by disparaging and throwing mud at gifted fellow-travelers." [58] Editors and critics were classified as "loyalists" or "capitulants," which created an atmosphere of hostility and of unscrupulous politics. The literary and political world was divided into two camps [59] by the stormy debates which ensued, and the struggle finally became so sharp that the Communist party intervened. On May 19, 1924, the Press Department of the Central Committee called a conference to discuss Bolshevist policy towards literature. This was the first active public interference of the Party in literary matters, and representatives of all of the antagonistic groups and many members of the Central Committee were present.

Nikolai Bukharin, at that time editor of *Pravda*, supported the theories but opposed the tactics of the At-the-Postists and accused them of trying to solve literary problems by force. "The cultural problem," he said, "is different from the military problem; it cannot be decided by blows or mechanical means." [60] He favored the encouragement of proletarian literary groups, but also consideration for peasant literature and the creative work of the fellow-travelers, and therefore opposed the At-the-Post group's claims to supremacy in the literary field. "I favor . . . a general leadership and the maximum of competition," he told the 1924 Party Conference, so that important questions of style and form could be solved on the basis of merit, rather than by political pressure.[61]

Anatol V. Lunacharski, Commissar of Education, was among those who supported Bukharin's policy of "the maximum of competition." He accepted both the bourgeois past and the proletarian future in art but believed that, since a writer must have a certain amount of education, the literature of the immediate future was likely to be created by members of the intelligentsia. "The only result of our discussion," he concluded, "is the realization of the fact that it is necessary to protect and support proletarian literature as our main hope, but under no circumstances must we estrange the Fellow Travellers." [62]

A resolution was adopted stressing the great importance of helping the creative work of the workers and peasants and the necessity for giving every assistance to Komsomol writers and poets. *Na postu* was censured for its criticism (directed against both the fellow-travelers and the serious work of the proletarians), which had estranged the most talented authors from the Party and the Soviet government and retarded the actual growth of the proletarian writers, while Voronski's policy towards the fellow-travelers was approved. His views triumphed over those of the "hatchet-swingers from VAPP" because they coincided with those of the government at this time, in spite of Averbakh's accusation that "in 1921 Voronsky was entrusted with a special task . . . the disintegration of the bourgeois writers, which he carried out in a short-sighted, most unsatisfactory manner . . . because he first disintegrated the proletarian writers." [63] It was further decided that *"no literary current, school or group must come forward in the name of the Party* [my italics]." [64]

The May Conference's resolution was incorporated in the resolution on the press adopted by the Thirteenth Conference of the Communist party. In 1925 a special commission was established to examine this resolution and to extend it, the enlarged version then being passed by the Politburo.[65] It marked the clearest expression of Party policy towards literature and the arts up to that time. "All frivolous and contemptuous" attitudes towards the cultural heritage of the past and towards "specialists in style" are opposed, the decree asserted.[66] "Such a thing as neutral art in a class society . . . cannot exist, although the class nature of . . . literature especially is infinitely more varied than that of politics." [67] The Party urged a tactful and guarded attitude towards fellow-travelers, peasant writers, and even towards bourgeois writers supporting the Soviet régime, so as to "hasten their approach to communist ideology." [68]

The resolution went on to say that "the proletariat may already possess an exact criterion of the social-political contents of literary works, but it does not possess definite answers to all questions concerning artistic form." [69] The Party should aid proletarian writers materially and morally but

cannot recognize the monopoly of any one group—even a group which may be the most proletarian in regard to ideology and subject matter. *To do so would mean the destruction of proletarian literature* [my italics]. . . . The leadership of literature belongs to the working class as a whole.

There should be free competition among the various groups and tendencies in the field of literature, the resolution stated. The Party not only condemns "any underestimation of the great importance of the struggle for the ideological hegemony of proletarian writers," but also "communist conceit" among them and all attempts to develop "purely hot-house proletarian literature." [70] Communist criticism "must show the greatest tact, care, and patience in regard to those literary workers who might join with the proletariat" and *"must avoid adopting a tone of command* [my italics]." [71] Finally, "the necessity of creating literature suitable for the mass of worker and peasant readers" was stressed.[72]

Formation of RAPP

This decree was a brilliant piece of NEP compromise, dictated by the political demands of the period for collaboration with the bourgeoisie while eliminating it and for the winning over of the intelligentsia; and it laid the groundwork for RAPP, although there seems to be a considerable difference of opinion as to exactly when the latter was actually organized. *Na literaturnom postu* (At the Literary Post) for May, 1932, says that RAPP was created "during the first years of NEP to strengthen the positions of proletarian literature under conditions in which there was still a strong influence of foreign elements in literature." [73] The *Literary Encyclopedia* states that in January, 1925, the First All-Union Congress of Proletarian Writers was called together and that it initiated RAPP.[74] An article by A. Selivanovski in the *Small Soviet Encyclopedia* gives this same congress of VAPP "in the territory of the R.S.F.S.R.," as the place of origin, but gives the year as 1928.[75]

One of the immediate results of the Central Committee's 1925 Resolution was a split in the At-the-Post group. The "impenitents," led by Lelevich and Vardin, refused to recognize the errors pointed out by the Party and joined the Leningrad Lefts whose leader was the critic Gorbachyov. This faction, to which Bezymenski, Rodov, and Dinamov also belonged, formed the RAPP minority. The majority, which accepted the Party's decisions, was composed largely of younger writers and critics and included L. Averbakh, Yu. Libedinski, V. Kirshon, D. Furmanov, A. Fadeyev, V. Yermilov, V. Stavski, and F. Panfyorov. They became the RAPP Right and took over the management of *Na postu*, changing its name to *Na literaturnom postu* to show a new point of view. "In *Na literaturnom postu* we continued the line of *Na postu* but corrected its errors," [76] Libedinski said. "We had to be ideological snipers" on the literary front.[77]

However, Polonski boldly gave as his opinion:

The latest period of activity of the leaders of the journal *Na literaturnom postu* shows that they have forgotten nothing and learned nothing. Those scandalous methods of criticism and impermissible methods of literary struggle, condemned by the Politburo's resolution, were reborn in this journal in still more unacceptable form. If in the first period . . . the harshness of their methods might be—not justified, but explained, by their minority position . . . so much the less can we justify the unprincipledness and unscrupulousness of the methods inaugurated by the journal, *Na literaturnom postu*. . . . Unprincipled alliances, now with the Rights, now with the Lefts; 180° changes of front; opportunism; cliquism; a low level of literary education combined with bragging insolence and self-advertising; contempt for the genuine interests of proletarian literature; slovenly and at times dishonest polemics; and, finally, they threw many prolet-literary workers off the journal and created a strong opposition within VAPP.[78]

Such was the group which dictated the policies of RAPP, an organization made up of a series of proletarian-writer district associations (APPs), the largest being in Moscow (MAPP) and in Leningrad (LAPP). It was headed by the critic Leopold Leonidovich Averbakh, a born organizer and a past master "in the truly creative art of identifying 'proletarian culture' with political machine loyalty."[79] According to Kaun, RAPP persisted in spite of the opposition of the leading authors and in defiance of official condemnation of its policy because: (1) Its members were shrewd politicians, who knew "how to pull strings within the Party and how to increase their power by means of alliances with other easily dominated groups, and by questionable means of swelling their own membership. Thus the RAPP issued a call for 'shock workers' to fill the literary ranks, relying on the docility of culturally immature factory hands whom the Averbakh gang could hold as a whip over recalcitrant members." (2) Grave inner conflicts existed within the Communist party during the 1920's and especially after the death of Lenin. The government was anxious to preserve the "general line" against threatening Right and Left deviations. "The Atpostists and Atlitpostists made use of the psychological moment for their vociferous clamor against non-Party elements. Their heresy hunt assumed the coloration of anti-Trotskyism at one moment, and of anti-any-opposition at another." The government regarded RAPP as a lesser evil and suffered it as a wartime nuisance while suspending various organizations suspected of Trotskyism and other oppositional tendencies:

The inauguration of the First Five-Year Plan, at the end of the 'twenties, demanded an even stricter policy against all tendencies that might imperil the success of the gigantic undertaking. *At the Literary Post* mixed its inquisitorial literary campaign with outcries against *kulaks* and doubting Thomases who dared question the feasibility of the Plan.[80]

By 1930 RAPP had about two thousand members, mostly beginners. It

accepted for membership only those who had proven themselves "creatively and by their creations able to organize the psyche of the toiling masses in the direction of the ultimate tasks of the proletariat," and it held them subject to expulsion "in case they violate the discipline of the organization, or manifest ideological unsteadiness (either in artworks or public speeches) or transgress the proletarian ethic." With these articles in its constitution and "the seizure of power in literature" as its slogan, it gradually but substantially monopolized the field of serious publication.[81]

Situation on the Eve of the First Five-Year Plan

In 1926 a number of fundamental literary organizations existed. The largest, numerically, was RAPP (Russian Association of Proletarian Writers), headed by Averbakh; then VOKP (All-Russian Association of Peasant Writers), which later became VOPKP (All-Russian Association of Proletarian-*Kolkhoz* Writers),[82] led by Zamoiski; and then VAPP (All-Russian Association of Proletarian Writers),[83] whose leader was Leonov and which united mainly fellow-travelers, both old and new, but also some proletarian writers. Lesser groups were: LEF, Pereval, and the Literary Center of the Constructivists. All of these societies were organized on the principle of democratic participation in VOAPP (All-Union Association of Proletarian Writers) and crowded into Herzen House, which had been given to the writers by the government in 1921. This resulted in a noisy literary life with a large number of periodicals and the *Literaturnaya gazeta* (Literary Gazette).[84]

The minor groups were liquidated or absorbed as control over writers became more centralized, leaving only "the big three"—RAPP, VOPKP, and VAPP—plus their federation, VOAPP. The fierce ideological battles which were waged in the arena of Soviet literature from 1926 on, were a reflection and a continuation of the class war which was raging throughout the U.S.S.R. "In the opinion of individuals was the behaviour of social groups reflected."[85] During 1926 and 1927 Stalin, with the majority of the Party, fought the Left Opposition, led by Trotsky, Zinoviev, and Kamenev.[86] The Left Deviation wanted accelerated development with higher tempos in industry and more intensive collectivization and *dekulakization* in agriculture. Trotsky preached the irreconcilability of peasants and workers and the impossibility of creating "socialism in one country" or of developing a proletarian literature. It was by violent opposition to this last theory that RAPP got into Stalin's good graces. Another episode of the class war was the discovery in the spring of 1928 of the "Shakhty Counter-revolutionary Plot" in the Donets Basin and the ensuing trial of fifty Russian and three German coal-mining specialists.

By the fall of 1928, three powerful figures on the left of Stalin had been disposed of: Trotsky, Zinoviev, and Kamenev. The struggle had really been a political one for control of the Communist party, rather than an ideological one. Differences and clashes in personality also played a large part in the conflict. In 1926–27 Trotsky was to the left of Stalin; but in 1928–29, during the fight against the Right Deviation, Stalin was to the left of what Trotsky had been in 1926–27. Bukharin (a member of the Politburo), Rykov, and Tomski,[87] leaders of the Right Opposition, believed that the industrial tempos and goals of the optimal variant of the First Five-Year Plan, which had been approved by the Sixteenth Party Conference in April, 1929, were not feasible; and that individual peasant farming, even by kulaks, should be tolerated for the sake of greater grain marketing. The end of 1929 saw the removal of these three powerful figures on the right of Stalin. The way was now clear for the attempt to build socialism in one country; the Soviet Union's active efforts towards world revolution were, for the time being, called off. Stalin's own future position of power and control, as well as the future of the U.S.S.R., would now depend upon the successful fulfillment of the First Five-Year Plan.

In November, 1928, the plenum of the Central Committee called upon

all Party members to concentrate their efforts on overcoming economic difficulties and mobilizing all the creative powers of the working class in order to maintain at any cost the pace set by us for industrialization and socialization, and to carry out the proposed economic plan.[88]

2. THE LITERARY FIVE-YEAR PLAN

The First Five-Year Plan, 1928–32

"SIXTEEN MEN IN MOSCOW," wrote Stuart Chase, "are attempting one of the most audacious economic experiments in history." As the presidium of the State Planning Commission, responsible to the Council of People's Commissars and popularly known as the Gosplan, they are laying down the industrial future of 146,000,000 people and of one-sixth of the land area of the world for a period of fifteen years.... Not only industry, but agriculture, transportation, superpower, exports, imports and the Government budget, all come within their purview.... It is an experiment so immense, so novel and so courageous.... It is something new in the world.[1]

Chamberlin considers October 1, 1928, when the Five-Year Plan (*pyatiletka*) of national development went into effect, the third outstanding date in Soviet history, the others being November 7, 1917, when the Bolshevik revolution triumphed in Petrograd, and March, 1921, when the NEP was initiated. Each of the three dates marks the beginning of a new era, of "a fresh act in the revolutionary drama."[2]

By 1928 Russian industrial production in most lines was back to prewar levels and the sown area of land, but not the grain crop, was approximately as great as before the Revolution (only about half as much grain was being marketed outside the rural areas). It was time to end the compromise period and to resume the socialist offensive.

"To change from the muzhik horse of poverty to the horse of large-scale machine industry—such was the aim the party pursued in drawing up the Five-Year Plan and working for its fulfillment," said Stalin.[3] He gave as the grounds which dictated the fundamental task of the Five-Year Plan:

(1) The necessity of putting an end to the technical and economic backwardness of the Soviet Union . . . the necessity of creating in the country such prerequisites as would enable it not only to overtake but in time to outstrip, economically and technically, the advanced capitalist countries.

(2) Consideration of the fact that the Soviet government could not for long rest upon two opposite foundations: on large-scale socialist industry, which *destroys* the capitalist elements, and on small, individual peasant farming, which *engenders* capitalist elements.

(3) Consideration of the fact that until agriculture was placed on the basis of large-scale production, until the small peasant farms were united into large collective farms, the danger of the restoration of capitalism in the U.S.S.R. would be the most real of all possible dangers.[4]

This fundamental task of the Five-Year Plan, according to Stalin, was:

to transfer our country, with its backward . . . technique, to the lines of new, modern technique . . . to convert the U.S.S.R. from an agrarian and weak country, dependent upon the caprices of the capitalist countries, into an industrial and powerful country, fully self-reliant and independent of the caprices of world capitalism . . . in converting the U.S.S.R. into an industrial country, fully to eliminate the capitalist elements, to widen the front of socialist forms of economy, and to create the economic base for the abolition of classes in the U.S.S.R., for the construction of socialist society . . . to create such an industry . . . as would be able to re-equip and reorganize, not only the whole of industry, but also transport and agriculture—on the basis of socialism . . . to transfer small and scattered agriculture to the lines of large-scale collective farming, so as to ensure the economic base for socialism in the rural districts and thus to eliminate the possibility of the restoration of capitalism in the U.S.S.R. . . . to create . . . all the necessary technical and economic prerequisites for increasing to the utmost the defensive capacity of the country, to enable it to organize determined resistance . . . to any and every attempt at military attack from without.[5]

Although the Soviet Union had officially given up fomenting world revolution, the Executive Committee of the Communist International hailed the Five-Year Plan as "an important part of the world proletariat's offensive against capitalism" and called it "a plan tending to undermine capitalist stabilization" and "a great plan of world revolution," [6] while Stalin himself admitted that "there can be no doubt that the international revolutionary significance of the Five-Year Plan is really immeasurable." [7] From the point of view of the *Berliner Tageblatt*, it was "a colossal defense plan, designed to safeguard and protect the unhampered realization of socialist ideas on Russian territory." [8]

The First Five-Year Plan went into operation on October 1, 1928, although not until 1929 was it actually endorsed by the Communist party (at the Sixteenth Conference) and the Soviet government (at the Fifth All-Union Congress of Soviets). Its basic policy was one of high-tempo industrialization with emphasis on the development of heavy industry. Supplements to the Plan, introduced on Stalin's initiative, were: (1) enlargement of the scale of reconstruction and fulfillment of the Five-Year Plan in four years (slogan launched in the fall of 1930), with the result that the Plan, which was to have run until September 30, 1933, was declared finished on December 31, 1932; and (2) all-out collectivization of agriculture and liquidation of the kulaks as a class.

The Five-Year Plan of Art and the "Cultural Revolution"

The purpose of the Five-Year Plan, however, was not merely to build a certain number of factories, railroads, hydroelectric power stations, etc., but also to create a new system of society and new men.[9] Centralized planning and control were therefore extended to cultural and other activities previously left untouched. In the literary sphere the various groups of Communist critics, led by Averbakh, began to agitate for the inclusion of art in the Five-Year Plan; and, flaunting the Party-backed slogan, "Literature Should Help the Five-Year Plan," they seized control of RAPP and of the editorial boards of reviews and journals. Then, as masters of the literary situation and with the tacit support of the Communist party, these proletarian critics started to issue "social commands," to lay down the uncompromising program that "the depiction of the Five-Year Plan and of the class war within its framework is the one and only problem of Soviet literature," [10] and to insist that creative work was a form of participation in the class struggle.

By a "Five-Year Plan of Art" was meant "a planned State guidance of art according to a programme, fixed beforehand, distributed over a period of five years and provided with a fixed budget." There was no intention of planning the development of geniuses, year by year, but only the ever more adequate satisfaction of the demands of the masses in the field of the arts. All forms of art must in every way help raise the mass consciousness and organize the mass will, mind, and enthusiasm for socialist construction and the great social reforms being carried out, and for international socialist education. Such were the main aims of art, according to the Five-Year Plan.[11]

The Plan was divided into sections dealing with the separate arts: theatre, circus, music hall, cinema, "self-activity art," plastic arts, music, and literature.[12] The paragraph dealing with the latter states that "literary art must be developed, its social contents must be made deeper, it must be made completely understandable for the mass reader, its circulation enlarged, etc. We must struggle for the hegemony of proletarian literature." [13]

The Fifteenth Party Congress had declared in December, 1927:

The Five-Year Plan of socialist construction must recognize the necessity of the decisive raising of the cultural level of both the city and the village population, the development of national cultures among the peoples of the Union, and the inclusion of the plan of cultural construction as an inseparable part of the general plan for the socialist construction of the Soviet Union.[14]

Two years later, Averbakh announced that the Five-Year Plan of economic construction made necessary the working out of a Five-Year Plan of cultural work, a "cult-plan," which must be tied to industrialization so that it should be an inalienable part of the general plan of socialist construction.[15] "Having gained political power," he went on, "we should 'conquer' and 'rule' in the realm of culture." [16] And since the cultural revolution shows itself, not outside of class culture, but as a form of the class struggle, "we must fight for proletarian hegemony in the cultural revolution. All of our socio-cultural measures must have a class character. We must set the peasant masses going on the tracks of proletarian ideology." [17] Cadres of "cultural specialists" are needed as much as cadres of proletarian engineers or scientific workers.[18] The building and growth of the new proletarian, and then socialist, culture will enable the Soviet Union to overtake and surpass the cultural level of the foremost bourgeois states. "From illiteracy to the Magnitostrois of literature—such is the path of the cultural revolution." [19]

Attitudes towards the Five-Year Plan

To Communists and to members of the Komsomol, 1928 to 1932 was an exhilarating and heroic time.[20] The last remnants of private capitalism were being swept away and colossal schemes for the building of industrial "giants" and the formation of huge *kolkhozes* (collective farms) and *sovkhozes* (state farms) were afoot. Only by great constructive fervor and iron discipline could the very high goals set by the maximum variant of the Plan be attained. Psychologically, the age had all the characteristics of a period of war or revolution: terrific concentration and straining of effort towards a supremely important objective; utter intolerance for opponents, doubters, and skeptics; ruthless disregard for individuals or whole classes who blocked the march to socialism; fanatical enthusiasm on the part of the active Soviet sympathizers, generated and stimulated by every conceivable propagandist device.[21]

The working class had accepted the struggle for the Five-Year Plan as the peaceful war for freedom from economic dependence on the West, and the new methods of work were given military designations: "staffs," "brigades," "shock troops," "operations." Reports on the progress of work were written in the style of war reports; wall newspapers talked about "storming," about "battle fronts," "breaks at the front," etc.; and in the central "staffs" daily "summaries of operations" were made out.[22]

The following factory report is an example of organized enthusiasm expressed in military language:

We, the workers of the K. Marx factory, initiators of the first "industrial and financial counter-plan," which has been taken up by all the working class in the Soviet Union, and initiators of the first "collectivization day," have not lagged behind in the ranks of the battalions of the proletariat who are storming the heights of the Five-Year Plan.[23]

And the wall newspaper of the Morozov works, in speaking of the Plan, exclaimed: "Here it is, our big revolution! That's why our worker's heart leaps. Comrade, we are raising ourselves up." [24]

A considerable number of authors, especially the younger ones who had been war propagandists, commissars, or students of a political school, felt closely bound to the social, political, and economic life of the country. Moreover, it is not surprising that such militant RAPP members as the poet Bezymenski and the playwright and novelist Kirshon sincerely and zealously backed the First Five-Year Plan. It was, however, noteworthy when Alexei Tolstoy, prerevolutionary and former émigré writer,[25] stated with all the ardor of a convert: "In my consciousness the start of the Five-Year Plan illuminated with the light of a heroic dawn that life to which I gave my strength. Socialism became a visible, tangible goal." [26] Kornely Zelinski, principal theoretician of constructivism, gave his views thus:

The Five-Year Plan has seized our thoughts. . . . I might say that the "spirit" of the Five-Year Plan—its tempo, its ardent struggle against nature and against hostile classes—cannot pass the writer by unless he locks himself up in his study and draws the curtains.

. . . . .

I do not separate my work as a writer from the work which my country does—by which it lives. I made my choice freely: to devote my creative work to communism, although I am not a member of the Party.[27]

Sergei Tretyakov of LEF explained that

the closer a narrative is bound up with the biography of a human being, the stronger it is. The Five-Year Plan which catches the author in the whirlwind of its plans becomes, by this very action, his biography.

The part of the Five-Year Plan in which the writer worked becomes, to a certain extent, the result of his work; and the author, himself changed by the Five-Year Plan, becomes its product.[28]

On November 17, 1930, VOAPP called a meeting at its club in Moscow in connection with the trial of the "Industrial Party" (led by Professor Ramzin and involving eight leading Soviet non-Party engineers), which was charged with sabotage and plotting with France. A resolution was passed calling upon authors to take up a definite class position with the proletarian revolution, with the working class, with the Communist party, for socialism and against capitalism; and declaring that "we, Soviet writers and dramatists, heartily acclaim that true sentinel of the Revolution, the OGPU, and petition the Government to award it the Order of Lenin." [29]

There was an "ideological rejuvenation and reorganization" [30] among the intelligentsia, a mass going over to the proletariat, especially after 1930, which appears to bear out the saying that "nothing succeeds like success." However, not all authors "reorganized"; some Right-wingers like Seifullina, Sergeyev-Tsenski, and Klychkov ceased to be heard from. But Maxim Gorky [31] seems to have expressed the sentiments of the majority of writers:

Are we . . . to sacrifice ourselves to the revolutionary demands of the epoch? . . . Yes, we must re-educate ourselves so that serving the social revolution becomes at the same time a source of gratification to the individual. "Great is the joy of battle!" [32]

. . . The meaning of life is to serve the revolution. In our day it can have no other meaning.[33]

The "Social Command"

MAYAKOVSKY

Mayakovsky had been the first to hear the social command, and he responded "at the top of his voice," hurling himself into communism, as he put it, "from the heights of poetry above." [34] In the early days he glorified the Revolution, rousing men to battle or to celebrate victories with such poems as "Left, March!" (1918), which was written for the sailors of the Baltic Fleet. Nearly everything Mayakovsky wrote after October, 1917, was propaganda for the new régime—epics, lyrics, plays, and satires on the evils and issues of the day. "My main work," he said shortly before his death, "is criticizing all that I think is wrong, against which I must fight.

And twenty years of my literary work has actually been a literary boxing match in the best sense of the word." [35]

In answer to the social command Mayakovsky joined the Department of Fine Arts of the Commissariat of Education, drew caricatures and wrote propaganda captions for the "Rosta (Russian Telegraph Agency) Windows" posters, helped to popularize slogans of political and economic campaigns, wrote for the newspapers, produced couplets for the advertising wrappers of various government products during the NEP, and even contributed rhymes such as "Good and Bad" in the interest of better behavior for children:

> Little piggies
>   into big pigs
>   grow . . .
> neatness
>   in childhood
>   in grownups
>   show.[36]

He was not exaggerating when he asserted: "I have never refused to write on any theme, beginning by verses about the Kulaks and ending about cat's-furs at the 'Gostorg' [State Trading Store]." [37] And he made this request: "Name me with the builder, the weaver, whom work raises to joyous fever." [38] Proudly he announced:

> Whole ranks of books
>   march with my name,
>   proclaim
>   that the labor of
>   Mayakovsky,
>   poet,
>   cogs with the labor—of
>   the republic! [39]

Mayakovsky addressed public meetings and read his poems to soldiers and factory workers in every part of Russia and also in Europe and the Americas. He felt that "only the working-class auditorium, only the proletarian masses, those that are now building our new life, are fit listeners and readers, and I can only be the poet of these people." [40] His last public appearance was made at a literary evening held in the House of Komsomols to celebrate twenty years of his activity as a poet. He said in his talk that the main object of the exhibition of his work, then being held, was to prove "that a revolutionary writer takes a very active part in the everyday life and building of Socialism" [41] and to show

that a poet is not one who goes about like a curly lamb bleating on love themes, but one who in our sharp class battle gives his pen up to the arsenal of the proletariat and does not scorn any dirty and hard work, any theme about the revolution, or of building a people's management of agriculture, and writes propaganda on any of these themes.[42]

The first requisite for starting poetic work, Mayakovsky declared, is "the existence of a social task that can be accomplished only by a poetic composition. [There must be] a social command." And then he added parenthetically: "Here is an interesting subject for special research: the lack of connection between the social command and the command actually given." This was written in 1926, and one wonders whether he had Averbakh and the other At-the-Post critics in mind. Mayakovsky considered the second necessary condition to be "an exact knowledge of, or at least a feeling for, the aspirations of your class (or of the group which you represent) toward this social task." [43] He believed that Demyan Bedny's verses [44] corresponded to "an urgent, well-understood social command," that their purpose was clear, and that they were adapted to the needs of the workers and peasants, the words being "those of the daily life of the semi-peasant class, mixed with remnants of poetic rhymes." [45]

The creed professed by the "poet of the Revolution" is given in these words:

For my part, I believe that the best poetic work will be written in accordance with the social command laid down by the Communist International and that it will tend to assure the victory of the proletariat. It will be written in new, striking words comprehensible to everybody. It will be born in the hour when it is wanted and will be sent to the editor by express airplane. I insist on this last point, for the poetic way of living is also one of the most important factors in our production.[46]

In 1926 Mayakovsky had explained how he wanted his socially planned poetry to be handled:

I want the Gosplan to sweat while discussing the assignment of my year's tasks. . . . I want the pen to be put on the same footing with the bayonet. I want Stalin, in the name of the Politburo, to present reports on the production of verse along with reports on pig iron and steel.[47]

Alexander Bezymenski, Komsomol poet and leader of the extreme Left of RAPP, has been described as going from Magnitogorsk to Dnieprostroi and from Dnieprostroi to some *sovkhoz* or *kolkhoz* on the Don, "inexhaustible in energy, in enthusiasm, and in a knack for turning out rather simple rhymes." [48] Like Mayakovsky by whom he was strongly influenced, Bezymenski considered his literary activity an aspect of revolutionary work; and he boasted that he carried his Party card, not in his pocket, but within himself.[49] In fact, he looked upon his poetic talent as so much of a political tool that he used it to produce a report in poetry on the condition of proletarian literature, which he delivered to the Sixteenth Party Congress (June-July, 1930). He began with these statements:

> I am a worker of RAPP,
> But I am first of all a Bolshevik.
> A Bolshevik
>   is not accustomed to shilly-shallying!
> Therefore,
>   my short report
>   will be sharp
>   as a bayonet.[50]

A little further along, with a bow to the Party, he got to the essence of his report:

> The word of the Party correctly commands us!
> We have achievements of the pen;
> Our circles have
>   growth and solidarity;
> The forces of the worker kernel
> Become stronger.[51]

Then Bezymenski came out categorically in favor of the social command:

> RAPP is not a club! It is an army of words!
> Now the country
>   takes the offensive,
> And in time of battle

> The Bolshevik campaign needs words.
> It means that members
> of this army
> Must be given
> marching orders.[52]

1929 CONTROVERSY

In 1929 a heated controversy about the social command broke out in the Soviet press, in which a number of the prominent critics (O. M. Brik, P. S. Kogan, Gorbachyov, Pereverzev, Polonski) and writers (Gladkov, Pilnyak, Fedin, Kaverin, Selvinski) took part. It was to be expected that an author like Kaverin, who had belonged to the "Serapion Brothers," [53] would champion the artistic freedom of creative work; but the fact that even the Communist Gladkov argued against the expediency of giving writers social commands showed how unpopular this theory of RAPP's was.

Polonski, too, came out in opposition to it, writing in *Pechat i revolyutsiya*: "The theory of 'social command' marks an attempt on the part of a group of extreme left writers and artists, who are torn off from the Proletariat, to establish a link with it while preserving their own independence as creators of ideological values." [54] He felt that the demands of the reading public would bring about proletarian literature if the authors were socially-minded. As a result, Polonski was soon proclaimed a counter-revolutionary and removed from his editorial jobs on *Novy mir* (New World) and *Pechat i revolyutsiya*.

The theory of the social command received official approval in spite of the fact that Lenin had said, "Every artist . . . claims as his proper right the liberty to work according to his ideal, whether it is any good or not." [55] Trotsky believed that "the domain of art is not one in which the Party is called upon to command. It can and must protect and help it, but it can only lead it indirectly." [56] But of course he did not count any more. However, in the Communist party's 1924 Resolution the following statement had been made: "Communist criticism must avoid adopting a tone of command." [57] Now, it was convenient to forget this; times had changed, and literature must serve the First Five-Year Plan. These circumstances gave the At-the-Post group its chance to attain the hegemony it had so long craved, and RAPP's literary dictatorship began.

Just how the social command operated in practice was explained to the Western world by an authorized spokesman:

Leaving the author at liberty to choose any subject he is interested in, we consider it possible nevertheless to go over to planned orders for works on definite subjects possessing the greatest actuality for the present period, the more so, as the whole historic experience of the development of art convinces us that the prevailing majority of both great and lesser works of art are a result of a definite social order, made to the author by individuals, or by groups of individuals, in the interests of one or other social class. Thus the Five-Year Plan in respect to thematics provides, besides the utilization of the legacy of old art and of contemporary works possessing a high artistic quality and responding to the demands of the Soviet spectator (or reader), which have been created outside of the plan, also for a planned organization of . . . subjects for the various kinds of artistic produce [production] in the interests of the closest and fullest reflection of the most stirring problems of our times.[58]

The *Literaturnaya gazeta*, whose editor, Dinamov, belonged to Lelevich's faction, made the following editorial pronouncement:

The only place for the true Soviet writer is in the ranks of our country's revolutionary working mass, which is building socialism. He must, straightway and unconditionally, without prolonged hesitation and the intelligentsia's self-analysis, roll up his sleeves and undertake with the proletariat and its Party the great joyful work of socialist construction; he must occupy a firm position in a sector of the cultural revolution, which demands enormous strength and lots of work.[59]

Averbakh, a little more tactfully (he was not as dictatorial as he became later on), wrote that the author daily receives innumerable impressions from the outside world and that he is free to choose those which he needs for his work. Writers, he said, write about themes of our times. "One must not dictate directly, but it is necessary to help [the writer] to perceive the social command." [60] The social command of the proletariat is no burden to the proletarian writer who does not struggle against it but carries it out. "Such an author considers that, in producing artistic works, he participates in a definite way in social life, influences it." And he has this utilitarian approach to creative work because he is "a writer of the proletariat, the rising class to which the future belongs." [61]

"First of all, remember the task of depicting the worker, the new people, and also the new relations," Averbakh continued. The proletarian writer should write about whatever he wishes but should realize that he, better than anyone else, can reveal "the new in our way of life and the growth among us of the new man." It is for just this reason that his class lays upon him the duty of focusing his attention, first and foremost, on this theme. "The slogan of showing 'the living man' should be, at the same time, the slogan of showing 'the hero of our times'—the central figure of our epoch." [62]

Gorky's point of view is shown in the following paragraphs:

The writer is the eyes, ears, and voice of a class. He can be unconscious of this, deny it, but he is always and inevitably the organ of a class, the receptacle of its feelings. He perceives, formulates, and portrays the moods, desires, anxieties, hopes, passions, interests, and virtues of his class, of his group. And he himself is limited in his development by all these. He never was, and cannot be, "a man inwardly free," "a man in general."

This will be possible only in the future when there is a classless society.

But until that time, and while a class state exists, the writer—a man of a definite milieu and epoch—must serve; and he serves the interests of his epoch and of his surroundings whether he wants to or not, whether with or without reservations.[63]

It is hard to tell whether the appeal issued by a group of outstanding Soviet writers and artists "To All Men of Letters and Art" was written "with or without reservations," but it certainly shows that these intellectuals were deeply involved in the social command:

The builders of the Magnitogorsk blast furnaces demand a Magnitostroi of art.

We, the writers, poets, composers, artists and actors, consider it our vital duty at the present stage of development in Soviet art to reflect in our works the gigantic work of construction going on and, more particularly, the construction in the Urals.

This task should occupy the same place in Soviet art as the Urals themselves hold in the political and economic scheme of the Union. We appeal to all writers and artists to make the theme of their artistic work the great socialist construction now taking place in the Urals.

. . . . .

One of the greatest paths to the Magnitostroi of art shall lead through the socialist Urals.[64]

The appeal was signed by a number of writers including L. Leonov, V. Ivanov, A. Bezymenski, P. Pavlenko, M. Shaginyan, and V. Vishnevski; *régisseurs* such as V. Meyerhold and A. Tairov; composers like D. Shostakovich; and prominent painters. It may be that Lidin's frank statement explains why some of the signers subscribed: "Only those survived in our literature who had felt that they were an integral part of the common cause which all the country is struggling for with incredible efforts." [65]

However, apart from all question of social command, many Soviet authors undoubtedly did feel so thoroughly in harmony with the existing order of things that they were conscious of no repression. The majority believed that bourgeois-capitalist civilization (then in the grip of the 1929 depression) was disintegrating and were convinced that the Five-Year Plan was building a wonderful new world. Political and social problems would, therefore, naturally furnish much of the material for their novels and plays.

RAPP's Thematic Requirements

Libedinski quoted a Central Committee resolution delimiting the subject matter of Soviet literary works: "The broad scope of phenomena in all their complexity, not locked up within the limits of one plant; the literature, not of the workshop, but of the great struggling class which draws millions of peasants to itself—such should be the limits of the contents of proletarian literature." [66] He explained that this does not mean that one must write only about how the working class leads the peasantry:

One can write about whatever one pleases, depicting either worker or intellectual. But, in describing the most remote little corner of actuality, one must not lose that great feeling of the country in which we are making a social revolution; and it is this feeling of the leading role of the proletariat in relation to the peasantry which the resolution of the Central Committee points out. This is the first and compulsory condition for every proletarian writer.[67]

The transformation of the ignorant worker, not yet freed from elements of individualism, into the conscious champion of the worker-collective must be shown, as well as the path of regeneration of the backward elements of the working class. In conclusion, Libedinski said:

We consider all this work [present-day writing] a rough draft for the general theme of our proletarian literature, for a depiction of plant and factory; a moving picture of a production collective of live, dialectically developing people; a picture of the Communist alteration of the world, man's own alteration and the creation of the new Communist man—here, comrades, is the task of proletarian literature; here is our Five-Year Plan.[68]

Addressing the Communist party congress in the summer of 1930 (the same one at which Bezymenski recited his report in verse), Kirshon gave what might be termed RAPP's aesthetic code:

In relation to bourgeois ideology, as on all fronts, we must pass over to [a] decisive offensive, mercilessly liquidating the bourgeois ideology. . . . The class enemy on the literary sector becomes active. In a moment of sharpened class struggle any liberalism, any respect for aesthetic language, even though it may be directed against us, is direct aid to the class enemy.[69]

The writer, he believed, should understand and feel that

each figure of the Five-Year Plan, each figure of the reports presented by the workers and collective farmers to the Sixteenth Party Congress, is a battle landmark on our path. Never yet has a country lived so tempestuously; no other epoch has offered such stupendous material for creative work as has ours. Fellow-travelers, and those of them who are becoming our allies, should understand that we cannot consider as allies those who cannot be inspired by the fight and work which the Communist party leads—because, in just what would our union consist? The whole purpose of our activity and our work lies in the fight for the building of socialism, in its construction.[70]

These words, spoken before top-ranking members of the very same Party which had passed a resolution advocating a "tactful and guarded" attitude towards the fellow-travelers, "one calculated to hasten their approach to Communist ideology," [71] showed the *pyatiletka* attitude as contrasted with that of the NEP. Kirshon went on to say that the fellow-travelers

should understand that, if they want their work to play any kind of a role in our great construction and not be merely unfruitful, but in some degree inspire and teach the Soviet reader, they must break more decisively with old traditions, caste aloofness, intelligentsia individualism. They must throw themselves into the thick of the building program; they must go to the village and to the construction, abandon their urban studios and houses of literature so as to get material for creative work with, and amidst, the proletariat, so as to unteach themselves.[72]

Leonov's *Sot* and Shaginyan's *Hydrocentral*, which present the problems of socialist construction, were mentioned as the only exceptions to the fact that "a reflection of the present day is not found in the works of the fellow-travelers." [73]

But proletarian literature also inadmissibly lagged behind, although for different reasons than those which caused the fellow-travelers to lag, and the reconstruction period had not yet found an adequate reflection in the works of Communist authors, according to Kirshon:

Heroic workdays inspire us; like the proletariat, we are carried away . . . with enthusiasm for great building. But we have not yet the power to reflect this adequately in our creative work. We write, but we feel that actual events are much more interesting than those about which we write. We feel how the heroes of our productions pale beside the authentic heroes of labor. Reality surpasses our creative imagination. We promise to do our utmost to reflect in our work our class's offensive and to support it. However, comrades, we have . . . significant inadequacies.[74]

Some of these inadequacies are, he asserted: an insufficiently high level of Marxist world-view; the fact that proletarian writers do not yet really know how to apply the dialectical method to literature; and the fact that they have not yet been able to carry far enough the bolshevization of their ranks, still have not enrolled more workers in every level of their organizations. All these obstacles and difficulties "prevent our work from developing in the right way." [75]

Averbakh, too, complained about this lag of literature behind the general development of industry at a time when the Soviet

Union, which "has entered an epoch of constructive socialism according to a definite plan . . . is advancing at a furious rate."[76] Literary works ought to reflect "the fundamental themes of contemporary reality": Party life; the struggle for the general Party line; the creation of a new industrial base, established on the level of contemporary world techniques; the class war in the villages; the liquidation of the kulaks on the basis of all-out collectivization; new forms of workmen's activity such as socialist competition, shock work, and the industrial and financial counter-plan; the efforts of the Red Army chiefs; etc.[77]

"A cautious writer," reported Slonimski, "does not set to work until after having talked with the 'comrades' of the 'Gosizdatelstvo' (State Publishing House) who, if he is in their good graces, advise him on the choice of the subject for his novel, while tipping him off on the latest political word of the season."[78]

Literature must go forward at a faster rate so as to keep pace with socialist construction. Mindful of this, Averbakh advised writers not to spend too much time in preparing a book or in mulling over and improving its style. He implied that Tolstoys were not wanted during the First Five-Year Plan, that speed was what was needed —journalism instead of long drawn-out works.[79] Libedinski, however, did not quite agree and felt that the problem was one, not only of tempo, but also of quality. "We set proletarian literature on a false path when we demand that every man begin at once to describe *kolkhozes* and plants without requiring that it be done profoundly, when we stress that the people in these descriptions be, not 'live,' but standardized 'speaking trumpets of the spirit of the times.' "[80]

"Why all the shouting?" asked the level-headed Gorky. "Nobody can seriously bewail the fact that literature is lagging behind reality. It has always followed in the wake of life, it has always 'recorded facts,' generalized about them, given them synthesis. No one ever demanded of a writer that he be a prophet and foretell the future!"[81]

What Gorky did demand of a proletarian writer was "active hatred for everything which oppresses the human being and prevents the free development and growth of his abilities; and pitiless hate for parasites, commonplace people, boasters, and in general for good-for-nothings of all forms and sorts." [82] It is interesting to compare this with Averbakh's statement: "The artist-Marxist, standing on the foundation of a materialistic understanding of the world, not only in politics, but also in creative work—such should be the prolet-writer." [83] Also with Libedinski's intolerant admission: "The fact is, that the proletarian writer who does not feel the true relationship of classes in our country is not worth anything." [84]

All in all, there was probably a good deal of truth in the following humorous description of a RAPP censor's demands:

A Soviet author should jump out [of] bed at the whistle of the factory siren, go through ten minutes of setting-up exercise in "Stalinism," take a rub-down with Spirit of Lenin, breakfast on Marx and Engels, then go to the Institute of Statistics for the latest figures on the success of the Five-Year Plan, memorize the decisions of the recent Central Committee plenum and, inspired by Soviet needs and revolutionary hopes, work for six hours each day at his proletarian novel. Dreams? Sub-conscious mental life? Your material, your inspiration, the censorious Bolshevik would say, must come from observations in the new peasant collectives, in the industrial giants now rising throughout the U.S.S.R., in the struggle of the working class for a better world.[85]

3. DEMANDS MADE OF THE "SKETCHERS"

Final Objectives

MARX AND ENGELS claimed that "the exclusive concentration of artistic talent in a few individuals and its consequent suppression in the large masses is the result of the division of labor" and that "in a communist organization of society there are no painters; at most there are people who, among other things, also paint." [1]

During the First Five-Year Plan an effort was made to do away with the professional author, the observer of life, and to create a worker who, among other things, also wrote: "a type of author-fighter, who can take part simultaneously in production at his bench and in literary struggles, fighting pen in hand." [2] This was to be accomplished by a leveling process. On the one hand, the intellectual middle-class author must become a part of his public and participate actively in the social life of the masses so as to avoid being "cut off from life." He could not remain in a separate caste but must become a genuine member of the proletariat in order to act as its mouthpiece. "Only that author is truthful who really lives the life of his epoch in all its intensity, in all its range." [3] The ivory tower was to be converted into a machine shop. On the other hand, thousands of shock workers (*udarniks*) were "called into literature"; plain workmen from the factories were "mobilized" to write fiction and poetry.

This two-way leveling on the literary front also aimed at abolishing, in true Marxian fashion, the differences between intellectual and physical labor. At the same time, the dividing line between novelist and journalist was to be swept away, the hybrid result being the sketch-writer, or "sketcher," who was to be the publicist

DEMANDS MADE OF THE "SKETCHERS"

and propagandist of the Plan. In the words of the Communist essayist, Boris Kushner: "The proletarian writer does not work out the principles of his world-outlook in the process of writing his book. [The Party solves all complex problems.] He lives in the midst of his class; he works in the ranks of his Party; he participates in socialist construction." [4]

Averbakh told a plenary session of VOAPP that a type of writer must be formed who would be professional in the sense that Lenin spoke of professional Bolshevist revolutionaries. To this end, every proletarian writer must, first of all, become really acquainted with the practice of Soviet construction work and class war.[5] As examples of such proletarian authors Zelinski named Vladimir Stavski, author of books about the *kolkhozes* in the Kuban (*Station* and *The Run*), who began by writing notes for a newspaper; Panfyorov, former president of a village soviet; and Chumandrin, a worker who became an author and the leader of LAPP.[6]

In his speech at the Sixteenth Party Congress, Kirshon said:

Comrades, we proletarian writers not only wrote. We considered, and consider, that, in order to write, we ought to participate directly in practical work. We carried out a series of tasks assigned by the Party, following the instructions of our Party press. We fought with the class enemy, not only using our work as a weapon, but also face to face. This year [1930] it happened that we lost two leaders of our local associations, killed in the country by kulaks. We never lock ourselves up in our studies and are not going to do so; we want to be direct participants in socialist construction; we want our creative work to be a weapon in the hands of the Party against our enemies.[7]

Another objective of the Five-Year Plan for Art was collective literary work; proletarian literature was to result from the class activity of the masses. In the *History of the Construction of the White Sea–Baltic Canal*, itself an example of collective writing, we find this statement: "The support of the collective—oneness with the collective—without these, any work is extremely difficult in the Soviet Union." [8]

Professional Writers → Observers → Workers

CONTACT WITH THE MASSES

Mayakovsky felt that inspiration comes from contacts with the rest of the community and a knowledge of its needs, not out of the individual mind, and that the writer who has become one of the people will be best able to hear the social command. In 1918 he upbraided his "Brother Writers" for their lack of contact with life and asked what they could possibly have to write about. "If such as you are the creators, then I spit upon all art," he declared and reminded them that François Villon, "when he finished writing, did his job of plundering," while they "quake at the sight of a penknife." [9]

A similar sentiment was expressed by Marietta Shaginyan when she wrote that "if the artist were not a live and active member of his society, if he did not participate in the work of his society, he would have nothing to write about." [10] She found that when you are tired and worn out, Narzan baths [11] will not cure you, but there are some which will: "He only knows of them who has experienced their marvelous effect upon himself. These baths are the breath of the masses when they are all assembled in just such a hall before the Red table of the presidium." She concluded with the assertion that there is no tenderness stronger or sweeter than that which one experiences when coming in contact with the masses.[12]

Fyodor V. Gladkov, author of the "first modern proletarian novel written on a grand scale" (*Cement*),[13] summed up what the Soviet writer who was "in touch with reality" should be like:

It is not the lookers-on, the "independent," "free" writers who spend their day in passive contemplation, who create our best works: it is the writers who take an active part in various fields of socialist construction. The work will be valuable, deep, and rich in content only when the author can completely embrace one or the other side of life, one or the other side of creation; when he himself is actually fighting for different achievements; when he himself lives the life, in small things and in large, of the industry, the *kolkhoz*, and participates in their customs and culture; when he rejoices and fights together with the masses. In other words, the Soviet writer must be inseparable from the great collective body of our country, he must be a fighter in one of the shock brigades of the workers, he must possess a clear Communist ideology (without the latter he cannot comprehend the epoch). He must always be active in everyday work, in the whirlwind of events; he is never a witness, but one of those who is taking part in the fight. He cannot be an artist who participates actively and organically in the construction of the new world unless he watches the life of the Communist Party and studies its resolutions, which are historical documents giving a general direction to the development and struggle of our epoch, as well as the only true picture of the times. He must carry out these decisions. Only under these conditions will he be an objective artist.[14]

Readings and Talks to Circles. It has been said that the factory and the village reading room are the literary salons of Soviet Russia. The literary circles in factories, mills, *kolkhozes, sovkhozes,* and machine and tractor stations (M.T.S.) organized readings of artistic works, both those of qualified writers and those of their own members; and Communist and Komsomol authors could fulfill their Party obligation of civic activity by giving lectures and recitations to these circles.[15] As has already been mentioned, Mayakovsky went "like a troubadour of old . . . from town to town and village to village; from factory to ship, from meeting to theatre; from a tiny Soviet Council to the All-Union Central Committee." [16] Everywhere he declaimed his poems directly to his audience. One of these audiences, made up of peasants who had gathered at Livadia Palace, he described in "Miracles" and said that "they all knew where to laugh, where to ponder." Then he asked:

> Where else
>   are palaces
>   fit to be
> halls
>   where peasants hear
>   poetry? [17]

Outstanding writers such as Fadeyev, Panfyorov, Leonov, and Aseyev participated regularly in sessions of literary circles at which they told of their creative experiences; how they chose their subjects; collected their material; worked out plots, composition, language, etc. They also often looked over and appraised the work of the members while the latter, in turn, criticized whatever the novelist, playwright, or poet had read them from his own writings. It was a case of give and take, the audience learning from the writer and the writer, from his audience.[18]

There were probably very few Soviet authors who had not, at one time or another, subjected their work to the mass criticism of a literary circle. On the basis of their own experience, these worker-critics made suggestions about, for instance, the faulty technical construction of an engine, the premature sowing of winter corn, etc. in the story read to them. When Libedinski finished a novel on the life of a factory in which he had been staying, he read it to the workers and asked for their criticism. They did not like it. As the hero of the book was in the audience, he was called upon to get up and tell his story, himself. He did so, and the factory hands preferred his account to Libedinski's. They thought it more moving and convincing. Libedinski's ideology satisfied them, they said, but his art could be improved on.[19]

Tretyakov fared better when he read parts of his *kolkhoz* novel to the members of the collective where the scene was laid and who appeared by name as characters in the book. A public meeting adopted a resolution praising the work, and 181 of the *kolkhozniks* bought copies.[20]

Selvinski received a mixture of praise and criticism when, nine months after his arrival at the Electrofactory (Moscow Electric Works), having finished a rough draft of his poem, "The Electrofactory Newspaper," he read it at a meeting of the active factory workers. They passed the following resolution:

(1) The poem gives a politically true description of the life and customs of the Electrofactory and effectively agitates for the fight for socialist construction, for the Five-Year Plan, for the general line of the Party.

(2) Technically the poem represents a new and extremely daring form—the newspaper in verse—which gave the possibility to discover new kinds of poetry: the leading article, the essay on industry, telegrams, stenograms, resolutions, and up to [even] advertisements.

(3) We must particularly note that the material of the poem is to a great extent the result of Comrade Selvinsky's practical work at the factory: for instance, the section "Wastrel [waste] is the Five-Year Plan's enemy" is built up on those slogans and epigrams which are still

hanging in the departments and testify of Selvinsky's participation in the campaign for the struggle against wastrel [waste].

(4) Owing to its political actuality, its high artistic value, and its sharp innovations, the poem is a precious contribution to the proletarian literature, a new achievement of the poetry of the U.S.S.R., and a big step forward in the reformation of Comrade Selvinsky's own work.

(5) Considering the serious value of the poem, which has grown out of the factory and is dedicated to the factory, the Factory Committee is begged to take over the official patronage [21] of the poet and to confer on him the calling of an honorable shock worker of the Electrofactory.

(6) In summing up, we once more emphasize the very important agitational significance of the poem and note with regard to further prospects of Comrade Selvinsky's work that a whole series of the factory's problems—in particular the rebuilding of human material—has not been put by him and, if it had been put, could not have been solved by means of the witty but schematic form of a newspaper.

We expect of Comrade Selvinsky new accomplishments in other, more deepened kinds of work devoted to the analysis of the new mankind—the Bolshevist worker, the Komsomol shock worker, the active working woman.

President of the meeting LEBEDEVA
Secretary KOTOMIN [22]

This resolution gives a good idea of what the proletariat especially required of its literature: that it give a "politically true" documentary picture of the factory "drawn from life," that it agitate effectively for the fulfillment of the Plan, and also that it show the emergence of the new man.

Observation Trips and Visits. So as not to be guilty of losing contact with the masses and in compliance with RAPP's social command, writers left their studios and began to "study life." They visited new construction sites such as Dnieprostroi and Magnitostroi to collect material for their stories, poems, and especially sketches; they participated in the literary and social life of factories and *kolkhozes*; they even traveled to the remotest corners of the U.S.S.R. and went on scientific expeditions to see backward peoples and unexplored territory, and then wrote books about it all.[23]

In Leonov's novel, Skutarevsky's artist brother, who had lost his talent as a result of his "alliance with a dead class," [24] decides that he must go away and "get in touch with the real roots of all those things out of which the life of the future is being made."[25] He therefore leaves for a power station in Siberia where, by agreement, he is to paint "midday, construction, barricades, a procession, spring —in other words, all those epic words with which a class begins its history."[26]

Similarly, Yossif Arnoldov, the artist in Panfyorov's *Bruski*, decides that "art must go to the people, and the people's talents must come to art. . . . To write about our days, it is necessary to feel life with your own hands."[27] Consequently, he sets off for the metallurgical and tractor works, and then proceeds to the collective farm, "Bruski."

During 1929 and 1930 many critics spoke of the fact that most Soviet writers, both proletarian and non-proletarian, were town dwellers and were therefore unable to handle village themes and that, as a result, the important changes going on in the countryside had so far found little or no reflection in fiction. *Sot* (Leonov), *Bruski* (Panfyorov), and Sholokhov's *Quiet Don* were mentioned as almost the only exceptions to this remark.[28] Libedinski bewailed the fact that young authors did not show the leading role of the working class in relation to the peasantry but, when they did write about the country, usually produced "paisage" or "kulak" works.[29] Tretyakov said, "The writer of today's connection with the country is limited to the ten-kopek roll which he buys himself for breakfast."[30]

Soon, however, literary men began working energetically to eliminate their ignorance of the country, and "in some manner or other the writers' fraternity was disentangled from their desks and from the maze of established routine and enticed out to the collective farms" where they found themselves in the midst of the social struggle.[31] "Over their [the collectivized peasants'] socialized bailiwicks," remarks Ostap Bender, "now wander multitudes of literary and musical brigades that are collecting materials for agrarian poems and truck gardening cantatas."[32]

Brigades of writers were often sent out with explicit social and political, as well as literary, tasks to perform. The First Brigade (consisting of V. Kazin, V. Lugovskoi, K. Minayev, and S. Groman) came back to Moscow in the fall of 1929, having carried out the mission assigned to it by the All-Russian Central Council of Trade Unions, according to an agreement with the Central Committee of Metalworkers. During the three and a half months of its tour, the brigade conducted sixty-five literary evenings and visited about forty enterprises; in Rostov and in Taganrog it took part in "Five-Year Plan evenings." The brigade, on its return, gave the Central Committee of Metalworkers an exact report of work performed, which was approved; and RAPP was requested to send out another group of writers to the metalworkers' districts during the fall and winter season.[33]

The best-known brigade trip appears to have been the one which Leonov, Vsevolod Ivanov, Tikhonov, Lugovskoi, Pavlenko, and Sannikov made in 1930 to Bashkiria, Uzbekistan, and Turkmenistan to see the rapid industrialization and cultural progress of these vast undeveloped stretches. The visit is said to have resulted in "the organizational consolidation of the national literary forces" and in the springing up from among the poor peasants of the remotest Tadjik villages of "national writers who portray the new life and progress of the people under Soviet culture." [34]

As a result of this journey, Lugovskoi wrote two volumes of poems entitled *To the Bolsheviks of the Desert* and *Spring*, and Pavlenko gave his impressions in a novel, *The Desert*, and in a collection of sketches, *A Journey to Turkmenistan*.[35] One of the latter, "Notes on Spring," describes how the writers' "bony Ford" stopped at the political headquarters of a sowing campaign which was being run by a dull-witted, verse-writing, Communist bookkeeper, mobilized to carry it out. A heavy fog closed in, the tractors lost each other, and "on several occasions we [the visiting authors] fell into ditches, became mired in irrigated plots, ran into trees and walls of houses." [36] The brigade's sightseeing was evidently not always a pleasure!

The following year Pilnyak also went to Tadjikistan, apparently non-collectively, "to observe a national minority passing from feudalism to socialism." [37] Selvinski, meanwhile, had gone all the way to Kamchatka and returned with this recommendation:

So that the working class of Kamchatka
Will not be the "Kamchatkist" of the working class—
*Open lyric workshops
Whose pathos is locked up!*
Such is my poetic report
To the secretariat of the Central Committee.[38]

Polonski paid a visit to the "Magnitogorsk metallurgical giant" near iron-rich Magnet Mountain, with Gladkov, Malyshkin, and the artist Svarog. The brigade toured the construction site of the coke-chemical plant on several days and reported that "the building grew literally by the clock." [39] Polonski afterwards set himself the task of giving a general picture of the huge enterprise in his sketch, *Magnitostroi*.[40]

In 1929 the ice-breaker "Sedov" left on an arctic expedition, led by Professor Otto Yu. Schmidt, to confirm the Soviet Union's possession of the Franz Joseph Archipelago and to collect scientific material. On board was I. Exler, a journalist representing TASS (Telegraph Agency of the Soviet Union), who described his adventure in a book called *At the Edge of the World*.[41] The following summer, when the "Sedov" went back to rescue the old and leave a new party of colonists, she had in her company the reporter Boris Gromov, special correspondent to *Izvestiya*, and the writer Sokolov-Mikitov, who was to record the details of the expedition in diary and notes.[42]

The superficial results of all these literary peregrinations were criticized, as follows, by Boris Kushner in an article which appeared in *Pravda* on October 4, 1930:

The opportunity to see, to make observations, to study, and to collect material is given to our writers, especially the proletarian ones, with such lavishness that at times it becomes almost wasteful. Unmindful of the distance and sparing no expense, just where do we not send them? —to old and new enterprises, to construction works, to *kolkhozes* and *sovkhozes*, on far-off cruises, on polar expeditions, on record-breaking flights. And one must do our writers justice—they go willingly. Our writers as a whole, however, are entirely inadequately prepared to understand and to master what they ought to see on these trips. With only a few exceptions, writers are not acquainted either with industry or with economics, and the level of their theoretical preparation and practical experience far from qualifies them for the tasks to which they are committed. In an overwhelming majority of cases, therefore, the application of their experiences to literature is either entirely absent or is extremely unsatisfactory.[43]

This lack of technical training and consequent reluctance and inability to cope with what the critics demanded is humorously shown by Ehrenburg in his novel about the Kuznetsk construction, *The Second Day*:

The author Gribin had to write a new novel. The critics harried him. They declared that Gribin eschewed contemporary themes. Gribin got from a magazine editor an advance on a novel about a construction works and reserved a sleeper in an International car. He now stood outside the administration office. . . . He thought of his wife, of his study with a picture of Pushkin on the wall, of his snug home now so far away, and he was depressed. But work had to be done. He drew a notebook from his pocket and wrote down, "A large structure. Called 'Cowpers.' Gives an impression of striking grandeur. To put in the chapter where a shock worker falls in love." [44]

Georgi Vasilyevich, the famous novelist in *Time, Forward!*, is another technical ignoramus who wanders about a construction site (Magnitostroi) taking notes. He admits to the TASS correspondent: "In a way, I'm thinking things over and observing, but, generally speaking, I'm not busy. . . . You know, to tell you the truth, I'm absolutely lost here. The newspaper expects a sketch from me, and literally I don't know where and how to begin." [45]

Failure to comprehend what has been seen is again shown in the case of Yuzov, the newspaper editor of Ilyenkov's novel, *Driving Axle*. After he has written an article ("The Steel Heart"), the plant manager says to him: "Listen here, Yuzov, you've got it wrong. Samples of casts are not taken from ingots. . . . Can you tell me what you saw: an axle or an ingot, or was it a cow? Oh, you writers . . . !" [46]

Mayakovsky's opinion of writers' observation trips to factories is further proof that these visitors probably drove the management almost crazy:

It's often said that an author must go and study production. But it does not mean that some fellow . . . having bought a sixpenny note-book, goes to the factory, gets into everybody's way, gets into a mess amongst machinery and then writes all sorts of rubbish in the newspapers. Then the factory organizations start swearing about misinformed writing of factory life. I believe that you have got actually to work in production, but if that is not possible at least to take part in all the everyday occurrences of the working class.[47]

Participation as Member of an Enterprise. The theory became current that a writer should participate directly in the practical work of building socialism; that he could not, as a mere onlooker, gain the knowledge necessary for the solution in literary form of the problems of industrialization, collectivization, and the creation of the new life.[48] Even Gorky agreed that

we remain obstinately behind and very little and very badly do we study real life with its phenomena which are so rich in meaning. Certain writers go to visit the awe-inspiring constructions of which our young Soviet power is justly proud. Naturally, this is a very good thing because these visits put us in touch with reality and help us to show it to our readers just as it is, without exaggeration or fantasy. But this is not all. It is not enough to learn the results of work—one must also examine this work's method of operation, its springs and its wheels, since only in this way can we keep constantly up to date.

One must participate in these multiple processes, study them closely and attentively, even lovingly. If we do not do so, we shall write nothing, that is, nothing that reproduces reality by means of a vigorous art such as compels recognition and which our epoch deserves.[49]

This personal participation is seen in the report of a member of an authors' brigade which worked at a paper mill. He and his fellow-writers unloaded timber, taking part in *subbotniks*,[50] loaded paper rolls onto trucks, and went to Petrozavodsk to report to the Karelian government about the breakdown of machinery. At the factory "we exchanged our pen for the painter's brush and wrote on cardboard with soot slogans, composed by our brigade's poet for the shock-workers' conference."[51] They also joined in production conferences, etc., and did literary work such as organizing wall newspapers, literary circles, and literary evenings.

In *Time, Forward!* the famous novelist, the TASS correspondent, and the poet Slobodkin are all put to work during the cement-pouring crisis. The first two tend the sand and rock carriers while

Slobodkin first gets a train for the additional cement by swearing and arguing at "that viper in the dispatching department" [52] and then is given the job of setting up and printing Komsomol membership application blanks.

Vladimir Lidin wrote a book called *Spawning Time* in which he gave an account of his work at the Volga Delta "for the purpose of becoming acquainted with the methods of fishing of that region at the time of the spring spawning of the fish," [53] but it is hard to make out just how deeply involved in the fish business he became or to what extent he "personally participated."

Leonid Leonov and Marietta Shaginyan both gathered material for their novels (*Sot* and *Hydrocentral*) by spending time in factories. However, in Leonov's case, it was felt that by his year's sojourn he did not really come to know the worker, that to him the factory was only a temporary stopping place, and that he always remained "a tourist to the proletariat." [54]

Shaginyan,[55] on the other hand, for four years lived with the workers in their barracks on the river Dzoraget in Armenia, working herself as an ordinary laborer in the construction of the hydroelectric power station so as to "comprehend the human motives underlying superhuman achievements." [56] She proved her ability to "modernize genuinely" [57] and produced an industrial novel which Mirsky called "a thoughtful and searching study of the main motives of the Socialist worker and engineer, and of the spirit of collective work." [58] According to Zelinski, "her small figure, dressed in a leather jacket, wearing a big cap pulled down over her eye-glasses, modestly popping up at construction jobs" had been noticed by the proletariat, which appreciated in her the honest, conscientious work of a sincere artist.[59]

There were three well-known literary Communists who could be said to have matched three types of mass writers: Selvinski corresponded to the *rabkor*, Tretyakov to the *selkor*, and Vishnevski to the *voenkor*; their respective places of work were the factory, the *kolkhoz*, and the Red Army and Fleet.

At the beginning of the second year of the Five-Year Plan, when his works were having their greatest success, Ilya Selvinski [60] felt himself on the wane. He had said all that he had to say and could only repeat himself—that is, he had reached the limit in the expression of his "intellectual's impenitence, groundlessness, solitude, and individualism." [61] He therefore left his writing and plunged into "the tremendous storm of life on board one of the best ships of the revolution—the Electrofactory." His aim in so doing was "to enter into the thick of the factory proletariat, to catch its revolutionary enthusiasm, its Bolshevist shock nature, to become its poet." His first impression of the factory was stupendous—it consisted of several independent factories and fifty-two departments, each worthy of study. The poet finally chose the transformer department, which he entered as a welder. In this position he was able to see all types of workers: "workers who endeavored not to swear in order to resemble the intellectuals in this respect, and intellectuals who swore in order to be like the workers"; welders who, after work, put on fresh shirts, ties, and even gloves, and went to a literary circle or to an evening workers' university, looking through geometrical propositions on the streetcar; people who came to the factory on their free days to roam about and gossip but who, in the end, could not resist putting on their working clothes and helping their comrades; stokers who took part in the debate following a report on the outcome of a philosophic discussion; and old women "who actually wept when a wooden elephant, the symbol of shameful sluggishness in work, was hung in their department." [62]

Selvinski's social work at the factory was rather varied. He was the artistic director of a circle, worked in the factory press, made speeches in the Red corners during the lunch hour, was an active member of the Party cabinet, and also composed slogans in verse about the struggle for quality production. Those written during his first six months at the factory were judged in the factory newspaper to be weak and ineffective, but his later ones were approved. His journalistic poem, "The Electrofactory Newspaper," has already been discussed.

Selvinski joined the ranks of the shock workers of the Electrofactory in order to reflect in his work "our struggle for the speed," stated the factory newspaper.[63] At the works "I palpably felt, for the first time, the growth of socialism," he said. "Here I found that practical fulcrum resting upon which I began to see the world from a new point of view," that of bolshevism.[64]

Before 1928 Sergei Tretyakov, as an "honorable observer," merely "narrated" what the country was doing; from that time on, he became "the man who kept the logbook of the Five-Year Plan." [65] After his first trip to a *kolkhoz* two things became very clear to him: that no matter how much of a trained observer or how talented a writer may be, he is bound to be superficial if he does not make a thorough study of a question before writing about it; and that one must be deeply concerned with a subject before venturing to write on it.[66]

Acting on these principles, Tretyakov began in 1928 to study thoroughly and from the inside all the phases of life on the *kolkhoz* "Lighthouse" (in the Tersk District) instead of jumping around from one farm to another. As a jobholder he studied any subject relating to the work of collective building, from scientific agriculture to bookkeeping, and also read everything that he could find about it in papers and magazines. When a combine was established in 1930, uniting fifteen smaller *kolkhozes* (including the "Lighthouse"), he was elected a member of the combine's council and put in charge of all the cultural work. Tretyakov has given this detailed description of how he kept busy:

My work was varied. I took part in the meetings of the management where we discussed every conceivable question concerning the life of the farms. . . . I organized mass meetings of the members of the farms, collected money to be used as the first installment for the purchase of tractors and seed grain. I made reports to the members of the farms about the progress of the combine, argued peasants into joining the farms, and even reconciled quarrelling mothers in the day nursery. I spoke at all of the meetings when we purged the farms of kulaks and anti-collective elements. I was a member of the inspecting commission which reviewed the various clubs and libraries, and made a census of all the children in order to organize the day nurseries. I was chosen to act as guide for the visiting delegations and excursions. I organized the wall newspapers and tried to work out a clear, intelligible account of socialist competition on the steppes.

We worked out a plan for establishing cultural-educational organizations by means of permanent and traveling clubs, and I purchased a portable radio and a good library in Moscow and a moving-picture projector in Georgievsk. I even organized an exhibition of wall newspapers. And all of this time I wrote regularly for *Pravda*, *Socialist Agriculture*, and other magazines about our experiences and difficulties in organizing socialist agriculture. We even had our own regular newspaper—the *Challenge*, which put out some 51 issues under my editorship.

In addition to the articles, official reports, sketches, and other written material, I also tried to keep a complete photographic record of this epoch-making transformation of the countryside. So far, I have secured nearly two thousand negatives recording all phases of this historic event. We even secured the services of a group of motion-picture photographers sent by the International Workers' Film Company.[67]

All of this activity, Tretyakov declared, proved to be absolutely invaluable and furnished him with an abundance of themes. Whereas he began his reports of the work of the collective with superficial and inadequate sketches, they gradually changed into dynamic expressions of the life of which he was a part. "A writer making operative sketches [those with 'direct practical efficacy'] takes the place of the one who made informative sketches." [68]

In 1934 he was still working with the same group of North Caucasian *kolkhozes*, from time to time publishing books which were, for the most part, collections of articles and sketches that had previously appeared in newspapers. One of these, *The Challenge*, describes how an author becomes a *kolkhoznik* and is written, "as usual, in a somewhat dry but extremely clear style." [69] Another book of sketches called *A Month in the Village* and the plays, *The Communist Lighthouse* and *We Will Feed the Globe*, all deal with the organization of collective farms and the class struggle in the country.

The sailor-author Vsevolod Vishnevski had no literary training but had spent many years serving in the ranks (navy, infantry of the Guards, Budyonny's cavalry, and underground revolutionary work), which gave him a huge stock of personal war memories and an excellent knowledge of the military milieu. Although he became known as a successful playwright, he remained a "non-professional" and even liked to emphasize the fact that he carried out his literary work, like any other battle order, at the command of his military chiefs or of a public organization. Vishnevski wrote with a clear political purpose, and his writing was only a new link in his military service work.[70] His novel, Sailors, and his plays, *The First Cavalry Army* and *The Last Decisive*, are all concerned with warlike themes. The latter drama, especially, the title of which was suggested by the line in the "Internationale" about "the last decisive struggle," was very popular, running for several seasons at the Meyerhold Theatre. At this period Russia feared and expected an attack (by France or England up to 1931; by Japan after 1931). *The Last Decisive* served to rouse a martial spirit in its audience, which is left to carry on the fight when the last surviving sailor asks, "Who will defend the Soviet Union? . . . The performance is finished. The continuation —on the front." [71]

SOCIALIST COMPETITION

Early in 1929 "socialist competition" was organized among the factories and works of the U.S.S.R. to replace private ownership and personal gain as an incentive to increased production.[72] RAPP was not slow in transferring this method of economic stimulation from the industrial to the literary front, and soon writers found themselves "challenged" in newspapers to turn out poems and sketches on definite industrial or agricultural topics. Great social pressure was exerted on the author so challenged to comply. Groups of writers also swore public oaths to fulfill certain "shock tasks" within a specified time, as a part of the literary Plan.

The best successes of socialist competition were obtained in the realms of the theatre and the drama because these are communal arts. Theatres challenged each other to improve and increase their repertoires and competed in sending out groups of actors to give performances at construction sites and *kolkhozes*. This led to an increased demand for topical new plays, which stimulated the dramatists.

As part of their cultural work, authors were urged to learn the languages of the national minorities and to undertake the task of translating the works of the national writers into Russian, and the Russian classics into the minority languages. This was a pet project of Gorky's which was more widely taken up after 1932, but a start was made under RAPP's dictatorship. Translations of the Georgian poets by Pasternak and Tikhonov were published in 1934.

Workers → Rabkors → *Literary* Udarniks

WORKER AND PEASANT CORRESPONDENTS

At the same time that the professional writer was being driven down from his isolation and made to mingle with the masses, the worker in industry and on the farm was being raised up by the cultural revolution and urged to express himself in print. In May, 1924, the conference held by the Press Department of the Central Committee had declared:

The basic work of the Party in the field of literature should be concentrated on the creative work of the workers and peasants, who are becoming worker and peasant writers in the process of the cultural development of the wide masses of the Union of Socialist Soviet Republics. Worker and peasant correspondents constitute a new social force which participates actively in the political and economic structure of the Soviet State and is organically bound up with the masses of workers and peasants. The worker and peasant correspondents should be regarded as future journalists and as a reserve from which will arise new worker and peasant writers.[73]

During the First Five-Year Plan, mass participation in newspaper work by *rabkors* (worker correspondents), *selkors* (peasant correspondents), *voenkors* (military correspondents),[74] and *yunkors* (correspondent-members of youth organizations) grew by leaps and bounds until there were two million such journalistic novices in the field at the end of 1931.[75] There were even *foto-rabkors* who went about snapping items of interest or of criticism to send in to their papers. These worker and peasant correspondents became one of the Soviet government's direct links with the masses and have been called the "barometer of daily life"[76] and "pulse-feelers" for the Party.[77] They are considered part of the mechanism by which the people "control the life of the country, act as a check on bureaucracy, and voice their complaints, needs, achievements and aspirations."[78]

DEMANDS MADE OF THE "SKETCHERS"

Rabkors were elected from the ranks by "the builders of socialism themselves" [79] and were usually the best workers, actively participating in social life and in socialist competition. We read in the *History of the Construction of the White Sea–Baltic Canal* that "the camp correspondents who wrote of victories and heroism were the best shock workers and leaders, and the work of a camp correspondent was a responsibility." [80] Three thousand five hundred and seventy registered prisoner correspondents and many more of whom no record was kept wrote to the Belomorstroi newspaper, *Reforging*, which was the organ of the cultural-educational section of this G.P.U. labor camp and whose special work was to broaden the worker's necessarily limited vision by giving him a picture of the entire workings.

The correspondent's position was an influential one as he controlled mass public opinion in his enterprise. He not only acted as the eye of his newspaper, but also carried on propaganda for government drives and slogans and fought with his pen against kulaks and wreckers. In the class struggle a number of *rabkors* were killed as government spies and agents.

Worker and peasant correspondents appear frequently in First Five-Year Plan literature, not always in a very flattering light, although it is more often the editor of the local paper who is depicted as a fool.[81] In *Time, Forward!*, Semechkin, correspondent of the regional newspaper, has the water pipes disconnected in the middle of the drive to beat Kharkov and has to be locked up to keep him out of the way. He is portrayed as a clumsy, clammy-handed figure in "large, impenetrably dark, disapproving goggles" and yellow shoes, wearing "a knitted tie in a large brass tie-holder," a cap with the back cut off and the visor "as long as the beak of a goose," and three badges on his lapel: "the Communist Youth International, the Chemical Aviation Society, and the Sanitary." [82]

Semechkin would appear suddenly, now here, now there—bobbing up everywhere. Along his way, he would approach people, stop beside various machines, peer into excavations, feel the stacked materials with his long fingers. Throughout this inspection trip, he mooed vaguely in his bass voice. He would clasp his hands behind his back, droop his head, and stand thus in profound thought, slapping his brief case against the back of his knees. His knees would jerk in reflex action.

* * *

Semechkin was energetically calculating how to take this world in hand, how to set everything in the world right, how to arrange everything, to organise it, and, by means of the regional newspaper, connect it with the largest sections of public opinion—in a word, to do everything that a clever, exemplary, militant special correspondent should do.[83]

However, "this world would not give in"; and the last time we see Semechkin he is writing a dispatch for the regional and central press, "exposing everything," especially the disgraceful treatment accorded him as a representative of that press. "He . . . wrote and wrote and wrote. He wrote at length. He wrote extensively. He wrote insinuatingly. He wrote without scratching out, with a multitude of parentheses, quotations, and dots," [84] all the while making through his nose thick noises of dissatisfaction.

"SHOCK WORKERS OF THE PEN"

An *udarnik* is a man who has not only learned to work fast, well, and in a disciplined way, but one who also tries and knows how to tell of his experience in the worker's world,[85] wrote Gorky, himself sometimes called the "first *rabkor*" or the "first shock worker" in literature.[86] He felt that "we should make it our business to initiate the literary youth into our experience without delay and to attend first of all to the young literary sprouts which are blossoming out abundantly and spontaneously in all Soviet works and factories," and was especially keen on this task because it was a method of increasing "our active army." [87]

So as to fill the ranks of Soviet literature and make it truly proletarian in spirit and also, perhaps, in the hope of submerging the work of the fellow-travelers under a torrent of *rabkor* texts and of creating a sort of inflation of the established literary values, ten thousand *udarniks* were "conscripted into literature." [88] At the end of September, 1930, a joint decision taken by the secretariats of RAPP and of the All-Russian Central Council of Trade Unions resulted in the formation of literary shock brigades among the workers. By March, 1931, about fifteen hundred "shock authors" were enrolled in Moscow and more than a thousand in Leningrad. Although a similar decision was taken soon afterwards by the Union of Peasant Writers, the drafting of collective farmers for literary work got started much later.[89] "Shock work," said Kushner, "having established a pattern of proletarian activity, mobilizes the forces of the proletariat for the needs of the literary front also. . . . An indispensable and adequate basis for mass literary work following the Party line is being created." [90]

In 1929 *Pravda* had invited several shock brigades of a Kharkov factory to correspond regularly in its columns. This laid the foundation for the gradual transition of *rabkors* from individual to collective newspaper work. By the end of 1931 the majority of newspaper contributions from workers were in the form of big articles written collectively by traveling brigades of *Pravda*, *Izvestiya*, etc. There were only five hundred press *udarniks* in 1930, but twenty thousand in 1931, an increase which made possible the development of new forms of mass work such as the "raids" by *rabkor* brigades (periodic shock investigations of some section of socialist construction).[91]

In the Leningrad rubber factory "Red Triangle," for example, the *rabkor* brigade conducted a campaign to improve the quality of production, drawing the engineers and technical personnel into the drive. They then participated in the organization of communal feeding at the plant, etc., which enriched their experience. After that, the "Red Triangle's" *rabkors* left the limits of their factory and, as an *Izvestiya* special correspondent brigade, traveled all over the country investigating the situation in the rubber industry. During 1930–31 *Pravda* brigades made 1,062 raids in different parts of the U.S.S.R.[92]

At the same time that this collective activity in the press was going on, the *rabkor* movement was being given new tasks. The 1931 decision of the Central Committee of the Communist party on the "Reconstruction of the Worker and Peasant Correspondents' Movement" noted that before socialist competition had brought about an enormous change in the attitude of the masses towards labor, the participation of workers and peasants in literature was limited to their contributions of raw material to newspapers, as members of their local networks. At best they could be factual writers, reporting various achievements or revealing and unmasking "petty defects of the mechanism." Now, said the decision, the *rabkors* and *selkors* are to become "commanding officers of proletarian public opinion," doing their utmost to direct it "to the aid of the Party and the Soviet government in the laborious task of socialist construction." [93] They must not only reveal the defects, but simultaneously illustrate the more outstanding positive sides of the achievement of socialist construction in all its fields of work, entering more deeply into its many important problems. This means, in the first place, making known to the masses the foremost mills, *kolkhozes*, factory shops, and shock brigades. Thus the press "must help to develop to the greatest extent an exchange of experience at the front-line of socialist construction." [94]

The following appeal, issued in the fall of 1931 by the Publishing Office of the Council of Syndicates, was obviously a result of this directive:

To all workers,
Peasant correspondents,
And members of literary circles.

Worker correspondents, peasant correspondents, and worker writers, you should all pass on the experience of your enterprise to those who still lag behind. Tell how your factory, your mine, your station, your *sovkhoz* fulfills and overfulfills the production plans. Show the heroes and the enthusiasm of your enterprise.

Set to work at once; gather together material immediately; study the subject collectively.[95]

The mass Soviet press was regarded as forming the channel along which new forces would pour into literature. The worker and peasant correspondents' movement was the first phase of proletarian literary development from which those who were capable of proceeding from factual reporting to thinking in images, from casual journalism to creative writing, would rise to the next phase—literary art. They would not, however, break with production, but would make their writing an artistic presentation of their experience at the workbench and in the field. This worker-author who, after a hard day at his factory, took up the composition of a technical book, a piece of fiction, or a poem was hailed as the living proof that in the course of socialist construction the boundaries between mental and physical work were being swept away.[96] RAPP's leaders believed that such a writer would be able to give "the correct Marxian illumination to life"; and, "dizzy with the success" of their recruiting program, they launched the slogan: "The *Udarnik* Becomes the Central Figure of the Literary Movement." [97]

The period 1930–31 marked the reign of the shock workers of the pen in literature. The number of books by fellow-travelers decreased; the quality of the proletarian writers' work sank; and a mass of "mobilized" volumes erupted onto the scene. "These books," said Gorky, "are aflame." [98] Polonski described the movement as follows:

Into literature . . . are coming men from the very depths of the working class, from the lathe, from the furrow, from the tractor, the mine, the village collective. Yesterday an unskilled laborer, a metalworker, a glazer, a tailor, a farm hand, a shepherd, even an inn waiter—today, having overcome tremendous obstacles, he acquires the technique of the writing craft (with difficulties, to be sure, and with interruptions), he stubbornly masters the art, and carries his conceptions, his tastes, his habits into a field which only recently was inaccessible to him.[99]

The first books by worker-authors originated as an expression of the exemplary workers' desire to share their experience with others, to help them master the most rational and productive methods of work. Many technical books and pamphlets were written by worker-inventors in order to make their discoveries the common property of the entire mass of workers, technicians, and specialists. Thousands of shock workers wanted to describe factory life and how they were building socialism.

It was asserted that the attributes of an *udarnik* author, which the professional writer usually lacked, were: a genuine understanding of the processes of production, a "sound and sober realism," an ability to see and to show the main tendencies of real life without bogging down in a mass of insignificant details, an organic knowledge of the people and their surroundings, enthusiasm for constructive work, the youthfulness of class, and sincerity and lack of pose.[100] It was felt that these new authors were backed by the collective experience of the masses whose vanguard they were, that their writings were "clinched with hammer blows."[101] It was claimed that all these qualities gave their books a great convincing power not found in the works of most literary men.

New subjects and new proletarian literary genres, such as the factory sketch, industrial tales and poems, etc., resulted. The leitmotif of the shock writers' productions was the freed and joyous labor which had become "a matter of honour, of glory, of valour, and of heroism";[102] and the main themes dealt with were the new socialist relations between individuals and the new psychology which prompted people to solve vital problems in a new way. The titles of these books, alone, give an idea of their contents: By *Force of Example*, *The Brigadier of the Hot Department*, *Meat Factories*, and *In the Fight for Metal*.[103] The author of the last volume, N. Mikhailov, was a paper layer at the "Sickle and Hammer" metalworks. He tells how a brigade became shock workers by engaging in socialist competition with another brigade and by fighting to carry out the industrial and financial counter-plan of the sheet-rolling department. Here is a sample of his style:

Six o'clock sharp. The signal bell rings from the motor. The huge flywheel swayed, shaking the dust from its iron shoulders. The couplings moved with a chime, and the spindles began to sing their song. The sheet-rolling mill moved along, to fight FOR THE METAL, FOR THE FIVE-YEAR PLAN, FOR SOCIALISM.[104]

An *udarnik* at the "AMO" works (called the "First State Automobile Factory") came out with this metaphor, somewhat reminiscent of the Smithy poets: "If we call mining and technical crops the roots and trunk of industry, then metallurgy is its flower, and the automotive industry its steel fruit."[105]

The following excerpts from "Industrial 1931" by Vassili Semyakin, worker in the Moscow Co-operative Candy Factory, give an idea of the new poetry:

> Who will impede
> our whirlwind speed
> of Construction?

Proudly arises,
  'mid victories won,
    the year nineteen-thirty-one
    of Production.

    . . . .

thousands of toilers,
  feeding the boilers,
    an industrial city they build.

Down on the Volga—
  acres unbounded
    of bounteous soil
rendered more fertile
  by machinery and tractors,
    by rational toil.

Dig,
  work on, and never retreat.

    . . . .

Strong and unyielding,
  with unfaltering feet,
we are a-building
  our country of steel and concrete.[106]

It was considered that such works were laying the foundation for a completely new literature, closely tied to socialist construction and growing as the culture of the masses increased. Towards the end of the First Five-Year Plan the toiling authors were gradually passing from small sketches and verses to novels and longer poems, but it was conceded that they were still in process of formation as artists and needed a great deal of training as writers. Their outstanding defects were addiction to standardized forms and inability to handle material.[107] However, although these new authors were admittedly raw material, they needed only polishing, and not "regeneration," as did the old authors belonging to the intelligentsia.

Kirshon, a member of the Moscow committee for summoning the *udarniks* into literature, at a Paris conference in 1931 recognized that proletarian literature was still in an embryonic state. He said that the names of the shock-worker authors would undoubtedly be forgotten because their writings were only the first chronicles upon which a future literature of the proletariat would rise and that, in this sense, the proletarian literature of this period resembled the chronicles of the Middle Ages from which history drew its primary materials.[108]

Sketch-writing

The sketch "arose as a significant phenomenon"[109] during the First Five-Year Plan and was certainly this period's most prevalent and most characteristic literary form. The majority of *rabkors* and *udarniks* did not have sufficient writing experience or technical mastery to attempt more complex types of expression, while the fellow-travelers found social photography easier than the social analysis now demanded of a novel. The literary results of the journeys made by brigades of writers to industrial constructions and collective farms were usually semi-imaginative descriptive sketches written for newspapers and magazines.[110]

Gorky wrote in 1931 that,

the broad flow of sketches is a phenomenon such as has never before existed in our literature. The extremely important work of knowing our country has never and nowhere evolved so fast and in such a successful form as now among us. The sketchers tell the multimillioned reader about everything that his energy is creating over the whole huge expanse of the Soviet Union, at all points where the creative energy of the working class is being applied.[111]

A group of talented sketchers such as Tikhonov, Lapin, Gleb Alekseyev,[112] Pavlenko, and others little by little has given the sketch the form of "high art." They "correctly feel the socio-pedagogical significance of their work and see its aim very distinctly."

Its goal is the depiction of the diverse and general process of the cultural-revolutionary construction, the depiction of the furious work of the masses, the heroism of the groups and units, of the work which is successful in spite of the stubborn and malicious obstacles placed in its path by all kinds of idlers, idiots, self-seekers and saboteurs, passive and active wreckers, and other scoundrels.[113]

Gorky thought it unfortunate that several of the young writers did not understand that "the sketch with us is a great, important work." This was probably because "our criticism does not find time to notice the significance of the sketch." In conclusion, he emphasized the fact that it was necessary to treat the work of the sketchers seriously, to stop considering it as the "lowest form of art," and to help it in every way "to grow and develop to the limits of possible perfection." [114]

One of the sketches to come out of the 1930 trip to the frontiers of Persia and Afghanistan, made by a brigade of well-known writers,[115] is "Cotton" by Sannikov. We learn how the Soviet agronomist Artemiev of Tadjikistan planted twenty seeds of the Egyptian cotton plant in the yard of his house as an experiment; how, although a donkey devoured fifteen of the twenty resulting bushes and there were wreckers on the Cotton Committee and kulak agitation, the remaining five plants opened "a new page in the history of cotton growing in Central Asia, converting it into Soviet Egypt";[116] how the Komsomol's "inimitable, unprecedented feats" increased its membership by 500 per cent within a year; and how the railroad was built at such a rate that the Afghans failed to notice the construction and were flabbergasted when the first train whistle blew. In a nutshell, Sannikov's story tells how "five bushes, saved from the donkey, did their duty." [117]

Kaverin's "The Return of the Kirghiz" is one of his Five-Year Plan sketches which were gathered into a volume called *The Prologue* (1931).[118] It describes the starting of a collective sheep farm for the nomad Kirghiz, with a garage for their camels.[119]

In "The Conquerors" Ivan Katayev relates how Vassili Smetanin, one of the twenty-five thousand industrial workers mobilized by the Central Committee for work in the countryside, arrives in the Kuban in July of 1929 and how he organizes the Cossacks into the "October" *kolkhoz*. The great part played by agricultural machinery in persuading the peasants to organize collectively is graphically shown in the following scene:

The time for voting was at hand . . . when suddenly a rattling was heard—far off but distinct, foreign, a rattling not belonging to the village sounds. . . . The sound grew louder until it became a triumphant thunder, rising up to the sky, and there at the gate, in a cloud of rosy dust, stood a tractor—strange, low-built, humpbacked, gold and green as a lizard, and after it another and yet another, until there were five tractors swinging ponderously into the yard. . . . A vote was taken: for and against the "Giant.". . . The victory was assured. And the hero of the day was the tractor.[120]

Evgeni Gabrilovich is a proletarian journalist who in January, 1930, was sent on a mission from the Bread Center to the *kolkhoz* "Dawn" at Sargar. The title story of *The Year 1930* describes in capsule form the transition of the farm from its poor condition, when it was run by a former telegraphist, "rather at sea where the class and economic policy of the collective movement was concerned," [121] to the successful carrying through of the communal sowing campaign. The principal character is Safatdin Kasimov, an old Tartar peasant who, at the age of forty-nine, decided to learn Russian grammar in spite of his sons' beatings. He becomes an active *kolkhoz* worker and organizer; because of his great ingenuity and energy, he is then elected manager of the farm. When he is finally shot by the reactionary son of a mullah, his death only strengthens the *kolkhozniks* in their resolve to follow the path which he pioneered. The administrative inefficiency and kulak agitation of the early days is contrasted with the final drive to fulfill the sowing plan; and a vivid account is given of the collective enthusiasm with which the other *kolkhozes*, newspapers, agriculturists, political workers, Komsomol groups, and even the factory in Samara help "Dawn's" all-out effort. The author concludes his story with these remarks:

I wished to compress this story. I did not wish to drag it out with politics and people on any pretext. I understand the essence of the great literature of the Five-Year Plan thus: Stop gossiping.

I wished to write this story, the story of a real man—honestly and without gossip.

An enormous labour. I set down phrase on phrase, exactly. . . . I like gossiping.[122]

It was not exclusively collective farms, however, that the sketch-writers depicted; industrial enterprises, too, were recorded. Marietta Shaginyan did a series of sketches of the Soviet Transcaucasus: Armenia, Azerbaidjan, and Georgia, which she hoped would serve as "a first beginning to a tale of a thousand and one constructions through the length and breadth of the Soviet Union." She felt that the story of the Five-Year Plan's best achievements would be a better stimulus to socialist competition than an endless dwelling on the defects.[123] One of the successes took place at the Dzorages in Armenia where an ordinary hydrostation was transformed into "a pioneer experiment in the building of a great roller and a pressure tunnel" [124] and served as a valuable precedent for Dnieprostroi.

Shaginyan's sketches are by no means mere objective journalism. She gives us her own interpretation of beauty:

Industry is destined to follow an original line of construction out of which will arise the highest form of beauty which the world has known —the beauty of expediency. This will be expressed in her depots and elevators, in the giant pipes of her power stations—the pyramids of our era—in her bridges, her underground railways, her workshops and factories.[125]

and also of the First Five-Year Plan's economic goal:

To us the sight of factory chimneys belching smoke is of more value, as a symbol of pulsating economic life, than the glitter of gold. In other words, what we are after is the concrete organization of the national economy, and not profit for its own sake.[126]

Polonski's *Magnitostroi*, too, is much more than a factual report of his visit to a metallurgical giant in the process of construction.[127] First, the importance of the enterprise is shown as being determined by the character of this century, which could well be known as the "metal age." So-called "modern culture" is built on metal, and socialism must therefore tear it from the hand of capitalism. Under the conditions of today's class war, the fight for metal is the fight for life; independence from capitalist countries must be secured. "With the building of the Magnitogorsk and the Kuznetsk plants, we shall overtake, and in the near future will surpass, the largest, most powerful capitalist countries." [128] Success in the fight for metal means success in the fight for bread: without metal there would be virtually no agricultural machine building. Fuel (oil and coal), transportation, and the industrialization of the country demanded by the building of socialism—all depend on it.

An expanding picture is given by Polonski, each construction described being only part of a larger unit of the whole Plan. The city of Magnitogorsk, which "grows out of nothing, as if alive, on the spot where, a year and a half ago, there was only the wind playing with the steppe grass," [129] is shown to be only a minor section of the vast and extremely complex metallurgical enterprise with its auxiliary electric stations and dams. This largest metallurgical plant in the U.S.S.R., in turn, is linked by a twenty-three-hundred-kilometer railroad with the country's biggest coal basin (the Kuzbas) to create one organism with one spirit—a combinat for the exchange of ore and coal.

"At Magnitogorsk, not only the mountain and the steppe are being rebuilt, but also man, himself." [130] Polonski was stunned by the work of the *udarniks* and amazed at the heavy labor performed by girls, and at examples of collective, mass heroism. Here, the right to life was acquired by work; and there was no room for holidays, for vodka, or for a church.[131] The Komsomol was everywhere—"Magnitogorsk was built by young hands." [132] These new methods of work and this proletarian creative enthusiasm could only be created by the Soviet Union, a country building socialism. Magnitogorsk was not only a metallurgical giant, but also a technical school of socialist work, preparing cadres of toilers who, "disciplined and rich in experience, will be able to go on to new construction sites after the building here is finished." [133]

Unlike Shaginyan, Polonski does dwell on the defects of the construction because he believes that the Party and tràde-union organizations must be made to do something about them. He advocates the creation of an organization "to study the experience of our constructions," to systematize it and make it available to others, "so that we shall profit by our mistakes." [134] For instance, the Magnitogorsk dining halls could learn a great deal from those at the Chelyabinsk Tractor construction.

No attempt is made to gloss over the fact that Magnitogorsk's plan was not nearly fulfilled for January, February, March, or April of 1931. Polonski analyzes the factors preventing the raising of the tempos of construction as: (1) fluidity of labor due to (a) bad living conditions and inadequate recreational facilities, (b) poorly organized dining halls (dirty dishes and long lines) and badly prepared food,[135] and (c) unrationally organized and unfairly paid wages; and (2) ignorance in the handling of imported machines, which are not put to full use. The factors retarding the tempos of construction are listed as: (1) systematic slowness and tardiness of other enterprises in filling Magnitostroi's orders; (2) inaccuracy in the filling of these orders; and (3) inefficiency of transportation, which slows up deliveries. Polonski concludes his pamphlet with the idea that there must be collective responsibility for each unit of the Five-Year Plan because all the parts are inextricably bound together. "Magnitogorsk construction, just like every other construction in our country, is the general, collective work of our whole social organization.[136] . . . Magnitogorsk is the whole country's responsibility." [137]

Collective Writing

In industrial work emphasis was placed, not on the deeds of single individuals, but on the "mass exploit" of the shock brigade; an effort was made to transfer the habits of collective work to the production of literature. Not only did all worker-authors read and discuss their manuscripts with fellow-members of the literary circle, but actual collective writing was attempted. A number of collective novels were turned out, but not published; and at the Theatre of the Revolution a group of actors, under the guidance of the dramatist Pogodin, wrote a play on the exposure of pacifist ideas.[138]

At the end of 1930, 257 of the best *udarniks* from 123 industrial enterprises were rewarded for their work in production with a month's cruise around Europe on the Soviet ship "Abkhazia." Many, on their return, rushed into print with impressions of the trip. The most comprehensive account was *The First Cruise*, written collectively by six workers from different factories, but with each individual passage signed by its author.[139]

Tretyakov, peering enthusiastically into the planned future, foresaw

the operation of literary workshops where the functions are divided. . . . That is, the workshop will contain specialists of an extra-literary order, having valuable material at their disposal (voyages, investigations, biographies, adventures, organizational and scientific experiments); alongside them fixators will be at work gathering necessary material, happenings, notes, documents (this work is analogous to newspaper reporting). The mounting of the received materials in this or that sequence, the working up of the language in dependence upon the public for which the book is being written—this is the job of the literary formulators. . . . The testing out of the social political effect —that is the work now carried out in embryonic form by our Gublit [Provincial Department of Literary Affairs] and Glavlit [Central Department of Literary Affairs]. . . . We can't wait forever while the professional writer tosses in his bed and gives birth to something known and useful to him alone. We assume that book production can be planned in advance like the production of textiles or steel.[140]

Although Gorky was one of the principal advocates of collective writing, he did not go quite this far and excluded works of the imagination from the category of mass production. However, he insisted that "writers and critics must find and work out a method of working collectively in the interests of the toiling masses." Gorky was convinced that these proletarian masses and the new, free workers on the land would "speedily come forward to delve into all phases of art" and that "we are about to witness the creation of a new form of collective art." He felt it incumbent upon writers and critics to extend them a helping hand.[141]

The *History of the Civil War* [142] and the *History of Factories and Works*, huge collective literary series based on factual data, which were undertaken in 1931, were inspired by Gorky. "It is not for nothing," wrote Valentin Katayev, "that Gorky constantly repeats: Write the history of factories and plants. Write the history of the Red Army. Create the history of the great Russian proletarian revolution." And Katayev exclaimed: "May not a single trifle, not even the smallest detail of our inimitable, heroic days of the first Five-Year Plan be forgotten!" [143]

The compilation of the *History of Factories and Works* was regarded as one of the most striking manifestations of the cultural revolution because every volume was written on the basis of data gathered from thousands of persons who had been directly involved in the history of the enterprise. The Central Editorial Board, headed by Gorky and directed by Averbakh, consisted of the most prominent men in politics, literature, and science, as well as representatives of the biggest Soviet factories and plants. Local editorial boards were soon formed at more than a hundred large enterprises, which attracted shock writers, *rabkors*, and members of literary circles. In answer to Gorky's appeal,[144] tens of thousands of old and young workers started to write the history of their works, of their lives, of their revolutionary struggle, of their participation in the construction of socialism." [145] Socialist competition was inaugurated for the composition of the best volume on the history of the plant. Entire factories competed, as well as the brigades working on the *History* and the individual workers writing their memoirs.

The task of producing the books of this series served as a training school for "the new generation of worker-intellectuals, the future sociologists, writers, historians." [146] It gave a political education to a new strata of the working class, said Gorky; it developed the revolutionary class-consciousness of the proletariat and mobilized the masses for a further struggle for socialism. Workers' meetings dealing with the history of the factory helped them to assimilate Bolshevik traditions and the revolutionary experience of the old workers. Finally, while putting the vast material into literary form, brigades of young writers learned the methods of work employed by well-known authors.

A resolution of the Central Editorial Board stated that "the gist of the programme must be a comparison and a concrete juxtaposition of the two systems—the capitalist and the socialist." [147] The volumes of the *History of Factories* were intended to be scientific works of art "distinguished for the theoretical profundity of their statement of the technico-scientific problems, factual authenticity, completeness of data, and vividness of presentation." [148] They were to inaugurate a new literary genre: "scientific-artistic historiography." [149]

The diversity in the books of this collection is occasioned by the historic, economic, and technical individuality of the enterprises dealt with. In some, the main attention is centered on life and manners; in others, on the revolutionary movement or technical developments. The first three volumes of the series to appear were the *History of the Izhorsk Plant* (the oldest in the country),[150] *People of the Stalingrad Tractor Plant* (the first factory of the First Five-Year Plan, completed on June 17, 1930), and the *History of the Construction of the White Sea–Baltic Canal* (a laborious undertaking performed by criminals and wreckers re-educated in the process).[151]

People of the Stalingrad Tractor Plant [152] is a collection of autobiographies of the best *udarniks*, technicians, engineers, and inspectors, a number of whom had worked at well-known tractor and agricultural machinery factories in the United States. A collective of thirty-two writers and journalists, grouped around Yakov Ilin and working under the leadership of *Pravda*, organized the material. Work was facilitated by the fact that the main staff of the collective was already familiar with the life of the factory and of its people, having been connected with the plant long before the history was begun.[153]

This book shows how people built the factory and how the factory re-educated the people, for, says Gorky, "a Soviet factory is a school of socialist culture, and not a capitalist slaughterhouse." [154] Through the stories of individuals we see the struggle of the plant as a whole to master complex techniques. Ilin confesses that their greatest error lay in the fact that at the new factory, under new conditions, they continued to work in the old way.[155] The writers do not conceal their shortcomings, but show how these were overcome and "how the meaning of social and state work penetrated into the individualistic consciousness." [156]

The last chapter of *People of the Stalingrad Tractor Plant* is a critical evaluation by the omnipresent Averbakh. He classifies the work as a new type of book "which shows the overcoming of literature's lag behind life" [157] and whose task is to give a really artistic picture of the building of socialism. In his opinion, the book as a whole is better than many of its separate parts.[158] It "transmits the experience of the fight for productive work, for reduction in production costs, for quality of products" [159] and reveals how workers are combined with work tools, how the socialist method of production grows stronger, how new work stimuli are formed, and the paramount advantages of socialist production relations in raising the labor efficiency. The main value of *People of the Stalingrad Tractor Plant*, Averbakh decides, lies in the fact that it answers the question: Just how was a system of work created which demanded the "collision" of the people of a socialist country with American machine tools, the last word in capitalist science and technique? [160] "We did not have a tractor industry. Now we have one," [161] said Stalin. This book tells how it happened.

Ilin not only edited *People of the Stalingrad Tractor Plant*; he also wrote a semi-fictional industrial novel of his own describing his experience at the plant. "In this book I am greedy, hasty, and indiscrete," he writes. "I wanted to put into it everything that I had seen and heard in recent years." [162] He goes on to say that, although *The Great Conveyer* [163] is not free from "lengthy, tedious discourses and long-winded descriptions," he thinks that the reader will find in it "the pulse of our life and a reflection of his interests, thoughts, and deeds." [164]

Like the collective history, Ilin's book tells how the Stalingrad Tractor Plant was put into operation and draws a contrast between socialist and bourgeois industrial methods. It deals with three basic themes: (1) the alteration and reconstruction of the petty bourgeoisie into conscious builders of socialism, (2) the grasping of technique, and (3) the young generation of Bolsheviks.[165] Raw human material from villages and borderlands is shown being made over in the course of the construction and mastering of the plant. *The Great Conveyer* was praised by a group of Ilin's comrades for its intense *partinost* and for being among those works of proletarian literature which "most fully reflect great deeds and show the great people of our epoch." [166]

In the *History of the Construction of the White Sea–Baltic Canal*, people are also shown being reforged by socialist labor, but this time they are political and civil prisoners. This third volume of the *History of Factories and Works* series is a collectively written, collectively illustrated, and collectively printed book about a collectively built canal. Thirty-four authors (including L. Averbakh, E. Gabrilovich, V. Ivanov, Vera Inber, V. Katayev, D. Mirsky, V.

Shklovski, A. Tolstoy, K. Zelinski, and M. Zoshchenko) helped and corrected one another, with the result that just who wrote the various sections could not be indicated. The work of this "first literary *kolkhoz*," presided over by Gorky, was welded into "a single seamless whole." [167] After a trip through the Canal, the writers studied all types of official and private documents relating to its construction and interviewed G.P.U. men, engineers, and prisoners. The method of group composition made it possible to write the history in three months; shock workers printed it in five weeks.

The White Sea Canal, itself, was built during the last year of the First Five-Year Plan in twenty months, through 147 miles of Karelian swamps and forests. Man's struggle to subdue nature with nineteen locks, five dams, and many dykes is vividly described. The brief northern summer, the short cold days and deep snows of winter, quicksand, rock, mud, marshes, floods, rain, and frost—all these obstacles had to be overcome. In addition, almost no metal could be used; lock gates and flood gates had to be of Karelian pine. There was also a shortage of the skilled labor such as the Five-Year Plan enterprises needed. Stalin had therefore proposed that the construction of the Canal be entrusted to the G.P.U., under whose supervision this ticklish engineering job would be carried out by the forced labor of "tens of thousands of enemies of the State." [168]

The camp was certainly a very strange place! The designing here was done by wreckers. The financial department was run by embezzlers, and the administrative department by people who had been sentenced for offences committed while in office.[169]

The first part of the book is made up of biographies and autobiographies of various individual worker-prisoners. We are shown the points of view of the imprisoned engineers as well as that of the Chekists who supervised the project. These officers of the G.P.U. and its assistant commander, Comrade Yagoda, are naturally depicted most favorably. As the story progresses, personal histories are overshadowed by the account of the final dramatic push when the Canal itself becomes the hero.

The fact is stressed that the digging of the Baltic–White Sea Canal was an old project dating from the eighteenth century but that nothing was ever done except to talk fruitlessly about it until after the Revolution. It took the Soviet régime to carry out the plan.

The principal theme of this history of construction is the political and moral reconstruction of socially dangerous individuals through collective socially useful labor and study. The prisoner by working as a Canal soldier finally earns the right to be called a comrade. One of the engineers imagines that the Party and the G.P.U. are telling him through the Special Construction Bureau:

You were a criminal, a wrecker, a counter-revolutionary. . . . But the Government exposed you and the secret intrigues of your associates, and now, it takes . . . a part of the socialist plan—the Belomorstroi—measures a tiny dose for you and it will cure you, the criminal, with the truth of socialism.[170]

By his work the criminal at Belomorstroi was, willy-nilly, helping to build a social order where there would be no crime. Their biographies show that the prisoners were the products of their environment and that capitalist conditions are responsible for robbery and murder, which are committed from a desire to acquire some other man's goods. Engineer Budassy's methods of reasoning and tricky character, for example, are considered "phenomena of a social order. The [corrupt] engineering circles of the capitalist era, in which Budassy lived and worked, must bear the full responsibility for him." [171] When he swindled the Karelian government out of ten thousand rubles for the benefit of the construction, it was hailed as proof of a certain psychological reconstruction because for the first time in his life he had cheated entirely disinterestedly!

Socialist competition between brigades is shown as one of the new methods of work. Hot pies were served as incentives to those who had raised their norms and shock workers were rewarded for high production indices by having their portraits painted in oils, while shirkers and loafers were caricatured. Other measures of encouragement towards better work were higher wages, decorations, and reduction or abrogation of sentences.[172]

The *History of the Construction of the White Sea–Baltic Canal* ends on the optimistic note characteristic of Soviet literature: "The hands of thieves, bandits and counter-revolutionaries had opened out a new way, not only for the ships but for themselves." [173] The Canal opened up new economic prospects for Karelia and the North. Its builders had gained self-respect and had become an asset to the country. As workers well trained and organized for socialist labor, they were invited to continue practicing their newly acquired skills on the Moscow-Volga Canal and other new Five-Year Plan constructions.

4. SOME LITERARY WORKS OF THE FIRST FIVE-YEAR PLAN PERIOD

Contents and Characteristics

"LITERATURE MUST UNDERSTAND that its role is to stimulate still greater energy," [1] declared Maxim Gorky. Averbakh believed that it was a "remarkably effective instrument with which to gain a knowledge of life" and that it helped readers to see "the actual and complete development of life phenomena," influencing their thoughts and feelings.[2]

The specific mission of Soviet writers in the struggle for the fulfillment of the First Five-Year Plan, according to Marietta Shaginyan, was to help the new man to perceive the Plan's unity and coordination by showing in their books "that dependence of one part of production upon the other and that unity which distinguishes our industries." [3] This is exactly what Polonski accomplished so successfully in his *Magnitostroi* in spite of the fact that he saw the construction only as a visitor and not in the way that Shaginyan considered mandatory—as a working member.

"The proletariat does not have the same attitude towards literature as towards a toy or a luxury," [4] Radek said. It regards literary works as weapons with which to bring about socialist competition, shock-brigade work, and the Five-Year Plan in four years. Ilin, who was certainly in a position to find out, felt that "our reader demands that a book answer his ideas, inquiries, and moods; our reader expects from it a new order of ideas, types, sensations, and thoughts. He does not like ruminations, insipidities, tiresome sermons, exclamation points, or the glazed dullness of thought." [5]

The reading public wanted an active literature filled with the clang of battle, "the symphony of creation," [6] and "the red blood of revolutionary Leninist journalism." [7] Such a literature eagerly served as the artistic chronicler of the economic transformation which was taking place and was characterized by its "conscious purposefulness and its conscious co-ordination with a collective existence." [8]

Writers took their subjects [9] during the First Five-Year Plan from life itself: the struggle of one class against the other, of the Revolution against reaction, and of the proletariat to build a new society. It was claimed by Averbakh that this new content required, and therefore created, new forms. Valentin Katayev's novel, *Time, Forward!*, and Vishnevski's play, *The Last Decisive*, were pointed to as examples.[10]

Literature reflected the new processes in Soviet reality: socialist competition, wrecking, grain collection, collectivization, and new trends among the intelligentsia; and in it the masses saw mirrored their strivings and aspirations. Mayakovsky had insisted that authors must even subscribe to a clipping bureau so as to be sure of receiving "a continual supply of material on subjects that are of interest to your district." [11] Such data would help the writer to present the required documentation of reality in his work.

In one part of his picture the writer must show how man changes history and is thereby himself changed from an ignorant and individualistic person to a politically "cultured" and collective-minded one. The new hero of our times in the epoch of socialist construction is

the builder, but he is still rather generalized than typical; he is depicted by external signs rather than by internal characterization; he is still the representation of his occupation rather than a living personality; he has a dangerous tendency to flash across the pages of a story, also a tendency to appear as a mere product of conditions; as the "leather jacket" or rubber stamp.[12]

The difficulty seems to have been that, since life had not yet fully crystallized a typical Communist or a typical worker and since there were no historical precedents for such a character, how could literature portray him?

Polonski classified Russian authors by their heroes. The émigré writers depicted the old intellectual hero while the fellow-travelers vacillated between the old and the new. Tradition often defeated the Revolution in their novels. "To the extent that the new proletarian hero triumphs, the work of the poputchiki [fellow-travelers] approaches the category of proletarian literature." [13]

The Soviet writer must also show in his picture of socialist reality the new man's unceasing, Party-led struggle: (1) a political and economic fight against the class enemies (wrecker and kulak), (2) a productive fight against the forces of nature, and (3) an educational fight against the bad habits of human nature (laziness, absenteeism, drunkenness, illiteracy, etc.).

While the typical Five-Year Plan literary work may not always have a "happy" ending, it is generally an optimistic one which looks forward to a better future.[14] Mirsky described this characteristic trait in the following words:

> The Soviet novel is an epic of purposeful effort. As a rule it has no definite plot in the traditional sense of the term. It is the story of a series of successive engagements in one and the same campaign, every hard-gained victory raising new tasks and demanding fresh victories. "The fight goes on" is the refrain that ends every novel. . . . The new Soviet novel usually ends on a victory, but a victory which demands new exertions in order to gain new victories.[15]

Industry

The Fourteenth Party Congress in the spring of 1925 had passed a resolution "to transform the U.S.S.R. from a country importing machinery and equipment into a country that manufactures machinery and equipment." [16] On the basis of this directive, the First Five-Year Plan concentrated on heavy industry, and especially on machine building. Thus, from 1929 to 1932 the foundation was being built for industry as a whole, as well as for the transportation system and agriculture.[17]

In the field of literature there appeared the industrial novel, which dealt with the problem of turning a backward agricultural country into a country of advanced industrialism. The theatre repertory was flooded with dull plays glorifying machinery and industrial construction; "machines, tractors, building projects, rather than flesh-

and-blood characters, came to dominate the stage."[18] The usual plot, with slight variations, concerned a new industrial plant built at record speed and triumphantly completed ahead of scheduled time, "despite the machinations of a villain in the shape of a sabotaging engineer or a kulak who has sneaked in as a worker and plays the part of a wolf in sheep's clothing."[19]

Cement (1926) was the first novel depicting the proletariat, not at war, but as a constructor and organizer. The author, Gladkov, considered this book and his second big novel, *Energy* (1933), "in reality documents of the epoch of socialist construction." *Energy* tells the story of the construction of the Dnieprostroi Dam and deals with "new people and the new methods of work created by the system of socialist competition and shock work."[20] The role of the proletariat as the organizing vanguard of the masses is shown, as well as its ability to infect them by example with its own enthusiasm for struggle and building. In the scene of the "storming of the granite" the peasant workers have run away, oppressed by the great granite cliffs. Kolcha saw "how nature enslaved feeble folk who were used to work with their muscles alone. Such people were always afraid of nature."[21] He and other Komsomol *udarniks* win over the peasants, arousing their labor pride with praise and encouragement and shaming the lazy ones by example.

The joy of creative socialist labor which makes over, not only backward and indifferent peasants, but also the old intelligentsia, is the theme of the chapter in which brigades of engineers are at work. "Amazing spectacle! The Russian technical intelligentsia, with its high reputation, was rolling stones like mere labourers, was loading and pushing trucks."[22] One of the engineers, Kryashítch, who had joined the others at first only because of the force of public opinion, began to change:

Without noticing it, he fell into the swing of the work, grew warm, his heart beat jerkily and elastically, and a physical joy swept over him. The blood thickened and sang in his ears, youth flowed into his muscles, everything became strangely interesting and lost all repulsion. . . . There was a moment when he felt with amazement that he was working with satisfaction, and that he was, in that instant, another person, in no way resembling the Kryashitch who had been so fastidiously putting on airs an hour ago.[23]

. . . . .

"What's happened to me?" he wondered, looking round. "The world and the people in it seem different to me now." [24]

In depicting the complex interrelations of the different groups and mass organizations at the construction, Gladkov also points to the "boundless future" into which a "mighty class" is marching. The proletariat "was building this hydrogiant as no mere dam, over a mile long and seventy yards high, but was raising the edifice of a new world which would live for all time and create a new race of men, free, daring, and audacious." [25]

THE OLD AND THE NEW

Gladkov, himself a member of this "mighty class," was interested primarily in the present and the future. On the other hand, the writers belonging to the intelligentsia were more likely in their industrial novels to stress various aspects of the conflict between the old and the new. Such is the case in Pilnyak's *The Volga Falls to the Caspian* (1930), Leonov's *Sot* (1930), and Ehrenburg's *The Second Day* (1933).

Boris Pilnyak was a fellow-traveler who had strongly opposed the social command; but, after his trouble with RAPP over the publication of *Mahogany* in Berlin, he rewrote it as a gesture of penance and appeasement, and it appeared as *The Volga Falls to the Caspian*. However, it might almost have been called, *Time, Backward!* Even the plot never moves forward; at the end of the book one gets back to the point where the story began. The marital tangles of three construction engineers are given against the background of a dam being built near Kolomna. Much scientific data is superposed, but it never becomes an organic part of the plot. The purpose of this new socialist construction was to make the Moscow River flow backwards (symbolic?) and to create a new river, which would destroy villages, history, and archaeology.

The chief engineer of the construction, Sadykov, who had risen from the worker's bench, "looked like a master mechanic and . . . was not followed by secretaries." [26] He was a man of straightforward ideas and direct actions; towards his wife he had "acted cruelly and honestly in accordance with communist morality." [27] Another engineer, Poltorak, was a specialist who had been bribed by an Englishman to blow up the dam and who felt that "our government régime is choking from roguery, flunkyism, treason, moral dissolution. The government weapons are armies of controlling organizations. . . . the whole country is turned into a moral placard." [28] After his failure to satisfy the workers' production conference, Poltorak became "one of the hunted wolves who are surrounded but do not know that death is around them." [29] By the end of the novel this disciple of Solovyov loses Vera (Faith), Nadezhda (Hope), Lyubov (Love), and his wife Sophia (Solovyov's Wisdom).

Other symbolic names are those of the watchman Ozhogov (Man of Burns) and his half-crazy beggar Communists: Ognyov (Man of Fire), Pozharov (Conflagration Man), Podzhogov (Incendiary), and Plamya (Flame), "men for whom time had stopped with the epoch of War Communism." [30] Ozhogov personifies this romantic and heroic period of the Revolution, which ended in 1921 when he became insane and was expelled from the Party. However, he "had not forgotten his sense of honor nor lost his conscience," [31] and his drowning when the new dam is opened may symbolize, for Pilnyak, the death of these qualities in contemporary Soviet life.

The main theme of the novel is the conflict of the old and the new; of the colorful, memory-rich, and variegated past with the drab, monotonous, regimented present. Moscow of 1929, tensely living the life of an armed camp "with her gray, heroic, humdrum days," [32] is contrasted with Asiatic Kolomna, a provincial town which has been "receding into history" since the time of Nicholas I and which is now "far in the rear of the fighting line." [33] The ever-recurring image of the tower of Marina Mniszek constantly recalls this half-Asiatic, medieval Russia. "The men with the theodolites" are seen digging into "the Jura and the Perm epochs" [34] on Muscovy's ancient lands, where the Soviet Union is waging its socialist battle. Within the person of Professor Poletika, designer of the dam, there is also a struggle of the old, represented by his desire for a copy of the Menology of the Saints, and the new which, in his case, conquers.[35]

Pilnyak's preference for the past is obvious, and there are a number of characters connected with it, many of them vividly drawn. Besides an archaeologist, a second-hand book dealer, and a museum custodian, there are the antique dealers, Pavel and Stepan Bezdyetov. In the "medievalism and dampness" of their semi-obscure, cobwebby cellar these mahogany restorers look "backwards to the time of things." [36] Their friend Skudrin has a house, resplendent with mahogany, in which the spirit of pre-Petrine Russia reigns and which he wants to prevent from being flooded, by blowing up the dam. He believes that "it is memory that rules the world" and refuses to "go into socialism." [37] "The wretched old man was sticking his knife into the revolution in order to retaliate for himself, for Alexander, for Russia, for his Voltairean mahogany." [38] These are the figures which one remembers, and not the representatives of the new order.

The only example of collective enterprise in the novel is a case of collective rape, which causes the women to become collectively offended at their fate. Not only is there no building enthusiasm, but the reverse: "The humdrum work of construction was proceeding," [39] we read. Pilnyak phlegmatically describes the conclusion of the enterprise as follows: "The various jobs at the construction were drawing to a close. The new river, battle for socialism, was emerging into reality." [40] The only hint about the future and the continuation of the struggle is a vague plan of Poletika's "to throw the Volga into the desert." [41] It seems safe to assume that *The Volga Falls to the Caspian* provided no inspiration for shock workers of the First Five-Year Plan.

Sot derives its name from a river in the depths of the northern forest where grow "mushrooms, bears, hermits, devils, everything— save reason and purpose." [42] Leonid Leonov presents a psychological analysis of the class struggle which ensues when the Bolsheviks try to erect a giant paper mill in this corner of old Russia. The dark forces of the old world include kulaks and backward peasants, a "doomed nest" of monks, wrecker-engineers, and a strange former White-Guard officer who believes that "all humanity lives for is the hope of an Attila." [43] The resistance of nature, in the form of a flooded river and shifting seas of silt, has to be overcome as well. "From the moment when Uvadiev stepped on to the bank, a challenge was cast at Sot, and at the whole ancient manner of life in the bed of which it flowed." [44]

This Communist hero is described as "not made of flesh and blood, but some kind of metal, red pig-iron." [45] In approved Soviet fashion, he feels the joy of physical effort when helping with the work during an emergency, but his fault lies in not paying enough attention to what the masses are thinking. Burago, one of the old *spetsy*, might be called a fellow-traveling engineer; he does his work loyally and well, even when feeling doubts: "Socialism . . . yes . . . I don't know. But everything's possible in this country . . . !" [46] Renne, on the other hand, is a "befogged intellectual" who has outlived his time and cannot change his way of doing things. "The conscientious little railway engine from the ancient Russian narrow-gauge had proved quite unsuited to the rails of the new main lines." [47] By contrast, Potemkin, the head of the enterprise, is "a citizen of the epoch and a son of his class." [48] So when he develops leukemia, the Soviet government lavishes every care and attention on him: X-rays, a trip to the Caucasus, etc.

The peasants are depicted as very backward indeed. An incubator is considered a "violation of nature" which will hatch some sort of a machine-bird whose flesh will smell of iron. In the new huts, to which the construction has moved them,

it was dull without the warm domestic bug, without the dirt, without the pervading calfy stuffiness; they were sad for their free and preposterous past, mercilessly trampled by Sotstroi, but yet more were they frightened by the uncertainty of the future.[49]

When some of the younger peasants are won over to the new order of things and join the Komsomol, a modern "fathers and sons" situation develops, especially in regard to religion.

There is some very effective anti-religious propaganda in this novel, carried out largely by ridicule. The monks, leading "their age-old preposterous mode of life," hang on every word that their diviner and wise man, Eusevy, utters. When he began "thinly and fitfully to sneeze," they all exchanged glances, "unsure whether this too formed a part of the message." [50] The holy man is portrayed as a dirty, diseased, repulsive half-wit, whose dying words are: "There is no God!" Yet he is the link which holds the monks together, and after all the hocus-pocus connected with his demise, they scatter to become beggars and vagabonds. The monastery had also sheltered counter-revolutionaries, hidden beneath cowls and praying to God for the Soviet ruin. Although its site had been selected for a sawmill, the suggestion was made that it be kept as "a kind of man-preserve, so that even half a century later the citizens of Sotinsk might see for themselves with what comical sports their forbears amused themselves." [51] Besides this, the "nepman" whom Uvadiev's mother marries, a coarse and "scrimpy personage," and his relatives are all "in the ecclesiastical line": he sells colored pictures; one of his brothers is a coffin-maker; and the other, a deacon.

A scandal about Sotstroi, which reaches All-Union proportions, is started (we are not surprised to learn) by the completely inaccurate article of an ignorant correspondent from the provincial newspaper—this time, "an extremely young man in square inlaid spectacles." [52] As a result, the construction has to be slowed up because of a reduction in the allocated funds. The consideration which carries the most weight in the decision to resume building at top speed is not that a domestic paper industry is needed to serve the cultural revolution, but that the Sot area must be proletarianized.[53] The ancient darkness must be forced to flee before advancing industry.

Like Pilnyak, Leonov uses the Five-Year Plan as a background for his personalities; and, as in *The Volga Falls to the Caspian*, so in *Sot*, the most vivid and individualized characters are those belonging to the "old." The construction of the paper mill is described from a disinterested point of view; no enthusiasm is engendered in the reader. Nor is there any idea at the end of going on to a bigger and better building assignment. The future is foretold only by the statement that "the face of Sot was changing; altering also were the men upon its banks." [54] This novel's principal contribution to the cultural revolution is in the realm of anti-religious propaganda.[55]

The third novel stressing the conflict of the new with the old is *The Second Day*, written in Paris by Ilya Ehrenburg, an émigré intellectual who subsequently returned to live in the Soviet Union. His scene is laid at the construction of the blast-furnaces in the Siberian Kuznetsk: "In what had been a wasteland, an industrial plant was rising, and around the plant a town was blossoming as in other days towns had risen around the cathedrals—the shrines of the people." [56] The building was going on without songs, banners, or smiles; people were driven by columns of figures and "worked faster than men are capable of working." [57] They dropped from exhaustion, but they went on building; and the Revolution burned their hearts "as metal burns fingers in a fifty below zero frost." [58]

The two hundred and twenty thousand men engaged on the construction were of all kinds and had been drawn to it for all sorts of reasons. "Some were led here by hunger, others by faith. Others still [kulaks and criminals] were brought." [59] Some came for profit, for what they could get out of it (government coats, etc.). There were technicians from abroad; Komsomoltsy burning with "Kuznetsk fever"; shock workers, "pure and not so pure"; and expropriates who, although not themselves guilty of anything, were members of "a class which was guilty of everything." "Some of the builders were heroes, some were half-savage nomads and superstitious peasant-women, some were thieves and grafters." [60] But most of them were ordinary people, capable of perseverance and courage, yet treasuring their lives. They flared up for an hour or two, but "refused to burn with that lofty, even flare with which blast-furnaces burn." [61] "Everything is in a heap: heroism, graft, cruelty, nobleness," exclaims Irina. "It frightens one to think of the conditions under which the people work." [62]

This kaleidoscopic picture of a construction site appears to be a true reflection of reality. One feels that things must have been a good deal like that. The fact that Ehrenburg has not glorified the enterprise or glossed over its shortcomings, makes it all the more remarkable that the Kuznetsk plant did get built on schedule and did start turning out steel. It is against the background of this struggle that the biographies of a great variety of individuals are sketched.

"Humanity can be made over," believes Irina. "Everybody is rushing today, higher and higher. This includes all: blast-furnaces, poetry, love." [63] Her change of attitude symbolizes the growth of men and women during the First Five-Year Plan. Irina personifies the turning away from the old towards the new. As a student at the futile, quiet, and boring university town of Tomsk, she loves Volodia, a "Soviet Pechorin." [64] Then, when she decides to take up social work and becomes a teacher in the factory school at Kuznetsk, amidst the noise and hurry of the construction she falls in love with Kolka, a Komsomol worker. This "simple, gay man," always "in a hustle to learn," at 50° below zero thinks "not of degrees, but of the schedule," and is, of course, first into the icy water to repair a break in the dam. Kolka in his sentiments is "at one with all the others, and this knowledge filled him with joy. He rejoiced every time he felt himself to be in intimate contact with thousands of other—to him—unknown men." [65]

Volodia is not simple, not gay, and definitely not "at one with all the others." But he is the novel's most interesting character, a Dostoyevskian "double" anachronistically living during the First Five-Year Plan. "Of such as he they wrote novels in the old days," [66] comments Irina. He considers himself "an untimely phenomenon" with no future, who would have been perfectly adjusted among the "superfluous" men if he had lived a century earlier. As it is, he fears to face life and in his heart takes no part in it, but aloofly and solitarily leads his "second underground life" as "a bookworm and a skeptic." He considers the Revolution "utterly without sense" and the new world, an ant-heap: "There are ant-workers, ant-specialists, and ant-chiefs. But there never was an ant-genius. . . . You have eliminated from life the heretics, the dreamers, the philosophers, the poets.[67] You have established universal literacy and equally universal ignorance." [68] And it is with such dull people, Volodia complains, that he has to live. "You can't imagine what that means. . . . for me they are not human. All alike—it's called a 'collective.' " [69] One cannot help wondering whether similar sentiments at this time did not make Ehrenburg want to get back to Paris in a hurry.

Volodia, of course, finally hangs himself (symbolic of the liquidation of the exploiting classes), while Kolka and his stronger-than-iron comrades set off optimistically on a new campaign of wrestling with nature. "The taiga was obstinate—it withstood mankind. . . . More obstinate than the taiga were men." [70]

TEMPOS

The fight for higher industrial tempos is the theme of Pogodin's 1929 play of that name and of Katayev's novel, *Time, Forward!* (1933). During the First Five-Year Plan, American engineers were regarded as leaders who pointed the way in this struggle to break production records and overfulfill the Plan, while wrecker-engineers spoke of it as a "stunt."

As traveling correspondent for *Pravda*, Nikolai Pogodin was sent to visit and describe the Stalingrad Tractor Plant, then in the course of construction, and the rate at which work was going on astounded him. He thereupon decided to write his first play, about peasant workers under the discipline of American tempos. "To write a play," he said, "in spite of being completely ignorant of the technique of playwriting was possible if one had great inspiration and some fatalism." [71] In nine days *Tempo* was finished and was then read to a group of writers in Leningrad. "All the scenes that I had drawn from life met with approval and all those I had invented were turned down," [72] reported Pogodin.

On this basis, *Tempo* should be largely a reflection of reality. The scenes of mass activity are the best ones. When the play opens, we see a group of typical muzhiks, involved for the first time in the industrial process, "the human raw material of the Five-Year Plan." They are superstitious and ignorant, afraid of the hospital and afraid to ride in a car, but at the same time already class-conscious enough to realize that they are working for themselves. As a metalworker says at the production meeting: "After all, we are the bosses of our own country, and this is our plant. We accepted the Five-Year Plan and we are building it with our own hands. Socialism won't drop on us from Heaven." [73] This scene, in which the city-bred riveters challenge the masons and carpenters to socialist competition so as to increase their tempos, is very well done.

Less successfully drawn are the Communist director of the project, another believer in the effectiveness of personal example; the super-efficient and conscientious, non-political American specialist; and the chief engineer, of aristocratic origin, who tries to sabotage the construction and kills himself when exposed. *Tempo* was one of the first plays to introduce the "wrecking" theme, inspired by the Shakhty trial of 1928.[74]

"If we could only master Americanism and suffuse it with communist principles," [75] exclaims a Komsomol worker. Higher tempos are regarded as "our challenge and our blow at all our enemies" [76] and are shown to be hindered by the "Oblomov type of workman," [77] the wrecking engineer, and even by bedbugs (time is lost in scratching). After the program has been overfulfilled, the American engineer concludes with this unsolicited testimonial: "I am far from politics, but I am sure that such a record is outside the reach of any country with a different political organization from yours here." [78]

On June 23, 1931, Stalin delivered a speech in which he said that "to lower tempos means to fall back, and those who fall back are beaten." This was the history of old Russia which was continually beaten because of its military, cultural, governmental, industrial, and agricultural backwardness and because it was profitable to do so. "That is why we cannot be backward any more," he concluded.[79] These words serve as the text for Valentin Katayev's *Time, Forward!*, the one industrial First Five-Year Plan novel which was considered by everyone a success.[80] It was also welcomed as proof of the creative reorientation of its fellow-traveler author by "the actuality of socialist construction." Katayev catches the spirit of the *udarniks* and succeeds in imparting to the reader the excitement and contagious enthusiasm of socialist competition which takes place, not only between brigades, but even assumes the form of a personal competition between two boys painting slogans in the art shop.

Private lives and problems are insignificant and always give way to the demands of socialist competition.

Time, Forward! is a chronicle of twenty-four hours at Magnitogorsk during which an attempt is made to beat the world record for pouring concrete. Human stupidity and inefficiency, the forces of nature, and especially time have to be beaten by teamwork and ingenuity.[81] The swiftly moving narrative reads like a dime novel, and a movie serial could hardly afflict its hero with more obstacles than those which the members of Ishchenko's brigade have to overcome to win their short-lived record: they run out of cement and then out of gravel; two workers desert; there are whirlwinds and a rainstorm that doubles back to give the competitors, not one, but two drenchings; the telephone connection snaps, then the water is shut off; a worker gets his hand smashed, and an elephant even breaks loose to add to the confusion. "There really was no elephant. I made him up," Katayev confessed. "As for the rest, I stuck to the truth as much as possible." [82]

Since the novel is concerned primarily with the technical problems of efficient production, it is not surprising to find the characters described somewhat superficially, although vividly. They do not stand still long enough for a deep psychological analysis. Also, there are no peculiar individuals such as those who wander through the books of Pilnyak, Leonov, and Ehrenburg and no major struggle of the old and the new. The technical matter, which occurs in quantity, is an organic part of the story; the unfolding of the plot, for instance, depends upon what the latest newspaper article says about concrete mixtures.

"Our great god is Speed!" [83] was Mayakovsky's declaration in 1918, and it was even truer ten years later. Katayev's novel is in perpetual motion: time flies and races, and, because it has to be outdistanced, "six-armed" telegraph poles march "like Martians," a train leaps "like a ramrod from the gun-barrel of the tunnel," the sun glows "with the speed of magnesium ribbons," and the whole country rushes impetuously forward. "Time continually intersects the action as the track and trains intersect a construction job." [84]

Margulies, the able engineer in charge of the sector, is extremely time-conscious. He does not own a watch because he is by nature so in step with time, and his times, that he does not need one. To him, time is so precious that he hates to waste it in washing or in eating. Margulies' energetic purposefulness, modesty, and endurance are contrasted with the hot-headed enthusiasm, selfish ambition, and lack of self-control of Mosya, the foreman in charge of the shift. Margulies bases his work on the most careful preparation; he leaves no detail unchecked and has a rare regard for production quality as well as quantity. "First I'll make sure, and then I'll have faith" is his motto.[85]

Nalbandov, assistant chief of the construction, is a brilliant but hidebound specialist and a Party member. An opportunist, very concerned over his prestige and position, he is jealous of Margulies. The latter insists that science be regarded dialectically, that yesterday's scientific hypothesis becomes today's academic fact and tomorrow's anachronism. Nalbandov, on the other hand, does not go forward with time. He believes in traditional and immutable mechanical laws and accuses Margulies of doing violence to imported machinery with his "barbarous speed." The novel follows the conflict of the two ideas propounded by Nalbandov and Margulies, respectively: "The construction is not a stunt!" and "In the epoch of Reconstruction, tempos decide everything!" [86] Also demonstrated is the manner in which the raising of tempos in one part of the construction influences the raising of tempos over the entire construction.

Bixby, an honest non-partisan engineer, is the efficient exponent of American technique, but his incentives for working are wholly bourgeois. He labors, not to build socialism, but to accumulate money so as to retire in individualistic ease, surrounded by luxurious "things." How futile his motive is, we see when his savings suddenly vanish in a Chicago bank crash. On the other hand, a profitable and safe investment, according to a wealthy American tourist, is "the construction of this Babylon." [87]

Optimism about the socialist future is seen in Ishchenko's thoughts about his baby: "Time was life. . . . It flowed too slowly.

But it flowed for him. The past flowed for the future. . . . Oh, how good life was, after all!" [88] We are left, as the novel closes, with the news that the Chelyabinsk Tractor Plant has just beaten Magnitogorsk's world record and the certainty that a new epic of socialist competition is about to begin.

WRECKERS

There are no bona fide wreckers in *Time, Forward!*. On the contrary, *Driving Axle* (1932) is primarily a "wrecker" novel in which Ilyenkov deals with the various types of engineers to be found at the gigantic, age-blackened "Krasny Proletary" plant. The main theme is the counter-revolutionary sabotage carried on by the old specialists, who organize the production of intentionally useless engine axles. Defects and waste abound; engines either stop or cause accidents. The local conspiracy is connected with "the forces abroad" through a wrecker in the Supreme Council of National Economy who issues instructions. The peak of wrecking in the Soviet Union was reached from 1929 to 1931, and Ilyenkov undoubtedly got ideas from the Industrial Party trial involving engineers subsidized from abroad.[89]

The members of the sabotage ring are not all in it for the same reason; motives vary. One of the engineers is out for himself and perfectly indifferent to politics while another is heart and soul with "the cause." A laborer helps the wreckers because of his greed to build and furnish a house; another does it because of the "damned heritage of the handicraft worker" in his blood. Handicraft is "the enemy of labour discipline and the advocate of drink and debauch . . . from the loneliness of labour born at the individual bench." [90] When the workman is activated by the "hitherto unknown incentive of socialist consciousness," however, voluntary labor results.

Side by side with the saboteurs, Ilyenkov shows honest old engineers and workers, sincerely devoted to the Soviet régime, but, for the most part, still politically ignorant. Experience finally teaches them that "an isolated individual falls into disuse just as a bolt that has been severed from its machine"; [91] they learn the value of belonging to "that myriad-armed working collective, surrounded with the ring of metal, the smell of oil and smoke." [92]

The most memorable figure in the book is that of Kuzmich, the "boss," who has seen serfdom, joined the workers' movement when it first began, and slaved at the plant under the autocracy. "Seething class energy fills his worn-out body with strength." [93] Too old to work, he becomes the self-appointed guardian of the engines. One night, while spying on the wreckers, he is discovered and killed; his heroic death inspires the workers at the plant to greater efforts.

The third group of engineers consists of those who are Party members. There is Korchenko, the plant manager, who, lacking faith in the forces of the working class and falling easily under alien influence, completely trusts the specialists. Coequal with him in the running of the plant is Vartanyan, who has been sent from Moscow by the Party as the "political engine driver." The author here reflects the situation existing in many Soviet factories at this time: a peculiar dualism of control which created chaos and irresponsibility since the two heads often did not agree.[94] Senka Platov is the typical "Red specialist" of the First Five-Year Plan; a common laborer at the plant five years before, he has now become an engineer. "From moulding wheels I rose to moulding our new life," [95] he says. He is entirely different from the old specialists because he has an engineer's education "for the purpose of leading the workers, not for the purpose of increasing my personal income." [96]

After the breaking of an engine's axle causes a serious train wreck and the saboteurs are exposed, the plant indulges in self-criticism. Careless work habits and lack of a sense of responsibility for the spoiled axles, due to the lingering influence of the past, are held responsible for the situation in which "five crooks succeeded in getting round 16,000 workers." [97] Another reason is the fact that only the old specialists possessed a knowledge of science and technology (a widespread dilemma in the early days of industrialization). As Senka tells Vartanyan: "You must know their [the engines'] language and the trouble is that neither you, nor I, nor

Korchenko, nor any of our secretaries of nuclei, nor our workers have learned it. The enemy, on the contrary, knows it perfectly." [98]

"People united themselves into one general whole, like parts of an engine, merging into one great collective," [99] and, guided by the revolutionary workers, began to correct the plant's defects. "We shall vanquish the enemy!" optimistically declares Vartanyan. "Because there is no force which can break the driving axle of the revolution—the working class and its Party! And why? Because they are forged from the best steel in the world—indestructible bolshevik steel!" [100] Ilyenkov prophesies that the day will come when the Red Banner of the Soviets will be waving above the Eiffel Tower.

HUMAN RECONSTRUCTION

A very different type of story dealing with engines is *I Love* (1933), interesting as a product of the mass literary movement. Alexander Avdeyenko wrote this autobiographical novel while working as a machinist at Magnitogorsk. Like *The Great Conveyer*, it is semi-fictional in form but gives a realistic account of the author's actual experience at an industrial enterprise. Although the *besprizornik* in *Energy* certainly exaggerates when he says, "There are enough waif-and-stray writers to form a regiment. Every waif and stray becomes a writer," [101] Avdeyenko is an example of one who did.

The first part of the book describes Sanya's childhood in the "Dog Kennels" (so nicknamed because "the dwellings resembled those of dogs rather than men") [102] in an atmosphere of poverty, filth, drunken squabbles, and beatings. His grandfather, after years of uncomplaining and exhausting slave labor as a seasonal coal miner, suddenly revolts, becomes a notorious drunkard, and at last goes insane. His father, a smelter, is involved in a futile strike against the Belgian factory owners; then, half-blinded by sparks from a furnace, he is killed by a foreman. Sanya's older sister becomes a prostitute; his little brother and sister die of hunger and cold; and the older brother Kozma, losing his arm in the rolling mill, organizes a strike for safety nets and is sent to Siberia. On his return, he is killed by Cossacks in the February Revolution. Kozma personifies intelligent social wrath making itself felt as conscious class struggle, whereas his grandfather stands for hidden social hatred, as yet unorganized, which explodes ineffectually.

Sanya, at the age of eleven, becomes a bandit-*besprizornik*. After a lurid career, he is "re-educated" at a Soviet colony, a complex and difficult process, goes to a factory school where he joins the Komsomol, and eventually arrives at Magnitostroi as an engine driver's assistant.

Socialist labor, shown in the second part of the story, is strikingly contrasted with labor under former capitalist conditions. During the scene in which the workers, risking their lives, prevent a catastrophe on the job, Sanya reminisces:

> I remember the furnace where my father worked. . . . Once just such an uproar arose there. The molten river had rushed out, turning everything in its path to ashes. And the workmen had been glad to see the waste of iron, and had run away from it.
> Now the shepherd Lesniak, agile and daring, is beating at the heart of the fire and barring its way with his own breast. Alongside him stands the engineer and myself—who lost my father at the blast furnace and buried all of his clan in Rotten Gully.[103]

I Love is no worker's romance in the bourgeois sense. The object of Sanya's deep and personal affection is Engine No. 20, whose driver he becomes.[104] "It stands ready now, waiting for its load of iron, looking as if it were fresh from the works, new, bright, alert, proud and beautiful." [105] The wall newspaper challenges Sanya to make his engine the best model engine at Magnitostroi, and he concludes a contract of mutual responsibility and socialist competition with the furnaceman Kramarenko: to deliver so many tons of iron to the pouring machines in a given amount of time. (We are shown a reproduction of the district newspaper's special page giving the agreement.) Engine No. 20 is to compete with the furnace, but in a special socialist way because, as Kramarenko says to Sanya: "You've got to feel as interested in the furnace as if it was your own, and I'll try and feel like the master of your engine. Mutual responsibility, see?" [106] The book ends with the former waif's election to the Communist party as a "Hero of Magnitogorsk" and his cliché-like exclamation, "How good life is!" [107] He cannot help but compare the beautiful and healthful new socialist town where he now lives with his memory of the horrible "Dog Kennels," the only remnant of which is his grandfather's mud hut, which has been preserved as a museum of the "old accursed past."

Avdeyenko expresses the joy and enthusiasm of socialist labor, which developed the characteristic devices of the challenge, socialist competition, and the socialist contract and which made possible the fulfillment of the First Five-Year Plan. However, the reader, himself, is not made to feel it as he is in *Time, Forward!* But *I Love* serves as a convincing demonstration that human beings, as well as plants, were salvaged and rebuilt during the reconstruction period.

SELF-CRITICISM

The Little Golden Calf (1931) is outstandingly different from most of its fellow-Five-Year Plan novels and may be classified as "industrial" only because it satirizes industrial enterprises. But satire in the Soviet Union is expected to educate the masses and influence public opinion by its ruthless exposure of administrative abuses and the machinations of the class enemy. It is therefore not surprising to find such a genuinely amusing work criticized because Ilf and Petrov's laughter contains too little sarcasm, anger, and contempt. The authors were also frowned on for having permitted "a very clever rogue to go about in an unreal world in which there are only Philistines but no builders." [108]

The hero of this picaresque novel is Ostap Bender, the "great schemer." He is not interested in the Soviet government's desire to build socialism; the idea bores him, and he wants to go to Rio de Janeiro where "a millionaire is a popular figure." [109] But first he decides to become a millionaire himself. After many adventures, Bender finally succeeds in blackmailing an "underground millionaire" clerk who has acquired his wealth unscrupulously by profiting from public disasters. The authors then show the ridiculousness, futility, unhappiness, and almost pitifulness of a millionaire in the Soviet Union where nothing can be done with private capital. Bender cannot get transportation or a hotel room at any price (reservations are all for engineers, writers, etc.); as a private person he cannot buy a car, or build a house, or make large investments; he even discovers that all the bourgeois pleasures of town have given way to sanitary, educational, and cultural enterprises. "What can I do with it [his money] except get some Nepmanish food?" he asks plaintively when a restaurant turns out to be for trade-union members only. "There you have the hegemony of the class crushing a lonely millionaire!" [110]

"There is no doubt that [this] plot is genuinely Soviet," admitted Lunacharski, "and being unraveled as it has been in a talented fashion, presents an artistic proof for a genuinely timely thesis." [111]

Two covetous Roman Catholic priests are depicted trying to get a car by working on the driver's credulity. In referring to their intrigues, Bender does his bit of anti-religious propaganda:

I myself have a tendency toward fraud and deception. . . . But I do not embellish my dubious activity with the singing of hymns, with the roar of the organ, or with foolish invocations in Latin or Old-Church Slavic. And anyway, I prefer to work without incense or astral bells.[112]

Bureaucracy [113] is ridiculed in the descriptions which Ilf and Petrov [114] give us of two remarkable commercial enterprises. Bender, who considers himself "at heart a bureaucrat and a blockhead," decides to set up the Chernomorsk Branch of the Arbatov Office for the Collection of Horns and Hoofs as a "front" for his activities. With the help of a few blanks and a round rubber stamp, the establishment quickly goes into operation and works out its Five-Year Plan, "indicating on a graph the excellent attainments for the past two years and pledging itself to fulfill its program long before the allotted time." [115] On the third day of its existence, the office receives three requests to send a representative to conferences and sessions.

The "stupid, disgusting bureaucracy" and red tape of the Hercules enterprise revolts even Bender. Its chief has long ago given up signing papers and uses instead one of his thirty-six rubber stamps, which carry the most customary resolutions. The latter is also the proud possessor of a universal rubber stamp which can apply to any occasion in life and proves "an excellent substitute for the man." [116]

However, *The Little Golden Calf* also contains more serious comments on contemporary life. Just as Volodia in *The Second Day* may have expressed some of Ehrenburg's sentiments, so here the former attorney-at-law who seeks escape from Soviet justice by pretending to be crazy may be the oblique mouthpiece for Ilf and Petrov:

In Soviet Russia . . . the insane asylum is the only place where a normal man can live. Everything else is super-Bedlam. No, I cannot live with the Bolsheviks. I prefer to live here with genuine madmen. At least they're not trying to build Socialism. Besides, here you can eat, while there, in their Bedlam, you merely work. But I refuse to exert myself for their Socialism. Here at least there is personal liberty, liberty of conscience, freedom of speech.[117]

The one scene in the novel which deals realistically with First Five-Year Plan socialist construction is that describing the meeting of the rails of the Turkestan Railroad.[118] No humor or satire is used here, and this gives emphasis and importance to an impressive achievement. The workers of the two tent towns (construction enterprises on wheels) had moved to meet each other, laying tracks across 93,750 miles of desert cliffs, lakes, and rivers; socialist competition between them had hastened the meeting by one year. In comparison, the other events of the story seem rather futile and superficial, as does "the absurd figure of the great schemer, who was running along the platform." [119]

Lunacharski supposed that it would be "very, very difficult" for the ingenious, roguish Bender to become "a builder of the new future, although," he added, "the gigantic cleansing power of the revolutionary fire permits such phenomena." [120] Ilf and Petrov, on their part, thought that their hero should have ended up rebuilding himself at Belomorstroi.

Agriculture

"If the adoption of the Five-Year Plan, viewed in retrospect, is the outstanding event in modern Soviet history, marking the beginning of a definite new epoch, the substitution of state and collective for individual farming is the most important single feature of the Five-Year Plan." [121] By the end of 1931 collectivization was 65 per cent completed, and twelve million little peasant homesteads had been absorbed into *kolkhozes*.

The Sixteenth Conference of the Communist party (April 23-29, 1929) had set before the Five-Year Plan the task of "drawing the millions of peasants into the work of socialist construction on the basis of social co-operation and collective labour, and of rendering all possible assistance to poor and middle individual farms in their struggle against *kulak* exploitation." This was made necessary by the fact that "it was impossible for long to base the work of socialist construction on two different systems, *i.e.*, large-scale socialist industry and private, technically backward, small peasant economy." [122] Agriculture, the base for the growth of industry, established a limit on its growth; instead of adapting industrialization to agriculture, it was resolved to reorganize agriculture and aim for higher tempos.[123]

During the summer of 1929 the decision was made to accelerate the socialization of agriculture on the basis of mechanization and to change over from a policy of "restricting the exploiting proclivities of the kulaks" [124] to one of "dekulakization"—elimination of the kulaks as a class.[125] (There was no deviation from this second policy, even after Stalin's "Dizzy with Success" article of March 2, 1930). The Party ordered twenty-five thousand industrial workers to the country to organize the poor peasants into *kolkhozes*. As Ilyenkov put it, "By its very impetus the driving axle of industry—class energy—would push the creaking wheels of the rural cart out of its rut." [126]

Stalin, on the occasion of his fiftieth birthday, declared that 1930 was to be the year of great change, and its first three months saw many excesses perpetrated in the all-out collectivization drive. Force, instead of persuasion, was used on the middle peasants, which resulted in tremendous confusion in agriculture: farmers slaughtered half of their livestock and crops were sharply reduced. It is with this dramatic period of class war in the villages that *Bread* (1930), *Bruski* (Volumes I and II [1930]), and *Soil Upturned* (1932) are all concerned.

COLLECTIVIZATION

Just as *Time, Forward!* was hailed as the industrial novel par excellence of the First Five-Year Plan, so *Soil Upturned* is considered its model *kolkhoz* novel. "Sholokhov has dismounted his Cossack heroes and is writing a long novel on collectivization," [127] noted Zelinski. We are given a vividly realistic picture of the first stage of mass collectivization (before the appearance of tractors and combines) in a Don village, which is of great documentary value because of its objectivity. The mistakes of the Communists and the resultant difficulties are not played down, and the tug of war between the forces of progress and of reaction for the support of the reluctant middle peasants is described with a wealth of truthful detail.

The struggle is shown, not by means of schematic, generalized figures, but from the point of view of a variety of living, completely individualized personalities. All poor peasants are not admirable characters; they are often coarse, avaricious, and vindictive. Nor can Sholokhov's peasants always be made to fit into one of the definite categories: poor, middle, or kulak; the dividing lines are often blurred, and a man may move from one group to another, or, belonging to one group, have a personal motive for supporting another. For instance, Titok Borodin, a partisan hero of the Civil War and poor farmer, by hard work and saving acquires property and is then dispossessed and exiled as a kulak.

The Communist hero of the novel is Davidov, a locksmith from the Red Putilov Works in Leningrad and one of the twenty-five thousand workers sent to proletarianize the country. Soon after his arrival at Gremyachy Village he explains the policy to be carried out:

> The Party proposes complete collectivization, so as to hitch you on to the tractor and lift you out of your want. What did Comrade Lenin say just before his death? "Only on the collective farm can the peasant find salvation from his poverty. Otherwise he is doomed. The vampire kulak will suck him as flat as a board." [128]

Like all good Communists of Soviet literature, Davidov is resolute, calm, and brave; and he believes, especially in an emergency, in leadership by "living example." However, his unfamiliarity with peasants and his inexperience in a new field of work lead him to place confidence in Ostrovnov's managerial abilities and to permit Nagulnov's exaggerations. Stalin's famous article, condemning the use of force and threats as a distortion which may lead to "the strengthening of our enemies and the discrediting of the collective farm movement idea," [129] makes Davidov realize his mistakes. "We've gone politically wrong in regard to the damned fowls," he tells Nagulnov. "You see, we've got a collective farm, and that's a cooperative association [an artel]. But we've been trying to turn it into a commune. . . . And that's a left-wing deviation." [130] The socialized chickens are returned to their former owners, the other excesses are corrected, then the middle Cossacks refuse to support the Whites' foreign-backed insurrection and swing back to the Soviet side. Having learned his lesson and acquired experience, Davidov proves to be an admirable organizer during the new *kolkhoz's* first sowing campaign.

The Cossack Nagulnov, Communist veteran of the Civil War and Left extremist, alone is not fooled by Ostrovnov but involuntarily helps him by using old partisan methods (instead of persuasion) in dealing with the middle peasants. He deviated from the Party line, he explains, because he was in a hurry for the world revolution and studies English so as to be prepared to go over and help cope with the class enemies when there is a Soviet government in England.

Sholokhov shows that the main difficulty in the way of collectivization lies in the very nature of the peasant, thereby exemplifying these words of Stalin's:

. . . in its development the mentality of man lags behind his actual condition. In status the members of collective farms are no longer individual farmers, but collectivists; but their mentality is still the old one—that of the owner of private property. And so, the "have-beens" from the ranks of the exploiting classes play on the private-property habits of the collective farmers in order to organize the plundering of public wealth and thus shake the foundation of the Soviet system, *viz.*, public property.[131]

The passion for private property affects not just the kulaks, but also the middle peasants like Ostrovnov and the poorer ones such as Maidannikov. Ostrovnov hates the Soviet government because it will not allow him to become a kulak and because, when the collective farm is organized, those who have worked hard are put on the same level with lazy people. "We each give what we've got, and we shall share the profits equally. And isn't that unjust to me?" [132] These sentiments lead him to join a counter-revolutionary organization and become its sabotage agent in the *kolkhoz*, of which he is also made manager because of his scientific initiative and efficiency. Ostrovnov suffers a strangely dual existence, simultaneously building up and breaking down the socialized village agriculture.

The most appealing character of *Soil Upturned* is the honest and self-critical Kondrat Maidannikov, a former Budyonny cavalryman. He joins the *kolkhoz*, convinced that it is the only possible solution for the poor farmer, and struggles valiantly to crush the "shameful regret" he feels for his own goods, but "a cantankerous yearning" continues for these possessions which he has himself renounced. "Each pines after his own horse and doesn't care a fig for the others," he muses. "Yet there aren't any 'others' now, they're all ours. But there it is. . . . And it's all come of the struggle we've had to get property." [133] Within Maidannikov the doctrine of communism battles the "peasant inborn psychology of ownership"; [134] and, until it conquers, his conscience will not let him join the Party.

At the end of the novel Ostrovnov says hopefully: "This time we weren't destined to say good-bye to the Soviet government, but maybe we'll have better luck next time." [135] The officers who had organized the conspiracy reappear in the village, and Sholokhov tells us that "the old was beginning anew." [136] However, in spite of this warning that the class war in the country has not yet been won, the success of the *kolkhoz* (which its enemies were not able to prevent) makes us believe that future attempts at wrecking will also be frustrated.

SOME LITERARY WORKS   101

PROLETARIANIZATION

Equal to *Soil Upturned* in documentary value for the history of agricultural collectivization is Panfyorov's four-volume *Bruski* (1930–37). It is a truthful chronicle of the development of a whole rural district on the Volga, from the end of the Civil War in 1921 to the twentieth anniversary of the October Revolution in 1937; and one feels that it could go on indefinitely, right on the tail of life itself. This voluminous epic of collective life may be said to wipe out the difference between country and town; it can, strictly speaking, be classified neither as a *"kolkhoz"* nor as an "industrial" novel because it is both. When the region and its inhabitants change under new conditions, so does the record of their struggles.

"Bruski," the estate of the late Sutiagin, is the object of a protracted struggle between the kulaks, who are totally unscrupulous in their efforts to get control of it, and the Communist Stepka Ognev, who wants to form on it a peasant artel. "Land," mutters the kulak Plakushchev.

Because of land Sutiagin's great-grandfather, Prince Ermilov, whipped the peasants; because of land the peasants threw the landlords in the Volga. . . . The peasants will not let go of the land, and so . . . everything comes from the land, the land is the cause of everything.[137]

At first the new *kolkhoz* has a very hard time of it and only gradually wins the support of the peasants, who are described as "eaten up by their cows, their horses, their allotments, their bits of bread, their lice." For all of this, they "cut each other's throats and work themselves dead." [138] But when Ognev finally succeeds in getting a tractor, its "iron song" lures those who have been reluctant to throw in their lot with the collective.

The subtleties and complexities of the class war in the country are revealed by contrast with the way Zharkov, the new secretary to the district Party committee, had imagined that villages were divided:

on the one side the enemy of the revolution, the Kulak; on the other side, the defender of the revolution, the poor peasant, while the middle peasant stood aside, biting his lips. But after he had lived in Shirokoye a few days, all his ideas and impressions grew blurred and confused.[139]

Although he has been a pre-revolutionary Party member, Zharkov longs "just to live, to throw off the burden of everlasting responsibility . . . for every action, every word, every movement." [140] Not unexpectedly, the holder of such un-Bolshevik sentiments, by Volume IV, is a friend of Bukharin's and has deviated to the extent of leading a counter-revolutionary group which aims to kill Stalin and restore capitalism.

Panfyorov, himself the son of a peasant, graphically presents various aspects of village conditions. We see what irresponsible, ignorant peasants held local government positions in the early days of the Soviet régime; how the father of the family no longer has autocratic power over his son; etc. Scores of characters appear for a short time, only to be replaced by new ones, but Kirill Zhdarkin persists. His development parallels that of the district.

Zhdarkin is first introduced as an energetic, progressive farmer, but a lone wolf who refuses to join the *kolkhoz*. At this time he is married to Zinka, the daughter of the leading kulak in the village; but he leaves her, perhaps symbolically, when he goes to work in a factory. True to family tradition, Zinka reappears later as a wrecker at the construction works.

After two meetings with Stalin and a trip to Germany, Italy, and France (where he encounters cafés for dope addicts and swindlers, prostitution, and unemployment), Zhdarkin becomes an organizer at the metallurgical and tractor works being constructed near Bruski, secretary of the Party committee of the surrounding town, and member of the Central Executive Committee. By now, he has married the Communist Ognev's daughter, Steshka, and feels that: "So far as I'm concerned, building socialism is the same as living." [141] Overflowing with "class instinct," he is constantly setting examples to the workers, studying to improve himself, and longing to raise everyone to a higher level—all of which finally gets him the Order of Lenin. At the end of Volume IV this very "positive hero" goes off, seething with enthusiasm, to head the Balkhash construction works.

Bruski, too, has changed unrecognizably. Its former poverty has given way to amazing fruitfulness: quadruplets are born and a cow breaks the world record for milk. There is now an abundance of food, innumerable tractors and combines, and all kinds of cultural and recreational resources. Zhdarkin's uncle, who had once left Bruski in search of "Muravia Land," [142] has returned and become a "Master of the Soil." At a Moscow conference he declares that the Bolsheviks and the people with their own hands have "turned human dreams into facts." [143]

GRAIN COLLECTION

However, these later realities were still dreams in the autumn of 1929. The First Five-Year Plan had greatly increased the number of wage-earners in industry and, consequently, the urban population. Several years of declining grain harvests and decreased government collections (which fell off 30 per cent during 1928–29) caused bread rationing to be started in the cities at the end of 1928. On the one hand, the peasants refused to part with their grain unless they got manufactured products in return; on the other, many of the laborers refused to work unless they received enough food. The kulaks speculated in grain, buying up all they could by overbidding the state, hoarding it, and then reselling on the black market at high prices. This situation led to the ruthless grain collections of the autumn and winter of 1929–30, the liquidation of the kulaks as a class, and the push for all-out agricultural collectivization.

As a Communist volunteer, Vladimir Kirshon took part in the sweeping drive and in the resulting intense class warfare in the villages. During the spring of 1930 he wrote *Bread*, a play "as topical as a news report." [144] This strict Party dogmatist produced a typical propaganda drama, agitating for the Party line on the agrarian front and attacking Communists who deviated from it, for whatever reason. His characters are dry and stereotyped, each one looking, talking, and acting "precisely like a wooden phrase in a *Pravda* editorial," reported Chamberlin, who saw a performance. He went on to say that the characters were like figures in a Communist morality play and that one felt they should have worn large distinctive labels: "General Party Line" (Mikhailov), "Left Opportunist" (Rayevsky), "Kulak" (Kvassov), "Class-conscious Poor Peasant," etc.[145]

"Russia needs bread!" [146] exclaims Mikhailov; and it is quite fitting that this incontestable fact, the play's mainspring, should be enunciated by the incarnation of the Party line. Mikhailov is a "stalwart, level-headed Communist" who handles situations decisively and can convince a meeting, putting over Party ideas as an efficient leader of the masses should. He believes that "unreasoned behavior . . . is always criminal" [147] and lets neither love for his wife nor personal gratitude interfere with Party duty; brave and always one jump ahead of his enemies, he is able to outwit the kulaks. His wife accuses him of lavishing his affection only on resolutions, decrees, and regulations: "You're not a man—just a set of Party principles. . . . You never deviate. . . . You're a Party automaton." [148] "There are no two Mikhailovs," he tells her. "There is only one man . . . that man is the Secretary of the Regional Committee." [149]

"The embodiment of political heresy in the ranks," Rayevsky, is "a true and tried Communist, but with a romantic flare and a hankering for the fleshpots." [150] Just back after three years in Germany, he is a great admirer of European technical efficiency. Although brave and loyal, he is impetuous to the point of foolhardiness and feels that "there are times . . . when reasoned behavior borders on the criminal." [151] Rayevsky is sent to the country as District Delegate to collect more bread and proves completely incapable of handling the situation, by his actions driving the poor and middle peasants to unite with the kulaks. First he tries to collect the grain at a "military tempo" and then, upon receipt of a threatening note, increases the amount to be collected as a retaliatory measure. When he refuses to rescind his order because to do so would be cowardly and a discredit to the Party, Mikhailov declares: "The Party can be discredited only by insane orders and unwillingness to correct an error." [152]

Kvassov, the typical wily, sinister kulak, is, of course, bitterly and unscrupulously anti-Soviet. He orders the house in which Mikhailov has taken refuge to be set afire, even though he knows that his own son is also inside. He is described as "the main head of the whole hydra-headed serpent" and practices all the tricks of grain speculation and hoarding. Living with him and helping to spread the spirit of revolt throughout the countryside is the nun Mokrina. Kirshon stresses the alliance, for counter-revolutionary ends, of the church and the kulaks who are seen frequently praying and crossing themselves. The village priest does his share by whispering to the peasants at confession advice which will help the conspiracy. In this way, a desirable note of anti-religious propaganda is introduced into the play.

Bread also treats the relationship of the Communist party to its members and their attitude towards it. That Party demands are stern and discipline for failure merciless is well illustrated when Mikhailov orders a Communist in charge of a construction job to the country with these heartening words:

You, Gromov, will be responsible [for the work here]. If you haven't selected capable assistants, you will suffer the consequences. If your quota isn't fulfilled, you will suffer the consequences. If the construction work isn't finished on time, you will suffer the consequences. . . . And you must also go to the country. These are difficult times, Gromov.[153]

The member's attitude towards his Party has much in common with that of a Roman Catholic towards his Church, the object of his faith. Loss of Party card is on a par with excommunication.[154] When Rayevsky goes unwillingly to the country to collect bread, it is because he has never yet refused to carry out a Party order. He knows that the Party uses its members for whatever it happens to need most at the moment and that it is a case of "theirs not to reason why." He reveals the hold that it has on him when he says that "the Party is a ring. It's an iron thong which holds people together. . . . the thong often cuts into my flesh, but I can't live without it." [155] Rayevsky does not want to be one of a crowd of identical, standardized people, all acting and talking alike; but he is terrified at the thought of this crowd going by without him, excluding him, and leaving him alone with his thoughts and doubts.

Their measured steps are merciless. And precisely because I myself am filled with thoughts which are not attuned to those of the others, with emotions which do not correspond to those of my companions, I cannot step out of the ranks. I dare not leave. I must feel another shoulder next to mine. I need someone to give me orders, someone to discipline me. I can't get along without those iron fetters which weld together the diverse sides of my "I." [156]

When he is asked, what if he were not being led in the right direction, he replies:

I'll follow and die with the rest. I fought for the Party. I'm its soldier. . . . It's impossible for the proletariat not to conquer. Victory is inevitable, as inevitable as death. I'm not sure that we—that Russia—will be the final victors. Perhaps we are but another Paris Commune which has managed to hold out for twelve years. If so, I shall know how to stand up against the wall. . . . No . . . I don't like the country. But I leave tomorrow.[157]

The antagonism between the country and the city,[158] and the peasants' jealousy of the proletarians as the pets of the Soviet government are well brought out in the following questions:

Why is the peasant burdened with so many loads? Why aren't the city people troubled? Why are the factory workers the favorite sons of the State, while we peasants—we who provide the food for all of Mother Russia—are the stepchildren? [159]

When Rayevsky speaks of the sacrifices that all must make for the industrialization of the country, a kulak answers:

It seems, then, that large sums of money are needed for industrialization. And that is why we peasants are ordered to contribute more bread? . . . But why the peasants . . . ? Why not reduce the salaries of the workers and the government employees? Why should the factory worker get new houses, clubs, theatres, and the peasant keep only his bitter fate? [160]

Another peasant grievance, which sounds like one that Kirshon himself may have had to answer, is voiced at the general meeting: "We used to receive manufactured goods. Where are they now? What's the matter? Have the factories closed down out there? Or have all the workers died?" [161]

The play concludes with an agitational technique similar to the one employed at the end of Vishnevski's *The Last Decisive*. When Kvassov tells Mikhailov that there is not room enough in the world for both "you" and "us," that one or the other must disappear, Mikhailov replies:

I'm afraid it will be you. . . . You wanted to kill Mikhailov, but you made a mistake in your reckoning. You thought there was only one Mikhailov—but there are so many Mikhailovs they can't be counted. Look at all the Mikhailovs! (*Points all around him; then points at the audience.*) And here are some more Mikhailovs! You can't destroy us by fire! [162]

At this point, the flattered audience was no doubt ready to run right out of the theatre and start liquidating kulaks.

Intelligentsia

A third major group of First Five-Year Plan literary works deals with the intelligentsia and its adjustment to the new Soviet order. The old intellectuals in industry—the engineers—have already been discussed in connection with industrial novels.

The intelligentsia was regarded by Marxists as a rather unstable group because of its position between classes. It was actually neither bourgeois nor proletarian; therefore no one was surprised when it wobbled in its attitude towards the Revolution. The government was forced to handle the intellectuals tactfully at first because they held a virtual monopoly of scientific and technical knowledge. The problem was, as an old scientist remarked: "You cannot dispossess us as you did the kulaks; you cannot expropriate us. . . . All my wealth is here!" (striking his forehead).[163] By 1931, however, the hope of a capitalist restoration or of another capitalist-socialist compromise (as during the NEP period) was virtually dead; and the successes of the first years of the Five-Year Plan caused the intelligentsia to make a rush to get on the band wagon.

The fellow-travelers were better fitted than the proletarian writers to handle, both artistically and realistically, the adjustment problems of the intelligentsia since they belonged to this category themselves. They had had personally to conform to the Soviet principles that the greatest growth of the individual occurs only through socialist participation and that individualism is a protest against the *status quo* in society. Leonov was a fellow-traveler. Alexander Afinogenov, although a Communist writer, was the son of a village schoolteacher and of a writer, and was under political suspicion from 1934 to 1940. Both chose to handle the problem of the intellectual in the realm of abstract science, and even in the laboratory we again find the class struggle going on between the old and the new.

In *Fear* (1931) Afinogenov demonstrates that socialist science cannot remain neutral and apolitical, that it must inevitably become either a weapon of reaction or an instrument of the Revolution. He also shows the process whereby an honest, individualistic old scientist, Professor Borodin, learns this lesson and adjusts to the demands of the masses, realizing that: "I lived a phantom life. I did not understand real life. And life penalizes those who shun it—with loneliness." [164]

At the beginning of the play, however, Professor Borodin is completely out of touch with reality and does not at all understand what is going on at his scientific institute: "Kirghisians with protruding cheekbones expel scholars, professors are put in jail, graduate students become professors, talented graduate students are crowded out by vydveezhentsy.[165] . . . What has come over people, I ask you?" "People are carrying on a class struggle, Professor," [166] his favorite pupil tells him.

Among the participants in this struggle at the Institute who belong to the "old" are (besides Borodin): the Professor of the History of Ancient Oriental Religions, discharged because he has "no Marxian basis"; Kastalsky, a graduate student who feels that his generation is "paying for the sins of the past that it does not even remember" and who is determined to avenge all those who, like him, "have been crushed by the weight of their social origin"; [167] Tsekhovoi, another graduate student with the wrong social origin, son of a military prosecutor, who has succeeded in concealing this fact and in joining the Party, but who comes to a bad end for having "deceived the working class"; and Professor Bobrov, who adapts himself to the new spirit of science with relative ease because he already believes human behavior to be the concern of politicians and because principles are more important to him than old friendships. The two main representatives of the "new" are: Kimbayev, a Kazak Communist student and *vydveezhenyets*, who shows the insatiable thirst for knowledge of the backward national minorities and their determination to catch up; and Elena, the semi-cultured, naïvely enthusiastic Red scientist who eventually replaces Borodin as director of the Institute because of her correct political outlook.

There is also the Communist managing director of the Institute, fresh from the Leather Trust, in whom Afinogenov satirizes bureaucratic interference and red tape in scientific work. His speech is peppered with Marxist clichés as he seeks to avoid inevitable (as it seems to him) deviations and tries to manage "in general and as a whole."

Kastalsky persuades Borodin to accept Elena's proposal to organize a laboratory for the study of human behavior but actually to use it to discredit her and to prove that "the Soviet system of governing people is good for nothing." [168] She thinks that the transformation of people under socialism is being studied. Borodin is then tricked by the foreign-directed counter-revolutionists into giving a public lecture revealing the results of his research: 80 per cent of the people are dominated by fear; the other 20 per cent are the masters of the country and have nothing to fear but suffer from a persecution mania. "We live in an epoch of great fear," [169] he asserts. Klara Spasova, an Old Bolshevik who works at the Red Rolling Mill, answers him: the fear of the oppressed turned into the fearlessness of revolutionists. Now only those opposed to the Soviet régime (the bureaucrat, the saboteur, the kulak) show fear; the class struggle is fearless.

Borodin finally realizes that the conspirators were able to use him as a tool because of his misconceptions about the meaning and place of science and because he studied life sitting at the window of his study. He is ready to criticize himself and his lecture publicly, and, turning over a new leaf, to resume his work from Elena's political viewpoint.

Like *Fear, Skutarevsky* (1932) reflects the process of the intelligentsia's transition to socialism; and, like Professor Borodin, Professor Skutarevsky at first considers science a privileged sphere and at the end descends from the heights of his scientific aloofness and detachment into the lower regions of practical communism and active adherence to the Soviet system.

The physicist and electrician Skutarevsky, although of proletarian origin, had become famous and wealthy before the Revolution. He has the ironic attitude towards the class struggle "which was a general characteristic of the whole class of 'intellectuals,' "[170] and the old conception of morals—"antiquated and sham conceptions of loyalty, of blood ties and social relationships"[171]—that prevents him from exposing "the dirty business in Siberia" where his son has built a defective power plant. He is not a sociable creature, he admits, and is "somehow scared, even repelled" whenever he comes in contact with the broad masses. He works away in the solitude of his laboratory, trying to find a solution for the wireless transmission of energy; and his assistant Cherimov can no more find out exactly what he is doing than could Elena in the case of Professor Borodin. After the failure of his experiment in the Caucasus, however, Skutarevsky realizes that his work has been "divorced from practice" and that it should be assisting socialist construction and defense. Leaving "friends and family and old habits behind him,"[172] he resumes his research, not alone as in the past, but surrounded by a group of pupils. At the close of the novel he is about to speak at the general assembly of the factory which has just taken over the patronage of his High-Frequency Institute.

Leonov shows the condition of science in Skutarevsky's youth under the autocracy when bourgeois industry exploited the inventions of young scientists, who were forced to exchange their "burning talent and scientific vision for roubles"[173] so as to live. To this he opposes a picture of the Soviet government's support of Skutarevsky's work for which Lenin provides a new institute, built to the professor's own specifications.

The Red scientist of *Skutarevsky* is Cherimov, son of a glass blower and former student at a workers' university, who has been sent to draw the Institute into closer touch with the actual practical application of its researches. Science, in his eyes, is his Party duty, and his approach to any truth is "in direct dependence on the echo it finds in the opinion of the masses."[174] Cherimov is a typical efficient young Communist, but he has an uncle who is rather remarkable. From the "former haughty, savage isolation" of his job as a bath attendant he suddenly flings himself into social reconstruction and has his beard cut off, as a result of his unexpected election to the district soviet. He becomes a new socialist man with the speed of a lightning conversion.

Most of the interesting characters of the book, as is usually the case in Leonov's novels, belong to the "old," the unusual, and the more or less subversive. There is Mrs. Skutarevsky in whom "a rotten microbe of grab got established" [175] and who constantly buys pseudo-antiques from Struff, the second-hand art dealer. Then there is Skutarevsky's brother Fyodor, museum expert and artist, who painted a portrait of the mysterious Zhistarev and who fakes old masters for Struff.

Skutarevsky's brother-in-law, Petrygin, is a great admirer of things European and believes that the world can be changed only by applied science and technology, which depends on the perfection of machinery and not on the class struggle. Leonov contrasts the "corpulent body" of this diabetic engineer with Skutarevsky's "wiry, mobile body," just one example of the way in which the physical appearance of a character is made a clue to his moral state.[176] (One might almost suppose that the author had intended his personages to be seen on the stage.) Petrygin, who occupies an important position in the administration of electrification, heads an industrial sabotage ring organized from abroad and financially backed by his father-in-law Zhistarev, a wealthy émigré. Leonov made something of a scoop in this matter as his novel was published only a few months before the Metropolitan-Vickers trial (April, 1933) in which seventeen electrical engineers, six of them British, were convicted of espionage and sabotage.

Just as Petrygin is set against Skutarevsky, so Arseny is set against Cherimov. They had fought together as partisans during the Civil War, but then their paths separated. This unsuccessful experiment of Skutarevsky's is the image of his uncle, Petrygin, and has the same large, flabby red ears (Cherimov's ears are normal). He has become a bored victim of bourgeois luxury, calls planned economy "enthusiastic hysterics," and speaks of "our crazy nigger-driven working days." [177] Finally, thoroughly sick of Petrygin's "conspirational world," Arseny shoots himself.

Although the social command is more evident in *Skutarevsky* than in *Sot*, we still find many colorful and devious old-world personalities in Leonov's story. He tells us that "the class which was irresistibly rising found no difficulty whatever in mastering the obstruction of a petty handful of people," [178] but it is this petty handful that he makes memorable.

Poetry

Although the period of the First Five-Year Plan was primarily one of prose, its poetry should not be entirely overlooked. Poetic creation was regarded as a definite form of social activity governed by the laws of social development, and poetry, as a social product "reflecting and expressing in a specific form the specific features of its time and . . . of its class." In its social role as transmitter of experience and educator of character, poetry at times becomes "an extraordinarily active militant force." [179]

In proletarian poetry after 1923 the cosmism of the Smithy gave way to the political realism of the At-the-Post group. Subjects were drawn from the life of the Communist party and of the Komsomol and from the concrete actuality of the daily life of the workers. This poetry was one of "gladness, profoundly buoyant and optimistic . . . reflecting the tremendous creative impulses, the struggle, the building of a new world." [180] It was also one of rhymed slogans of the day and of newspaper items paraphrased in verse.

All of the Komsomol poets were strongly influenced by Mayakovsky. Perhaps most prominent of this group was Alexander Bezymenski, "the poet, primarily, of the 'light cavalry' in struggle and labour," [181] who boasted:

> The factory is my father; the Party branch is my home,
> My family books, labor, and comrades.
> We live in Communist Youthland,
> A great and rich country.[182]

His poetic report to the Sixteenth Party Congress has already been mentioned; and he also versified as a Party publicist about socialist competition, shock brigades, the Five-Year Plan, and all the crucial up-to-the-minute problems in the economic and political life of the

SOME LITERARY WORKS

U.S.S.R. It was while working in the ranks of the proletariat that he wrote the poems published as *Poems That Make Steel*. One of them, "The Stoker's Song," is about the Donbas and has the refrain: " 'Tis the coal of our Soviet land." [183] At the same time Bezymenski wrote big works: a dramatic poem entitled *The Shot*; a long one about Dnieprostroi, *Tragic Night* (1930); and *The Night of the Head of the Political Section*, a poem about the successes of the *kolkhoz* movement.

Another Alexander, Zharov, like Bezymenski a Komsomol poet who came from the Smithy, proclaimed enthusiastically that:

> The destiny of building
> Not only songs but an epoch
> Is yours and mine! [184]

His poems dealt with themes intimately linked up with the life of the masses; and one of his collections, concerning socialist construction in the Ukraine, clearly revealed its propagandist nature in the title: *Poetry Helps to Produce Coal*.

In "Pyatiletka" Semyon Kirsanov spurred the workers on with a promise:

> To Five-Year Plan forests
>   go, peoples,
> with fires
>   into depths
>   of a thousand lands;
> in work,
>   in stress,
>   in smoke,
>   in drone,
> out of NEP Russia—
>   will come,
>   will come—
> Russia
>   socialist.[185]

When the Plan really began to roll, the following rosy picture was presented:

> With rising sun the factories
> And mills begin to throb

> And in the fields the tractorists
> Get early on the job.
> The farmers work collectively,
> Their common land they till;
> And in the town effectively—
> The whistles shrill . . .
>
> No money-grabbers niggardly
> The workers to despoil!
> To work we hasten eagerly,
> With song and zest we toil.
> We build our future commonwealth—
> One aim, one plan, one will!
> What we create, is common wealth.
> The whistles shrill . . .[186]

Even Selvinski's ape, Pao-Pao,[187] became human when he discovered the true socialist ideology in the harmonious environment of a Soviet factory. His testimonial was given in these words:

> U.S.S.R. rings with the ring
> Of golden Socialist melody.
>
> .   .   .   .
>
> I chased it as far as Tahiti,
> And at last understood this ring
> Only here, in this country and mill! [188]

With justifiable pride the former Futurist Aseyev pointed to one of the First Five-Year Plan's greatest constructions, the Dnieprostroi Dam:

> Well then, posterity, look at
> The universe of human miracle:
> There where lay the rock of ancient darkness
> Is erected the monument of Dnieprostroi.[189]

Finally, Vera Inber made a New Year's resolution for her fellow-poets:

> Today is the day of the rumbling mines,
> The triumphant day of the tractors,
> The joy of sirens shouting back and forth:
> "Long live the creative New Year!"
>
> .   .   .   .

It's the anniversary of the Five-Year Plan,
Hoisting up on buildings the figure "5";
And the proletarian brigades demand
Collective shock-work poems,
And we, poets, will give them!

. . .

Happy New Year, comrades!
Happy New Year, the Third!
Long live Next-to-Last of four years! [190]

Quality of First Five-Year Plan Literature

The First Five-Year Plan literary works mentioned in this chapter are exceptional, the *crème de la crème* of their period, and nearly all by authors who were already known. In general, one may say that the more interesting they are, the less they comply with the social command.

Almost engulfing these peaks was a vast flood of tendentious, sometimes illiterate and usually dull, descriptive scribbles by the literary *udarniks*, who possessed all the ideology but little of the ability necessary to produce a work of art. (There were, too, the writers' assigned "reports" on the achievements of the Plan.) This enormous literary Magnitostroi was uniform in its themes and in its treatment of them, "a monotonous literature of reportings interrupted by political hymns" turned out by "fountain-pen robots." [191] Lidin naïvely admitted in 1931 that "we write such a literature which in its essence can in no way be called entertaining or amusing." [192]

The literature of this period is characterized above all by the unity of its conceptual trends. The plenum of RAPP, said the critic Yermilov, examined all proletarian literary works from the point of view of how they met the demands of the reconstruction period,[193] that is, their success depended on RAPP's idea of their value in helping the fulfillment of the Five-Year Plan. The claim that Soviet literature was the best in the world was based, not on its superior craftsmanship, but on the fact that it, alone, portrayed great creation and great construction, presented correctly the death of capitalism and the birth of socialism, and provided an answer to the basic questions of mankind.

Literary quality ranked third after subject matter and social philosophy. As Engels wrote, "It is the old story: form is always neglected at first for content." [194] Style was "subordinated to the surge of construction going forward in the land," [195] while "often the content outstripped the form," stated Alexei Tolstoy:

> And often the reader's sympathy with the content, and his imagination, supplemented what was indicated by dotted lines in the book, or given only schematically; that which the writer had not enough force and experience to express.[196]

Many years ago the Russian novelist Saltykov warned propaganda writers against the danger of stereotyping characters: "One can count on one's fingers the 'types' required by a tendentious work and guarantee that they will all appear in each work of this kind." With unbelievable speed they take on the appearance of weather-beaten scarecrows, lifeless bodies, shadows. "It follows from this that anyone at all can write to serve a school if he merely has some notion of punctuation." [197]

How right Saltykov was, was proved by Leonov's account of the "books of nondescript colour and form" which appeared from 1929 to 1932:

> A standard type has been created for an individual sketch, a novel, a play (with the inevitable disaster in the middle and the heroism of the masses), for a collective farm epic (with the inevitable cunning peasant who is at first "for" and then "against"), for a current newspaper or magazine poem (where the revolutionary thought of the poet is replaced by the beating of some rather inaudible witch-doctor's tambourine). Titles are prepared in advance just as labels: the birth of a guild, the birth of a hero, the birth of a factory, the birth of an artisan, the birth of a woman: this sounds majestic and saves the author's mind all trouble. Many pages of such books are known to the reader long before they have been written.[198]

The typical Five-Year Plan hero is a man of action who reveals himself through the "historic deed of his people." But the deed is often so great that he is lost in the contours of the construction, and the real hero turns out to be the factory, the dam, or the mine.[199] "Labour," exclaimed Gorky, "is the real hero of our reality!" [200]

But even if some of the Soviet writers were too schematic, if some were armed "with the club instead of with the pen," and if others do not stand up under the criticism of time, said Alexei Tolstoy, in all of them there beat the pulse of an epoch not to be repeated: the building of the Five-Year Plan and the struggle for a classless society, an epoch which is instructive for all humanity.[201]

This period emphasized quantity at the expense of quality in every field of endeavor. In order to carry out the ambitious plans for the expansion of industrial production, a deterioration in quality was often deliberately tolerated: trimmings, colors, and designs were simplified; the choice of articles curtailed; thickness reduced; etc. Mass-consumption goods of substandard quality from virtually every branch of production came pouring out to help fulfill the Five-Year Plan in four years. With the Second Five-Year Plan (1933–37) the emphasis was shifted to quality of output. Exactly the same thing happened in literature. Themes were narrowed down and books of doubtful quality multiplied until here, too, the specifications were changed.

Even during the period of RAPP's dictatorship it was acknowledged by some writers and critics that contemporary literature had its failings, but it was still felt that the young inexperienced writers, promoted by the workers' circles, would soon perfect their literary technique (they were, of course, completely "in touch with the masses"). Not every generation produces geniuses, Lidin regretfully declared; but, he said hopefully, "our work is a preparatory work." [202] Gorky believed that, with few exceptions, this work was merely a temporarily successful experiment, not yet able to give "a synthesis of the most characteristic manifestations of our reality," [203] but that "never yet and nowhere" had literature kept so well in step with life as it was doing then in the U.S.S.R. However,

> the demands for "great" and "perfect" works of literary art are not only premature, but also, it would seem, intentionally aesthetic. Soviet literature cannot create a *War and Peace* because it, together with the whole mass of creative strength of the Soviet Union, lives in a state of war

against the old world and of strenuous building of a new world. Aestheticism is out of place in war. In war only an indifferent cynic can remain an aesthete.[204]

By 1934, it was officially admitted that most of the literature of the First Five-Year Plan period was fit only to be thrown into the wastebasket and that the Soviet proletariat, which in real life had already created Magnitostroi, Dnieprostroi, and Kuznetskstroi, had not yet created any works of prose or poetry commensurate with the greatness of its material and political achievements.[205]

The zealous Tretyakov had proclaimed:

Here the printed word is a toiler, with his sleeves rolled up. Here the pen is the brother of the tractor and the lathe. Here the only words that are bad are those that have nothing to do with deeds and those are bad which have not been made permanent in words.[206]

But Lenin's words at the Ninth Party Congress were perhaps remembered on April 23, 1932: "All aspects of literature are good except the boring." [207]

5. THE LIQUIDATION OF RAPP

The Class War in Literature

THE CLASS BATTLES which were raging in the Soviet Union became intensified when the First Five-Year Plan's socialist offensive began. The struggle to destroy the kulaks as a class, the all-out drive to collectivize the peasants, the conspiracies and wrecking activities of reactionary elements of the bourgeois intelligentsia—all this was reflected in a bitter literary class war which acquired an open and irreconcilable character. During this period "the class nature of literary groups and individual writers came to the surface as blood rushes to the face during a fight," [1] wrote Zelinski. The last vestiges of capitalism in literature must be destroyed; the cultural revolution required a crusade against all literary schools except the proletarian. There was a need for greater emphasis on revolutionary enthusiasm, socialist competition, and the direct collaboration of the writers in the struggle for the Five-Year Plan. RAPP became the Communist party's man Friday with a mission to organize such literary support and to "tear away the masks" from the enemies of the proletariat.

Averbakh and his adherents ("the oldest, most strongly interlocked, most intolerant, most authoritarian, and closest group of comrades, uniting . . . under the general sign: 'At-Lit-Post' " [2]) controlled the press, paper supplies, and editorial boards and began to exercise an inquisitional censorship.[3] Whatever aesthetic tolerance there had been, vanished. Proletarian writers such as Kirshon and Bezymenski zealously supervised, investigated, and denounced fellow-authors whom they suspected of heresy. At the Communist Academy it was declared that:

Literature for us is a weapon of political education. We are convinced that in regard to the great majority of the poputchiki we can exert influence by methods of ideological persuasion. In regard to those writers who are organically foreign to us, we do not renounce other methods of struggle, such as taking individual plays off the repertory, forbidding the printing of their works, etc.[4]

Authors who did not deal with contemporary themes were at once branded "counter-revolutionary." One publishing house even refused to print a novel because the time of action was three years behindhand.

"Detecting anti-proletarian tendencies in literature, RAPP called attention to their danger . . . (criticism of Pilnyak, Zamyatin, writers of Pereval, Constructivists)." [5] Three of the campaigns prosecuted by the At-Lit-Post critics were later counted to their credit: the exposure of the errors of Voronski's and of Professor Pereverzev's schools of criticism and the struggle against the Litfront.[6] Pereverzev was with malice aforethought accused of protecting art for art's sake while pretending to be an orthodox Marxist and of repudiating the ideological and political functions of literature just at a time when the proletariat of the world was engaged in a deadly struggle.[7] After he had been smashed, "the comrades understood," explained Libedinski, "that it was impossible to work outside of our organization [RAPP], that it was necessary to work within it." [8]

It was dangerous to oppose RAPP unless one was strong enough and had prestige enough to be beyond Averbakh's reach. In 1926 Demyan Bedny had publicly disassociated himself from the At-Lit-Post group; and, two years later, on his return from abroad Gorky had attacked the boastful and dictatorial claims of the At-Lit-Post clique and quarreled with RAPP about the education and professional training of young writers.[9] But few, if any, other writers successfully stood up against Averbakh and his followers during this period.

In 1929 a new campaign was started against the fellow-travelers. Pilnyak, their Moscow leader, was proclaimed a counter-revolutionary full of pernicious, Trotskyist, petty-bourgeois tendencies as a result of the publication of *Mahogany* in Berlin. Zamyatin in Leningrad was accused of unbelief and non-acceptance of the social revolution because of the publication, unknown to him, of pirated fragments of his novel, We, by a Russian émigré journal in Prague. A violent onslaught was made against him in the Communist press, and a vote of censure was passed by VAPP.[10] As a result, both of these novelists resigned from VAPP.

RAPP tried to destroy those who had not won its favor, even prominent writers such as Furmanov (Chapayev) and Sholokhov:

Naturally the right sector of Soviet literature was dealt the heaviest blow. Vsevolod Ivanov's and Babel's last works were not allowed to be published. Pilnyak had to make changes in his latest works and was prohibited from republishing his older ones. M. Bulgakov [Days of the Turbins] and many others were reduced to complete silence. In Moscow there was a distinct feeling that Maiakovsky committed suicide not only because of his disillusionment in the successes of Communism, but also because his two plays, Bathhouse [1930] [11] and Bedbug [1928], were banned by the authorities, who detected in them, not without reason, a satire on the Soviet government. Even the proletarian group of writers, to which belonged Libedinsky and his followers, was looked upon with suspicion. Next in turn to enjoy the confidence of those in power was Bezymensky, who for a while became the poet laureate of the Soviet régime.[12]

In February of 1930 (the same year as E. Bagritski, V. Lugovskoi, and "a series of literary scholars and Red professors" [13]) Mayakovsky had joined RAPP, presumably in self-defense. Libedinski gave an interesting version of this event. He said that Mayakovsky himself left LEF and "came over to our leadership in RAPP, and not to Gorbachyov."

When he appeared in our organization, he did not write such things as the Pereversevites did; he simply arrived at the conference of MAPP and declared: "Our opinions differ. You know me; I, you. I am joining you because I know that outside of your organization I cannot work further." [14]

On March 25 Mayakovsky read for the first time "At the Top of My Voice," the prelude to a projected poem on the Five-Year Plan, in which he confessed:

>   I'm fed
>   to the teeth
>   with agit-prop,

> I'd like
> > to scribble for you
> > > love ballads,—
> > they're charming
> > > and pay quite a lot.
> > But I
> > > mastered myself,
> > > > and crushed under foot
> > > the throat
> > > > of my very own songs.[15]

On April 11, he shot himself.

Mayakovsky's death was a most unexpected and severe blow to Soviet literature since the thoughts expressed in his poetry had seemed so much in harmony with the social command. He had only recently boasted that he would "lift up high, like a Bolshevik partycard, all the hundred books" of his "ComParty poems."[16] RAPP had attacked him before his death for insufficient closeness to, and concern for, the masses; and afterwards it succeeded, for a while, in preventing the publication of his works, delaying the opening of his museum, and removing his name from the school curricula. According to Averbakh, Mayakovsky fell by the wayside because he came from the petty bourgeoisie.[17] Bezymenski characteristically issued him a posthumous reprimand for his suicide and assured him that "a bullet means a deal in the life of a man, but *nothing* in the life of an age."[18] He told the elder poet, who had once influenced him:

> Your life, that fabulous tower,
> Stood up on stilts of mere straw.
> Cursed stilts of old-fashioned feelings,
> Thrust in your way by the old world![19]

Zelinski agreed that Mayakovsky "was overcome by the forces of the old world so passionately denounced by him," but added that he died "like a soldier in battle, 'struggling forward.'" His end "made us feel acutely that it was a struggle to the death, and that there were victims in literature, too."[20]

V. Ya. Kirpotin, secretary of the Organizing Committee of the Union of Soviet Writers, thought that the growth of the influence of proletarian literature and its leading role in all Soviet literature, which was attained with the help given by the Party and through RAPP, was the best justification for the support which the Party at that time gave RAPP. This growth could not have taken place without the struggles which were waged by this organization, under the leadership of the Party, against all sorts of hostile, anti-Marxist, anti-Leninist movements. Kirpotin concluded that, without the decisive destruction of Trotskyism and of Trotskyite contrabandists of the type of Gorbachyov, the successes of Soviet literature would have been impossible and that the struggle waged against the ideas of Voronski and the Pereval group,[21] Polonski, Pereverzev, the Litfront, formalism,[22] etc., wiped out the doctrines hostile to Marxism.[23]

According to I. M. Gronski, chairman of the Organizing Committee who presided at its first plenum, RAPP was a special organization, created to lead the proletarian writers and to strengthen the position of the working class and of proletarian literature in the general literature of the U.S.S.R. It represented the Party and guided literature on behalf of the Party, in general correctly, in spite of various errors.[24]

However,

the Party repeatedly gave the leadership of RAPP instructions about the necessity for a categorical reconstruction of its work, so as to bring it closer to the tasks of socialist construction. Repeatedly, it was pointed out that RAPP was not an administrative, but an ideologico-educational organization. The necessity for the development of self-criticism was pointed out, the necessity for the solidarity of all the forces of proletarian literature and criticism in the chief positions. However, all these direct and urgent instructions, to a significant degree, were not carried out.[25]

Bureaucracy flourished, the *udarniks* were an artistic failure, and literary talent dried up under regimentation and standardization. As under Napoleon's dictatorship, the peculiar "ambition to call into being on order masterpieces *of a certain kind*, prevented the appearance of masterpieces without a definite character." [26] We read that First Empire poetry created "a sinister boredom," that "if one is struck by the abundance of such a production, one is no less struck by its monotony," and that "no one work can be distinguished from the others; they all resemble each other." [27] The cause: the didacticism and disciplinary measures against writers which prevailed under Napoleon, and by his order, and which contributed to the literary sterility of the period.[28] "Why," Napoleon asked M. de Fontanes, "has our literature become so boring?" [29]

Evidently, the same question bothered Stalin and Kalinin towards the end of the First Five-Year Plan period.[30] Gorky spoke of the scholastic, barren, and wordy disputes; the confusion accompanying personal relations; and the "abundance of vulgar gossip on which we thrive" as characteristic of "our present life and current work." [31] In order to correct this situation, on April 23, 1932, a decree of the Central Committee of the Communist party abolished RAPP.

Decree of April 23, 1932

Whereas the Central Committee's 1925 Resolution had "legalized a situation which had arisen out of the literary disputes of the time and had given the Fellow-Travellers their full 'citizen rights,' " the new decree, creating a Union of Soviet Writers, brought about an "organic" revolution [32] and was considered a sign of Soviet literature's transition to a new, higher phase. This was possible because of the turning of a wide mass of the old intelligentsia to the side of the Soviet power, due to the correct politics of the Communist party and to the successes during the First Five-Year Plan on the front of industrial and cultural construction and on the collectivization front; and because of the leading role of proletarian literature and the growth of proletarian writers' cadres. In the words of the resolution:

Now that the rank and file of proletarian literature has had time to grow and establish itself, and that new writers and artists have come forward from factories, mills, and collective farms, the framework of the existing proletarian literary-artistic organizations (VOAPP, RAPP, RAPM,[33] etc.) is becoming too confined and impedes the serious development of artistic creation. There is thus the danger that these organizations might be turned from a means of intensive mobilization of Soviet writers and artists around the problems of socialist construction into a means of cultivating hermetic groupings and of alienating considerable groups of writers and artists, sympathizing with the aims of socialist construction, from contemporary political problems.[34]

It was therefore decided to liquidate the Association of Proletarian Writers and to "unite all writers upholding the platform of the Soviet power and striving to participate in socialist construction into a single Union of Soviet Writers with a Communist faction therein" and to entrust the Organizing Bureau with the working out of practical measures for the resolution's application.[35]

This decree was hailed as a realistic application to literature of the principles of Stalin's speech, showing the true dialectic, and as "a classic example of our proletarian criticism, classic by its conciseness, by its profoundness." [36]

One of the results of the Central Committee's decision was the following announcement, which appeared in the final number of *Na literaturnom postu*, May, 1932:

> The management of the Association of Proletarian Writers (RAPP) announces that the Association is liquidated and resolves to pass on to the Organizing Committee its journal, finances, and property.
>
> The literary circles in [business] enterprises are continuing their work.
>
> Secretariat of RAPP
> L. AVERBAKH, I. MAKAROV, A. FADEYEV,
> V. KIRSHON, F. PANFYOROV.[37]

This Organizing Bureau, or Orgcommittee ("the strong monolithic, Communist skeleton of the future organization of Soviet writers" [38]), represented various creative groups and movements but was not, in itself, a creative group. It was formed to unite the writing masses and to prepare for a congress of Union writers by the liquidation of the literary organizations' conflicts and clannishness, which had severed them from contemporary political problems.

VAPP, RAPP, and the various APPs were liquidated, as was FOSP (the union of *kolkhoz* proletarian writers). LOKAF (Literary Union of the Red Army and Fleet), which had brought cadres of Soviet writers into contact with the army to further the development of a defensive and military literature, was merged as one of the detachments of the new writers' union. Advocates of the policy of forcible proletariazation were replaced on editorial boards, publishing committees, and censorship boards.

A strong nucleus of Communists in literature was considered necessary in order to establish correct relations with the non-Party writers, to lead them towards the Party, and to control and help them in their work. Members of this Communist faction must not squabble among themselves, but must appear as a single group before the non-Party writers. Quarrels on literary themes should take place only within the limits of the single Party line.[39]

The six months between the April Decree dissolving RAPP and the First Plenum of the Orgcommittee were a period of great activity. Big new literary works were completed or being written, and groups of writers spent the summer at the new constructions and on *sovkhozes* and *kolkhozes* collecting material. Works of authors such as Sergeyev-Tsenski, Romanov, and Klychkov also began to appear again in magazines. They had lapsed into almost total silence after having been the victims of "Averbakh's literary poison gas," [40] "nasty criticism full of invective, but devoid of constructive thought." [41] Under the new conditions, however, the writer was no longer afraid to appear in print, knowing that he could already count on a sympathetic attitude on the part of the critic, who would show him his errors so as to help him change his old point of view.

During this half year "certain prerequisites for the liquidation of clannishness" were created, especially in relations between critics and writers, between organizations as a whole and individual writers, between editorial boards and writers, and, most important of all, between Communist writers and non-Party writers.[42] Former leaders and workers of RAPP were criticized and corrected "in a comradely way" to overcome resistance, incomprehension, and passiveness in carrying out the decision of the Central Committee and to create conditions for teamwork between them and the Orgcommittee. To facilitate their enrollment in the ranks of Soviet literature and to give them a chance to correct their mistakes, Averbakh, Makarov, Yermilov, and Subotski were included in its R.S.F.S.R. section.

Nevertheless, there had been certain problems in the criticism of the mistakes of RAPP, of individual comrades, and of the leadership as a whole. Many At-the-Postists clung to their old methods of work and tried to infuse fresh strength into the group by taking in new members, even fellow-travelers, in order to create an even stronger clique. There was often an absence of broad self-criticism. For instance, immediately after the Central Committee's April Resolution, there had been an attempt by the *Literaturnaya gazeta* [43] to distort this Party decision. In an article full of false and harmful statements no mention was made of the fact that the liquidation of RAPP had been ordered, and the whole thing was presented simply as an organizational reconstruction. Also, the fellow-travelers and allies were charged with fencing themselves off from proletarian literary movements when the truth was that RAPP had lost contact with this important group of writers who wished to take an active part in socialist construction. This matter was exposed by *Pravda*.

Neither did *Na literaturnom postu* co-operate actively and in a Bolshevik way to implement the Party's decree. The resolution itself and the article in *Pravda* commenting on it were merely printed in Number 12 of the magazine after one issue ignoring it had already appeared. In order to

liquidate clannishness, it is necessary to have consistent, all-sided, systematic criticism of the mistakes of individual comrades and of the whole leadership of RAPP, mistakes which created the basis for this clannishness, the danger of the cultivation of cliquish aloofness, and the separation from political tasks of a large group of artists sympathetic to socialist construction. Without criticism of the mistakes of the leading literary organizations, a situation cannot be created which will be guaranteed from relapsing into clannishness.[44]

Even after RAPP had understood the necessity for a quick and complete change in all of its methods of work, it "continued to roll by the force of inertia along its former paths," [45] hindering the Party itself which had started, in the form of the Orgcommittee, to reorganize the literary front.

First Plenum of the Orgcommittee, October 29– November 3, 1932

The First Plenum of the Organizing Committee of the Union of Soviet Writers met in Moscow from October 29 to November 3, 1932, and was attended by writers of the R.S.F.S.R.; the Ukraine;

Belorussia; the Transcaucasian Federation; the Karelian, Crimean, and Tartar Republics; Turkmenistan; Moldavia; Tadzhikistan; Uzbekistan; Kirghizia; Kazakstan; Siberia; and the Ural, Udmurt, Komi-Zirani, and Chechen Autonomous Regions—129 delegates in all. About five hundred authors and members of literary circles were present as guests.[46]

The purpose of the meeting appears to have been to expose and criticize the errors of the past, to report on the existing state of affairs in literature, and to discuss socialist realism and methods of creative work for the future. Since the plenum coincided with the fifteenth anniversary of the October Revolution, the results summed up there were also the results of the development of Soviet literature for the previous fifteen years. "This plenum will go down in history," predicted Bruno Yasenski, "as the first plenum of the consolidated forces of all the Soviet writers around the Bolshevik party and its Central Committee for the realization of tasks set by the Party before our literature as a whole and each individual writer." [47]

In an opening speech Chairman Gronski outlined the future plans of the Orgcommittee. "This program of work," he said, "demands the unity of Communists, correct relations with non-Party members, the solidarity of all Soviet literary men around the Soviet power and our Leninist Party, around the leader of our Party and of the international proletariat, Comrade Stalin." [48] Next, Comrade Kirpotin gave a report on "Soviet Literature to the Fifteenth Anniversary of the October Revolution," after which, Comrade L. M. Subotski told "About the Progress of the Reorganization of Literary Organizations." Then the general discussion began, to be terminated several days later by Kirpotin's concluding remarks and Gronski's concluding speech. These two speakers were the only ones who talked more than once; everyone else had one chance to make a speech and after that had to confine himself to shouting remarks from the floor.

There were speeches by writers and critics of all hues, from black reaction to Red bolshevism: Klychkov, Shklovski, Slonimski and Vsevolod Ivanov, Pilnyak and Olyosha, Berezovski, Bakhmetyev and Gladkov, Libedinski, Yermilov and Kirshon, and, of course, Averbakh. Representatives spoke for the Institute of Literature and Art, children's books, *kolkhoz* literature, the Komsomol, the trade unions, and the defunct LOKAF. Novikova, a delegate from the Moscow literary circles, testified that the workers of the Orgametal Factory had organized a circle and named it after "the first historic plenum of Soviet writers," while Pantiyeleva of the Red Proletariat Factory told how their circle-members had been thrown out of MAPP for pointing out inadequacies and carrying on criticism of the errors of RAPP. Friedrich Wolf greeted the plenum in the name of the German dramatists. MORP (International Union of Revolutionary Writers) was represented by Katsumoto of Japan, who was looking forward to a world-wide proletarian socialist culture; by Bela Illesh, a Hungarian Communist expatriate; and by the German-Polish Bruno Yasenski, who spoke of a special "MORPish" clannishness, which in some respects had been possibly even stronger than RAPP's and which had developed because MORP was led by a group of political-émigré writers who had partly broken away from the revolutionary movement in the West.

RAPP'S TWO PERIODS

Fadeyev said that there were two periods of RAPP's activity. During the first one, RAPP and its nucleus, the At-Lit-Post group (which was not so much a group as an ideological current) played a positive and progressive role in the development of Soviet literature. The culminating point in the development of the proletarian literary movement was during the fight against the Litfront, when "everything truly revolutionary in Soviet literature" in large measure rallied around RAPP, in spite of the groupish structure of the whole literary movement. To this period belonged the enrollment in RAPP of Mayakovsky and many other fine writers, while in Leningrad the fellow-travelers took part in the struggle against the Litfront, siding with RAPP.[49]

Gorky considered that,

at the time when the RAPPists acted in comradely harmony and were not yet ill with "administrative exaltation," although not distinguished for a wide and deep knowledge of literature and its history, they yet possessed the sharp-sightedness and sensitiveness of Party-line followers and saw well the enemy and the blunderer, saw the parrots and the monkeys who imitated the voice and the gestures of Bolsheviks.[50]

One of the merits of RAPP and the At-Lit-Post group was that they always stated questions sharply although they often ran the risk of making a mistake. Questions were pointed in discussion, thereby revealing their true solution. The elements of Proletcultism present in the Smithy group were uncovered in RAPP's fight against it; and other deviations were exposed during the struggles against Voronski, Trotsky, etc. However, Averbakh admitted that RAPP's leaders did not think over the "enormous positive experience" accumulated in these discussions and that the critics were too busy abusing each other and trying to decide who said this or that, and on what occasion.[51] As described by Gorky, "the critics are split into petty groups, quarrel furiously, and censure one another, bringing into this scarcely fruitful work much manifest partiality, ambition, many personal sympathies, antipathies, and, finally individualism." [52]

To Gronski, RAPP, in spite of its later mistakes, was a great mass movement in literature of thousands of workers and *kolkhoz* peasants, led by a small group of highly qualified literary men such as Averbakh, Kirshon, Fadeyev, and Afinogenov; and it gave many talented people of the working class to literature.[53]

Louis Fischer, writing from Moscow at this time, characterized RAPP as a censor, not a literary organization:

True, it encouraged young workers to try their luck at writing. In this wise, of course, much trash entered the literary field, and the trash was nursed because it carried the holy adjective "proletarian." But the opening of the literary door to factory employees and peasants is an achievement which may be booked to RAPP. In all fairness, however, I can think of nothing else.[54]

According to Chumandrin, Averbakh's Leningrad representative:

RAPP . . . did not lead the enrollment of shock workers in literature badly but did not know how to consolidate it fully. From the ranks of RAPP important writers arose who were widely known, even beyond the boundaries of the country. I am not inclined to forget that RAPP was the principal center of political literary life, and this secured for it a basically correct line in relation to the fellow-travelers. RAPP knew how to smash decisively, in a Bolshevik way and without mercy, all the anti-Party groups wherever they were formed.[55]

In the field of politics MORP, guided by RAPP, was successful in attracting a wide stratum of foreign writers to the defense of the Soviet Union.

It seems likely that during this first period RAPP had the Communist party's wholehearted support of its activities in mobilizing literature behind the socialist construction of the First Five-Year Plan, in broadening the base of Soviet literature by its enrollment of shock writers, and in its fights against ideological literary deviations. However, from here on, said Fadeyev, RAPP became a train that began to leave the tracks, although its leaders did not notice this. "That was when we should have made a sharp turn towards a really revolutionary Soviet literature" by liquidating RAPP at the time of its nearest contact with the Soviet writers.[56]

But RAPP was not dissolved then, and during the winter of 1930–31 its influence turned negative as a result of the ultra-clannish condition which began to develop, aggravated by the monopolistic position of the At-Lit-Post group. The slogans, "For a Greater Art of Bolshevism!" and "For a Genuinely Revolutionary Art!" which were launched by RAPP, were correct; but there was a great contradiction between them and the way in which they were applied. The discord became acute, not only between RAPP and the non-Party writers, but among the Communists themselves, with the At-Lit-Post group getting into an isolated position. Averbakh and Kirshon said that the difficulty lay in the fact that the At-Lit-Postists represented a creative group (with all of its loyalties and antipathies; with its own creative line, platform, and methods) and, at the same time, the leadership of the whole proletarian literary movement; and that the contradiction between group and leadership was the essence of the conflict:

. . . group sympathies interfered, became an obstacle; and we sometimes did not know how, because of our literary-clique discords, to give our hand to a writer, a class comrade. We approached such a writer

... by appraising his nearness to our creative method, not understanding that he with his creative path had brought positive benefit to the building of socialism, just as we had with ours.

Further, we definitely had group encirclement and group selection of personnel. We rebuffed a whole series of writers because they did not share our creative position and views, while they could have been attracted and should have been used.[57]

Fadeyev did not agree with this explanation because he thought, in the first place, that the At-Lit-Post had already ceased to be a genuinely creative group; that within it, too, there were already conflicts; and that people in it differed not at all from those belonging to other groups. In the second place, he said that Averbakh was wrong because

> our problem consisted, not in preoccupation with the maintenance and development of certain groups, but our problem was to transform ourselves as quickly as possible into a really genuine leading force for literature, attracting, of course, all the other Communist forces, increasing and strengthening Communist leadership, turning into a leading force.[58]

ADMINISTRATIVE MISTAKES

Clannishness (*gruppovshchina*) appears to have been RAPP's basic error and is blamed for causing: regimentation, bureaucracy, domineeringness, snobbishness, intolerance towards outsiders, inadequate development of self-criticism and the ignoring of Party and comradely criticism, loss of contact with contemporary political problems, an incorrect policy towards fellow-travelers, and self-isolation from the basic cadres of Soviet writers with a consequent weakening of influence on them, which hindered the fulfillment of the principal task set before RAPP by the Party—the correct leadership of non-Party writers.

Clannishness is a big impediment to artistic creation because it does not permit the objective appraisal of literary works. The leading writers of the group are hailed as geniuses, and the faults and artistic mistakes of members are readily excused. Many laudatory articles are written in praise of a writer who "belongs," while an outsider is ignored or often abusively berated for his slightest fault. Kozakov put the situation this way: "We ignored the growth of Soviet literature as a whole and came to be a little like some sort of restricted co-operative store in which fame, mutual understanding, talents, etc. were distributed to members only," with Averbakh, of course acting as manager.[59]

The monopoly of leadership held by the At-Lit-Post group caused other groups of an antithetical character to spring up in self-defense and for the preservation of their creative individuality. As a result of this, the leading section of RAPP and its critics were concerned primarily with the strengthening of their dictatorial position in literature. In order to do this, it was necessary to take devoted persons into the group, whether or not they had any real literary talent or had had any previous contact with literature. On the other hand, writers who were not members had to be boycotted. They were not studied critically and carefully from all sides; they were simply "silenced and destroyed."

In the matter of the literary *udarniks*, a large number of workers and peasants was shanghaied into writers' circles but then more or less abandoned to fate. These groups of would-be authors in many places, including Moscow and Leningrad, were not consolidated; and RAPP gave no theoretical, methodological indications for systematic work with them. As a result, from the time that they were high-pressured into joining until the liquidation of RAPP, the shock writers kept dropping out of their cadres. In Tula, for instance, 80 per cent of those enrolled fell by the wayside. In explaining this to the plenum of RAPP, Comrade Kirshon had blamed it on the fact that many of those who had joined had done so by chance and from a vague desire to be writers and that they really belonged in readers' circles. However, he failed to point out the basic cause of this disaffection: the undifferentiated, depersonalized approach. A circle member was not asked whether he wanted to be a poet, a prose writer, a journalist, or a dramatist; no account was taken of his desires, and he therefore soon lost interest in the work and dropped out.

The state of affairs in Moscow was, in a sense, typical of the general picture. Upon investigation it was discovered that more than half of MAPP's sixty-two workers' literary circles existed merely nominally, and only twenty-eight could be found that were really active.[60] Also, the number of consultations which MAPP's "Cabinet of Shock Workers" had held with young authors was obviously inadequate.

In the working literary circles, the academic program which was carried on, the time lost in futile conference-sitting, and the participation of the members in clannish fights resulted in a separation from concrete creative work and contemporary political problems. No connection or correlation existed between the work of the literary circle and the life and work of the whole enterprise in which it was situated, between its work and that of the Komsomol, of the Party cell, of the trade-union organization. The factory, *sovkhoz*, or *kolkhoz* could find itself in a serious crisis, but this would not be reflected in the work of its literary circle which took no interest in helping to fulfill the tasks set for the enterprise. Neither did the circle members show any enthusiasm about contributing to their wall-sheet newspapers, their "Ilych papers," or their local papers which consequently had no literary page; these beginner-writers were interested only in appearing in the large magazines and newspapers.

Besides these faults, regimentation and intimidation flourished in the literary circles. Certain comrades developed the practice of imposing on the members a system of disciplinary penalties in the form of reprimands, etc., which were carried out both in the circles and at meetings of the association secretariats. There were, presumably, even cases in which these reprimands were published in the press.[61]

RAPP had nothing in common with the peasant writers and was accused in its relations with them of bungling leadership, an underestimation of the alliance of the proletariat with the peasantry, clannish snobbishness, a failure to understand the problems of the proletarian *kolkhoz* writers, and a narrow conception that proletarian writers should write exclusively about factory and mill. The At-Lit-Post critics "turned up their noses at *kolkhoz* literature." They noticed only two works: *Bruski* and *Soil Upturned*, and that was partly because Panfyorov and Sholokhov belonged to the RAPP organization. When the former quarreled with RAPP, they tried in every way to insult him and to smear him.[62] MAPP's indifference is shown by the fact that it was not until the spring of 1932 that the first brigade of worker-writers was organized to go to the *kolkhozes*.

The Komsomol, too, complained of its treatment in a quarrel with RAPP, which had defended creative views opposed to the cultural interests of the young people of the working class. And among RAPP's most serious mistakes was its loss of contact with the older writers, who found that there was no place where they could even speak with its leaders.[63] Moreover, it had shown little interest in, and given no adequate help to, the various APPs. VAPP and RAPP were morely closely tied with the western part of the Soviet Union (Ukraine and Belorussia), less with the eastern part, and least of all with the literatures of the national minorities of the R.S.F.S.R.

To RAPP, neutrality and non-political views in an author were a mere excuse on his part for evading active participation in the tasks of socialist construction. The "politically false and contrary-to-the-Party-line slogan 'Ally or Enemy'" was adopted by the Fourth Plenum of RAPP in September of 1931 [64] and continued to be promoted as indispensable during 1932 in spite of the fact that as early as June 23, 1931, Stalin had stated to a conference of industrial administrators:

About two years ago [mid-1929] things were going on with us in such a way that the most qualified part of the old technical intelligentsia was infected with the sickness of wrecking. . . . That was a year or two ago. Can we say that we now have just exactly such conditions? No, this cannot be said. On the contrary, we now have entirely different conditions.

The old intelligentsia, and even an important part of the former wreckers, has begun to work beside the working class; as a result,

it would be incorrect and undialectical to continue the old policy under new, changed conditions. . . . Therefore, to change our attitude towards the engineering-technical forces of the old school, to show them more attention and care, to attract them more boldly to work— such are the tasks.[65]

RAPP misinterpreted the Party line as formulated in this speech of Stalin's and launched a leftist slogan which contradicted it. In January, 1931, B. Kor, writing in *Na literaturnom postu*, declared: "But in any case, only two possibilities face the fellow-travelers: either ally or enemy." [66] In a speech on "Greater Self-criticism," delivered at the plenum of RAPP in February, M. Luzgin of Leningrad said: " 'Ally or Enemy'—here is the basic formulation of the question which we now give. This statement of the question is true in principle and politically correct. It means that now we can speak only about the kind of writer who really accepts the reconstruction period." [67]

A resolution of the Fourth Plenum of RAPP, printed in the September 15, 1931, issue of the *Literaturnaya gazeta*, presented the following ultimatum although the slogan, "Ally or Enemy," itself, was not mentioned: "With the agents of the bourgeoisie and of kulakdom in literature, or with proletarian literature—thus stands the question before each of today's fellow-travelers." The resolution explained the approved line for the proletarian literary movement towards writers who were still fellow-travelers but who could approach the positions of the proletariat, as "a policy of decisive and uncompromising criticism of petty-bourgeois swaying and, together with that, of friendly help in genuine reconstruction by way of a *rapprochement* with the proletariat." [68]

Averbakh's book, *From RAPP's Diary*,[69] was received by the publisher on November 18, 1931. In it he again advocated the slogan, "Ally or Enemy," and the fight for the Party line, for Bolshevik intolerance, and for the line of most resistance. "To go today with the Revolution . . . means to be confident of the 'possibility' of building socialism in our country. Moreover, perhaps the name of 'fellow-traveler' suits whoever goes with the Revolution—unless 'ally' is better?" Any Soviet writer who did not fit this formula, Averbakh put into the camp of the counter-revolution; and about him he asked: ". . . perhaps this is not an adversary, not an enemy, not an agent of the class enemy?" [70]

The slogan, "Ally or Enemy," in reality basically contradicts the Party line towards the fellow-travelers, said *Pravda* on May 9, 1932;

THE LIQUIDATION OF RAPP

it is a schematization and a vulgarization of the Party line towards the intelligentsia.[71] RAPP's application of the formula had the following results:

When they scare a writer with this slogan, when he is threatened with the danger that any error on his way to us can cause him to be tagged "Class Enemy," then, by such a course of action they demand of the writer, not an ideological turning, not a true, well-considered, heartfelt turning, but a quick, full-gallop "reconstruction" which excludes a genuine, deep weighing of all problems and questions. This slogan produces reconstruction by magic formula, by RAPP's will.[72]

Chumandrin confessed that in their relations with the fellow-travelers RAPP's leaders very often engaged in regimentation and that in judging a literary work they were frequently influenced by the consideration of what group position the author occupied, and not always by what his book itself represented in a certain period of the literary development of the class struggle.

But it was not only the fellow-travelers who suffered during RAPP's second period. The atmosphere created at this time was bad also for the proletarian writers, not only those who were in disfavor, but also some of the leaders of RAPP. The themes and problems of literature were forgotten, the workbench was abandoned, and people busied themselves with organizational squabbles and organizational fights for power.

ERRORS IN CRITICISM

During RAPP's régime, "Dnieprostroyian clannishness" led to the over-praising of the At-Lit-Post writers and their narrow circle of friends, to the rude shoving aside or ignoring of outsiders, and to the constant heckling of many non-Party writers. The most negative phenomenon in this sharp publicist criticism was "the habit of denouncing a writer as a class enemy, as a Fascist, on every excuse or even without any excuse at all, thus excluding him altogether from Soviet literature."[73] Such intolerance could cause a writer to be called a class enemy and thrown out of literature on any pretext; for instance, if he did not put a comma in the right place. Utkin even went so far as to say that *literary* criticism did not then exist,

RAPP functionally was a critical organization which worked at social incrimination, at the classification of literary artists to whom it gave characteristics. The controversy was between the *social* criticism which RAPP produced, on one hand, and literature, on the other.[74]

Groups and clannishness lock a writer in a narrow compartment. He gets used to certain abstract principles and loses contact with life; he does not verify his ideas with changing life and, as a result, arrives at a conflict with it and loses his sense of values in appraising literary phenomena. It was because of just such a resistance to life and ignoring of reality that RAPP was liquidated. The basic deficiency of this organization's criticism was its dogmatism. "That is to say, this was criticism not issuing from life, but contrasting itself to life. The comrade critics tried to correct life, and, like everyone dogmatic, they carried out their views by administrative methods." [75] The problem of truthfully showing the new socialist reality in its typical manifestations was replaced by abstract scholastic demands.

Another result of clannishness in the field of criticism is a depersonalized approach to the writer when individualized work with him is indispensable. Critics read hurriedly and apparently looked only for an opportunity to pick a quarrel with the author, to "down" him.[76] The leaders of RAPP gave excellent reports; but, said Chumandrin, "it is one thing to give a good report and another, to carry on systematic work, day after day, on each book, on each production of each writer, uplifting and educating him. Many good writers appeared, not always thanks to us, but very often in spite of us." [77]

Over-simplification and vulgarization of the concrete complexities of art and of the literary process was also an error of RAPP critics. Only a wholly proletarian point of view, they asserted, enables the writer to produce works truly in harmony with the epoch. A decade later Alexei Tolstoy was to refer to these "theoreticians," who sorted literary works and writers into blacks and whites: the bourgeois, who had to be done away with, and the proletarians, who had to be glorified.[78] He blamed ignorance for this mistaken attitude and also "the direct work of fascist agents who had crept into literature."[79]

The following humorous example of RAPP's literary criticism was given by Vera Inber. A young writer complained to her: "I wrote a poem about the fact that busses should not run over people, but the editor crossed out this line and wrote: 'Busses should not run over proletarians.'" Thus, she said, was understood the question of the intensive class line in literary works.[80]

Within RAPP itself raged a controversy on matters of principle and problems of creation. There were two main factions: the one to which Fadeyev, Libedinski, and Chumandrin belonged; and the opposition,[81] consisting of several separate groups led by Bezymenski, Panfyorov, and Zharov, respectively, which was dissatisfied with the way proletarian writers were lagging behind the demands of socialist construction. The orthodox RAPP theory of art (which was based on Lenin's comment that Tolstoy "tore the mask from reality") called for an "objective-realistic, as opposed to a subjective-psychological method of approach to life,"[82] coloring nothing and revealing those objective forces which were embodied in it. The psychology of people must be understood against the background of this realistic interpretation of life. "To present individuality concretely, is now the principal task of the present epoch of proletarian literature,"[83] Libedinski told a VAPP conference.

It was Fadeyev who carried these precepts into practice most fully. His novel, *The Last of the Udegs* (1929-35, which depicts a semi-patriarchal tribe of the Far East, the local bourgeoisie, and the semi-peasant mass of Red partisans), was reproached by the opposition for its "superficial remoteness from the burning interests of the moment."[84] Another furiously attacked example of psychological realism[85] was Libedinski's "degenerate" novel, *The Birth of a Hero* (1930),[86] which portrayed a trusted Communist from the point of view of his love affairs, rather than that of his Party work; it was edited by Sutyrin, Yermilov, Kirshon, and Fadeyev. Libedinski was referred to by Yermilov as a sacrifice to clannishness, and all of RAPP was blamed for putting a brake on his development.[87] Kirpotin said that it was the substitution of subjective idealism for socialist realism in art that led to such mistakes as this novel, which became a weapon in the hands of the Litfront in the fight with RAPP. The quarrel arose because RAPP would not permit its mistakes in the matter of *The Birth of a Hero* and Bezymenski's *The Shot* (1930)[88] to be pointed out openly, and it narrowed down to scholastic discussions of these two literary works.

Among other writers named as victims of RAPP's unprincipled factionalism were the playwrights, Bill-Belotserkovski and Vishnevski; Ilyenkov for his novel, *Driving Axle*; and Panfyorov, who was first put upon a pedestal as a genius and later demoted and spat upon. Bezymenski was not taken to task for the series of foolish things that he had done or for the Litfront adventure, as he could and should have been. But he was denounced by RAPP's leaders in an inadmissible way for having echoes in his works of Zamyatin,[89] the name being used in the sense of "inside émigré." Zamyatin was not at all an inside émigré; but, even if he had been one, it would have been a profound political error to connect Bezymenski with him.[90]

Marietta Shaginyan considered the principal inadequacy of RAPP's criticism to have been its mechanicalness, which consisted, in the first place, in a one-sided application of the idea of the writer's personal development only; and, in the second place, in an inadequate knowledge of the planned development of reality and, therefore, insufficiently concrete historicalness applied to the analysis of an artistic work:

Criticism took the work of a writer, his latest book, compared it with the preceding one, with still earlier and even . . . pre-revolutionary ones, and on this basis determined progress or retrogression, movement to the right or to the left. Criticism turned its basic axis towards the disclosure of the artist's social personality. Thus, the book itself was put aside, and in the foreground appeared the active disclosure of the artist's personality. And the reader, receiving such an interpretation of the book, was first of all interested in the writer and not in the book written by him. . . .[91]

The other twist consisted in an inadequate historical concreteness. It resulted again from the critic's ignorance of the planned development of the economy. Thus, it turned out that a writer wrote a book in which he reflected entirely correctly such and such social relations. He could reflect them weakly or with a class tendentious deviation, but he took the situation as it was given to him. However, the critic reproached him for what the writer could not, and should not, have reflected. . . . that is, the critic borrows a phenomenon from an entirely different historical period and accuses the author of its absence.[92]

The Litfront had thought it possible to recommend for study only tendentious writers of the past, in its own simplified meaning of the term. As a counter-balance to this, RAPP advocated that only the realists of past literature be studied; and there was a tendency to identify realism with materialism, to interpret it one-sidedly and superficially, showing an uncritical attitude towards certain types of realism of the past. Alexei Tolstoy said that RAPP opposed proletarian to all human culture, denying Russia's literary heritage and purposely breaking "the ties which lead from the contemporary man to the historical past." [93] "We were . . . at fault," confessed Mikitenko, "when we propagated the slogan of proletarian realism; we were at fault because some comrades canonized the realist writers, while they anathemized all those who did not accept proletarian realism but adhered to the romantic heresy." [94]

In 1931, Averbakh boasted to a plenary session of VOAPP:

Our Association . . . is at present a center for all Communist forces on the literary front. Proletarian writers have already conquered the leading place in literature from an ideological and political point of view and are now conquering the leading place from the point of view of art. We must raise our literature to a higher level than any of the best examples of previous literature.[95]

And the false slogan, "To Overtake and Surpass the Classics," was launched—"a vulgar mechanistic transference from the field of economic relations into literature." [96]

Yet the attitude of RAPP's leadership towards lyric poetry was entirely negative; and, especially during its last period, the atmosphere created was such that "lyric poetry with its elements of the individual . . . as opposed to the social, could not find any place at all for itself." [97]

Kushner's *Pravda* article of October 4, 1930, deplored the fact that proletarian literature was slavishly lagging behind the tempos of socialist construction and that this hitch, which had manifested itself only recently, was a big problem. The most important reason for it must be sought in the traditions of literary work and in the creative habits established by many proletarian authors, he wrote. There have been, and are, a number of false, harmful theories and slogans such as, "Living Man" [98] and "Direct Impressions." [99] The path to a lasting conquest of the hegemony of proletarian literature lies in the mastery and consistent application by writers of the correct creative method, the dialectical-materialistic approach to reality; in the further bolshevizing of proletarian literature; and in the growth of the core of workers among the proletarian writers, which is impossible without truly Bolshevik tempos in the mass conscription of reinforcements drawn from the *udarniks*.[100]

A month later, at the Kharkov Congress, Averbakh announced in a "Resolution on Political and Creative Questions": "Every proletarian artist must be a dialectical materialist. The method of creative art is the method of dialectical materialism." [101] One of the basic errors of RAPP's leaders in the field of creative questions lay in the fact that, having correctly put before the writer the necessity for mastering this method, they dogmatized the problem and began to approach literature primarily from the point of view of the method used by the artist. A letter about the creative discussions in RAPP stated that

the At-the-Post group first raised the question about the dialectical materialistic artistic method in proletarian literature. Not one of At-the-Post's creative slogans can be broken away from this principal and decisive initial point: all the rest of the slogans are steps on the path to the mastery of the dialectical materialistic method of proletarian literature.[102]

In commenting on this position of RAPP's, Kirpotin said,

We are for dialectical materialism in art, but we consider the dialectical materialistic creative method to be an incorrect one. It simplifies a thing; it converts a complicated relationship, an intricate dependence of artistic creation on an ideological conception, a complex subordination of the artist to the world-outlook of his class, into an absolutely, automatically active law.

THE LIQUIDATION OF RAPP

An artist sometimes arrives at a correct and instructive deduction in spite of his world-outlook. This is a minus for art. But that this can be, must not be forgotten or ignored. To forget this, leads to forcible regimentation just when the writer needs to be given the chance to follow his own fruitful road to dialectical materialism under ideological leadership only, with help from Marxist criticism.[103]

The slogan of the dialectical materialistic creative method, combined with the slogan, "Ally or Enemy," under which the mastery by a writer of the method of *diamat* was often made a criterion of his classification as friend or foe, was a slogan of crude regimentation. It inevitably led to the academic application of dialectics in criticism itself. It did not teach the critic to analyze all the complexities of literary reality by means of dialectical materialism but taught him to use dialectical materialism as a rigid academic yardstick while ignoring all world-outlook. RAPP critics erred when they did not seek the elements of dialectical materialism in a certain concrete work, but took the conception of dialectical materialism itself and dogmatically tried to fit the work to a preconceived critical measure.

Yermilov advised critics to remember the classical criticism of the *raznochintsy*[104] which said that one must criticize artistic works for what is in them, and not for what is not in them. He continued: "We very often criticized artistic works chiefly for what was not in them, for the absence of adequate mastery of the dialectical materialistic method. And, proceeding from a plan, we often passed over what was in a certain artistic work."[105]

RAPP undervalued the significance for the writer of artistic mastery and failed to realize that form is an indispensable side. Kirpotin reminded the Orgcommittee that, when two works of art have an identical ideological content, the one with the more perfect artistic form will have the greater educational effect. Further, the more deeply, the more faithfully, a writer incarnates in his literary productions the essential side of reality, its perspectives, tendencies, and the aims of its development, the greater will be its elements of dialectical materialism.[106]

RAPP's leaders demanded that the writer should write according to the method of dialectical materialism, but they were never able to state simply and clearly what this meant. This was brought out in Gorky's condemnation of the At-Lit-Post critics:

I do not want to give our enemies the opportunity to laugh at us by emphasizing the coarseness, the lack of culture and, very often, even the ignorance of our critics. Perhaps our critics are very well equipped ideologically, but something seems to deter them from stating with the utmost clarity and simplicity the science of dialectic materialism as applied to questions of art. They quote Karl Marx, Engels, Plekhanov and Lenin, but they often obscure the meaning of these quotations by burying them under an avalanche of colourless verbiage. The demands made on literature and on writers are not clearly defined. It often happens that critics possessed of one and the same ideology make entirely different demands of a writer. Contradiction among critics is a usual occurrence, but the thing to be deplored here is that the contradictions grow and develop on the basis of the critics' attitude towards the most important question of all: the method of conceiving the phenomena of life.[107]

Averbakh admitted that,

when in RAPP we spoke about dialectical materialism, we methodologized abstractly a great deal; and perhaps often our discussions about dialectical materialism as a slogan were vulgarized and unhistorical. . . . Our critics very often did not know how to disclose the basic world-outlook of the creative method by an analysis of the structure of forms, their relationships, and the whole artistic tissue of production, together with its artistic technique.[108]

On the opening day of the First Plenum of the Orgcommittee, October 29, 1932, the *Literaturnaya gazeta* appeared with an article by Fadeyev called "Old and New Questions of Artistic Creation." Among the subjects discussed were dialectical materialism, the world-outlook of the proletariat, and its presentation by RAPP as the new revolutionary artistic method: the method of dialectical materialism in art. Fadeyev considered that "the elaboration of questions of artistic creation from this point of view had a revolutionary significance for our literature." He continued:

In the performances of a great many critics the so-called method of dialectical materialism turned into some sort of tabular and trivial conception, into a yardstick, into a "talisman" fitting the palm of the hand. Indeed, many beginning writers, and also some of the older ones (those who were fellow-travelerish), began to think that one could find an all-inclusive Marxist book or series of books from which one could grasp this dialectical materialism and apply it to creative works. On the other hand, in the performances of a great many critics the method of dialectical materialism turned into something self-sufficient, into an end in itself. The result was, that the principal aim of artistic work seemed to consist in achieving the ideal and neat dialectical "method," although nothing yet was known about writers who had achieved this method. But there was a certain insignificant number who had approached it, a certain number who were approaching it, and a large number who were either far from this method or who misinterpreted it and wrestled with it.

Meanwhile, every intelligent man understood

that the organic transition to the positions of the working class, the organic perception of its world-outlook, being both useful and indispensable, helps every true artist to grasp with the greatest fullness, depth, and truthfulness the whole richness of reality, the true essence of appearances, the main trends of the development of human society, and the stabilization of the new socialist society in its fight with the old exploiting society. (The organic perception of this world-outlook is possible, not by means of a book and bookish study of the basic positions of Marxism, but primarily by means of the living practice of life, which elucidates the revolutionary theories of Marx and Lenin, theories which condense the whole diversified, living, rich historic experience of humanity.)

Fadeyev came to the conclusion that "the true dialectical materialism in art is, primarily, the truthful artistic rendering of reality in its development, in its basic trends, in its living richness, in the diversity of problems and questions agitating new humanity." [109] It enables the writer to reveal the true dialectic existing in life. "When we say that the writer should write the truth, we say first of all that the writer should dialectically reveal the processes of life." [110]

The cultural and educational importance of literature, its role as "the traveling companion of history," and its critical attitude towards contemporary life were underestimated by the critics, declared Gorky. Although much was said and written about the class content of the novel, the short story, and the drama, no mention was made of the technical methods to be employed.[111] The critics were occupied, not so much with literature, as with "reciprocal education." They all "straightened the line"; and, as a result of their efforts, the line became "so capriciously bent and tangled" that it was hard to understand just where the "straight and single one" was.[112] Dissension and internal strife took up so much of their time and energy that, when a heretic did appear among them, they failed to notice him for a long time, and only when he went to extremes did they "sound the alarm and begin to chastise him." [113]

In his article, "A Revolution in Revolutionary History," which appeared in the New York *Herald Tribune* on November 27, 1932, Louis Fischer held RAPP responsible for the poverty of Soviet literary criticism. He wrote:

This association last year exercised dictatorial prerogatives. It considered itself the dominant element in Soviet literature and Soviet literary criticism. That was why Soviet literary criticism was so poor and so shallow. If the RAPP frowned on a writer his career was crippled. It persecuted the fellow travelers or poputchiki with a bitterness and relentlessness which merely indicated that it had no respect for art. . . . the Soviet critic was "a literary nihilist, not a literary Bolshevik." The Soviet critic took his key from RAPP. And RAPP wished to destroy all that was not "proletarian literature." It certainly has plenty of destruction on its conscience. I think it may be blamed for the death of Vyacheslav Polonsky, the most talented and cultured of Soviet critics . . . RAPP drove other brilliant literary figures into silence. RAPP critics never cared about artistic quality. They scarcely ever appreciated ability. Their only criterion was politics, and if a novelist deviated a hair's breadth from the orthodox party line they stamped him a "counterrevolutionary"—which finished him completely. Hundreds of manuscripts lay unprinted in the State Publishing House because RAPP disapproved of their contents and their authors.

If an author was visibly trying to do the right thing, but had slipped once or twice, the Soviet critics did not lend him a helping hand; they threw him to the lions. "They never guided or coached authors with delicate suggestion. They attacked maliciously with blunt weapons; they shot to kill."

RAPP had not only alienated men whose soul was with the revolution. It had become a sort of royal thumb on the hand of Averbach & Co., which went up when one or two authors entered the arena and down on most other occasions. It was an administrative organ which decided who and what could be printed.[114]

After the Central Committee's April Decree, the task of the new comradely criticism became: to criticize the writer cautiously and respectfully, without hooting and without condescension, and to help the old writers to join the ranks and attain a position in the working class. "It is impossible to transform the slogan of socialist realism into a schematic prescription," said Kirpotin. Individual artists will overcome their backward tendencies and will approach socialist realism in various ways and in differing degrees.[115]

AVERBAKH

Chairman Gronski, in his concluding remarks, divided the former leaders of RAPP into two groups as a result of their speeches, which were not all on the same level. Comrade Chumandrin did a model job of "manly Bolshevik self-criticism," turned around sharply, and burned all his bridges, thereby finishing entirely with clannishness and leaving no possibility of "maneuvering." Exactly the same thing may be said about the speeches of Libedinski, Fadeyev, and Yermilov. The other group is overcoming clannish habits of work with more difficulty, continued Gronski. Averbakh, Makarov, and, to a lesser degree, Kirshon failed to give an exhaustive exposition of RAPP's errors and their own. Although their declarations were not exactly unsatisfactory, yet the plenum expected more from them. "*These comrades left the possibility of maneuvering.* Whether they will avail themselves of these possibilities or not, the future will show."[116]

To the populist proletarian author, Bakhmetyev, it seemed that Yermilov "spoke well and sincerely, but—about anyone you like, only not about himself, not about his mistakes. Averbakh—about all, only not about himself; both, about everything, only not about literature; and Fadeyev—also, finally, not about himself." Fadeyev and Libedinski should have spoken, in the first place, not about the mistakes of their comrades, Averbakh and Kirshon, but about their own; they should have noted how much they were indebted to the At-Lit-Post's clannish support for their fame as writers, "in what degree, so to say, they used an administrative prop to become well-known figures."[117]

THE LIQUIDATION OF RAPP

In the case of Leopold Leonidovich Averbakh, literary critic, editor of *Na literaturnom postu,* and virtual dictator of RAPP, there was a very definite change in the attitude of the meeting towards him. He had been put on the Orgcommittee as one of the representatives of the R.S.F.S.R.; and the chairman, Gronski, in his opening speech called Averbakh his friend. But after the latter's speech, the feeling towards him appears to have been quite different. It was felt that he had repented of his errors just enough to get by, that he had shown his usual arrogance, and that he did not have a Bolshevik attitude towards criticism. Serafimovich asked what one can say to Comrade Averbakh and then, addressing him, declared, "Although your skin has changed, your heart remains the same." [118]

Averbakh in his speech said that the principal masses of non-Party comrades have been dissatisfied with the situation and the policy which had existed in literature under RAPP and that its leaders must take the responsibility for this. He considered it a pity that RAPP was not liquidated sooner, since this would have been beneficial to the whole of Soviet literature. However, in spite of all of its mistakes in its relations with the non-Party intelligentsia, in spite of its clannishness and of a series of errors in theoretical and creative questions, RAPP was an organization whose workers had no other aim in literature than those dictated by the interests of the Party. "It was a fine organization, which educated many hundreds of young proletarian writers," declared Averbakh, "and I am proud that I was a member of RAPP in its time." [119]

A review of the entire RAPP literary inheritance is full of meaning, Averbakh continued, because it reveals on the one hand what was correct in RAPP's activity, and on the other, its many mistakes. "It would be ridiculous to claim infallibility when we had errors connected with the theory of direct impressions, with an insufficiently critical attitude towards Plekhanov, with the slogan of Demyanization, and with a series of appraisals in concrete criticism, etc." [120] But it is also ridiculous when people try to fasten onto RAPP the tag of Voronskyism, on the basis of citations from individual members, because RAPP followed the line of fighting against Voronskyism, even though at times inadequately and not always with theoretical depth. In creative questions, however, RAPP became rather set in its ways, partly from having a fairly monopolistic position and partly from having committed a series of errors. Averbakh admitted that RAPP's leaders should have responded more quickly to the conditions and problems of the new period and that they must be punished for this tardiness, as well as for being too late in correcting their mistakes. He answered for this lateness and these mistakes, his own and those of his comrades.

In concluding his speech, Averbakh said that during the past six months he and his comrades have learned a great deal from the Party's correct criticism of them and that the principal cadres of former RAPP workers have a real desire to be included completely in the work of the Orgcommittee, to be loyal sons of the Party, and to fight for and follow the Party line in practice. He and the other RAPP leaders included in the Orgcommittee are entering it in order also to war against such revengeful attitudes as may yet remain among any of the former RAPP members.[121]

Chariyev of Turkmenistan followed Averbakh, and he wasted no time in declaring:

We did not expect from Comrade Averbakh a speech such as he gave; we expected a speech of self-criticism. (Libedinski and Chumandrin: "Correct!") We expected a Bolshevist speech. . . . He glossed over and did not acknowledge his mistakes like a Bolshevik. (Applause.) We are Bolsheviks and should speak in a Bolshevik way, acknowledge our mistakes, and fight against them. (Libedinski: "To the end.") But Averbakh did not do this, and I am not satisfied with this, and I think that others are not satisfied. The impression is that Averbakh has not reformed as he should. We demand a self-critical, Bolshevik speech and a Bolshevik acknowledgement of his mistakes. (Applause.) [122]

Berezovski said that, instead of speaking in general sentences, Comrade Averbakh should have come out and, with Bolshevik firmness, undressed as Chumandrin did. "I am deeply convinced that he would then have left this tribune with huge relief, instead of the heavy feeling which he must have carried away . . ." [123] But Buachidze of Georgia felt that, "in general, to undress is simply indecent," and that "Party self-criticism consists, not in undressing, . . . but in a Bolshevik postmortem of all elements of clannishness.[124]

Vera Inber remarked that Averbakh was such a good orator, he had made his comrades and himself appear much less guilty; while Reizin of LOKAF thought that, since he had had more than half a year in which to think over his errors, he should have given the concrete analysis of his literary-creative mistakes that the majority of those present had expected from him.

Gladkov considered that in RAPP Averbakh had been a strong force and a courageous man, but that he had betrayed this courage. The reflexes of clannishness had seized the upper hand over true self-criticism, and they would remain with him for a long time. Mikitenko, after noting the presence still in Averbakh's mind of remnants of the old methods of work, exhorted: "Leopold, reorganize with the Bolshevik tempos because neither time nor work waits. We expect from you intensive, concrete work." [125]

Klychkov, whom RAPP had called a "reactionary and feudal kulak," was naturally not very favorably disposed towards Averbakh who, he said, never had understood, did not now understand, and, judging by his speech, never would understand what an artist was; and who, in fact, had nothing in common with art. He characterized Averbakh as a verbal machine-gun who "could do very well standing at the entrance to any state institution and bring greater benefit than, for instance, here in the Orgcommittee. For us, sometimes, it is much better and more sensible when a man stumbles and is suppressed." [126]

Tarasov-Rodionov, a former member of RAPP, stated that "Averbakh does not at all understand the class significance and nature of art. . . . I consider that we should work a while with Klychkov, but that we should and must work much more with Averbakh. He is ours." [127]

Vishnevski, too, found Averbakh's great fault to be that he had not gone into the problems of art deeply enough. "His whole speech was a political speech, and we now are more and more demanding skill, quality, and specificity." [128]

Libedinski, another fellow-RAPP member, also saw some merits in Averbakh. While admitting that he might be prejudiced, he believed that

Averbakh is a man who sees well the perspectives of the development of literature and their ties with the general course of the cultural revolution, but who often makes mistakes in small details. This is his essential deficiency—to be mistaken in details and in concrete things, also, to see the wide horizons of literature, but to see very indistinctly. (Gronski: "Therefore he also missed the reorganization.")

Libedinski said that this strong and talented man, with organizational experience and the ability to see perspectives, is important capital belonging to the Party, but that his faults prevent his being used.[129]

Averbakh's speech shows that he does not know how to join in breaking up the old groups or how to use a comradely tone towards those who criticize him, continued Libedinski. Until now he has not wished to criticize his errors, and the central part of his speech was clogged up with individualism and "me-ishness." Libedinski warned Averbakh that he will not make progress until he roots out his errors and prophecies that he will have to start at the bottom, talking concretely with each writer about the problems of his work and helping him to grow—a thing that he never did in RAPP where he was monopolized by a small group of writers.[130]

Kirpotin, however, denied Libedinski's assertion that Averbakh has been taken into the Orgcommittee to do the drudgery of a common soldier and said that he has been brought in on the same level as the other members. Kirpotin considered that Comrade Averbakh most urgently needs a little revolutionary academism and that "there will be no harm if he pursues this study in the Orgcommittee," which is kind and does not object to teaching him.[131]

At great length, Kirpotin analyzed and criticized the speech in which "Averbakh, in very fine Ciceronian form (I give him his due), said nothing about literature." He should have talked about certain principles of the science of literature in more detail because a series of his basic standpoints entered into the principal directives of RAPP.[132] Averbakh had written in *Creative Paths*: "The artist-writer must not lose contact with ideology, with his (the writer's) world-outlook as a whole." This premise is perfectly correct, but he continued: "Moreover, the artistic method is *completely and totally* subordinated to his (the writer's) whole ideological point of view." This "completely and totally" gives a vulgarized idea of literary-artistic creation. The dependence of art upon political ideology is not as direct and simple as Comrade Averbakh imagined, said Kirpotin, although art is narrowly tied to other superstructures and is under the influence and leadership of politics, economics, and socio-political changes. (Such a simplified view of the complexity of art inevitably leads to regimentation over the writer, to pushing him when only an ideological influence is needed to guide him.) Not understanding this, Averbakh had to make his speech, not with literary material, but from a literary-organizational angle:

> He spoke about the danger of "neo-Proletcultishness"; he said that we should work less with a club and occupy ourselves more with ideo-educational work. He talked about replacement, about regimentation, about the necessity for liquidating, not only RAPP, but also the At-the-Post group; he spoke about the suppression of books. . . . All these are important things; but all this is on the plane of literary-organizational, literary-political questions, not on the plane of literary-creative questions. As a result, Comrade Averbakh cannot explain such an extremely essential thing as why we dialectical materialists declare that the slogan of dialectical materialism in art was not good enough, that it was a slogan of vulgarization; and why we replace this slogan with the slogan of socialist realism.
>
> If one does not understand the correlation of political, philosophical, etc. ideology with the artistic, one cannot understand the change of these slogans. . . . Comrade Averbakh, looking over RAPP's past, determining the obstacles which should be removed, cannot explain the replacement of the slogan of the dialectical-materialistic creative method by the slogan of socialist realism. It means that his transition to the slogan of socialist realism can have occurred only by way of a formal understanding, and not by way of a deep contemplation of the essentials on the basis of a study of the literary factors.[133]

Kirpotin finished his dismemberment of Averbakh's speech with the remark, "I say all this affectionately so that the Orgcommittee will get a valuable worker." [134] Apparently, however, this worker did not prove his value, for Averbakh and his clique lost their power and were gradually removed from all responsible positions and banished to posts in the Urals and in Siberia.[135]

PRINCIPAL CAUSES OF RAPP'S DISSOLUTION

Averbakh confessed that RAPP's leaders

did not know how to profit by those decrees which the Party (and, in the first place, Comrade Stalin in a series of talks) gave us, to the effect that our RAPP organization should have an ideologically educational character, that in it any elements of regimentation and domineering were inadmissible. In words we all understood this . . . but in practice nothing happened. . . . It was necessary to strike the leadership of RAPP because we underestimated the shifts among the intelligentsia and continued the line of group gathering-of-forces when all old groups and groupish partitions had to be smashed. This means that we proved ourselves unequal to the occasion.[136]

They continued to be a group instead of having in view the interests of the whole of Soviet literature. Yermilov gave a dialectical explanation of what happened during RAPP's last period:

That form of socialist attack in the field of literature which RAPP was in its time, outlived itself; we needed a new form of socialist attack. The achievements and merits of the old form began to change into its opposite—that is just what is expressed in the April Decree of the Central Committee. The leaders of RAPP became blind to this basic question, did not understand that the form of attack which they were leading had outlived itself and *does not work* in the new historical conditions.[137]

And Fadeyev rendered a self-critical judgment in these words:

And now, in looking over the experience of the past, one must say that the At-the-Postists, the leading detachment of RAPP, in large measure did not justify the hopes of our Party. We proved to be considerably smaller than the tasks which it set before us. If we really look at ourselves, clearly and bolshevikly, we must say that, if we called ourselves the nucleus of the Central Committee in literature, if we stood at the head of the proletarian literary movement in a land of socialism and proposed to head it further, then these claims are unusually high. . . . The inertia of the past lay on various groups, but more had to be demanded from the people to whom much was given, *whom the Party backed* [italics mine].[138]

The Central Committee did not deny RAPP's great services to proletarian literature in the past, but what was fruitful and reasonable during the early period outlived itself.

... in the new period of the development of Soviet literature, RAPP, which could not understand the changing conditions, began to cultivate clannishness, monopolistic snootiness, intolerance, regimentation and abuse, cliquish arrogance, and separation from contemporary political tasks. RAPP arrived at a clash with the demands of the radically changed conditions, and, instead of becoming a bond of solidarity around the Party and the Soviet power for all writers who wished to share actively in socialist construction, it turned into an obstacle in the path of important detachments of writers and of the Party. Clannish partitions, cultivated by RAPP, prevented the correct carrying out of the Party line in literature.[139]

It is these clannish partitions that Subotski gave as the basic cause of RAPP's liquidation. Other speakers offered different reasons, but they were all closely related to each other. For instance, the delegate from Kazakstan said that the Central Committee decided to dissolve RAPP because of its clumsy leadership of the national organizations and because it did not know how to lead a movement among the poor and middle peasants (who were becoming collectivized), at a time when the distinctions between city and country were about to be abolished.

Others believed that RAPP's principal error was the political one of attempting to substitute itself for the leadership of the Party in the literary field, of creating an organization outside of the government apparatus (somewhat as the Proletcult had tried to do during the period of War Communism).

The At-Lit-Postists, who had become the leaders of RAPP, finally overreached themselves and invented their own general line of RAPP ... and then created a general secretary of RAPP [Averbakh]. The comrades imitated the Party, forgetting that they were working in literature and that there is one line, the correct line of the Party. Turning RAPP into an organization with a general line and a general secretary, these comrades led it into a whole series of errors.[140]

Gronski, the chairman of the Orgcommittee, put the matter thus: RAPP did not remember the altered circumstances, was not able to draw all the conclusions from the changed situation, could not face towards those writers who were coming over to the side of Soviet rule, did not know how to make the change of policy in literature. RAPP and the leadership of RAPP are guilty of this fundamental and important mistake. . . . The Party cannot wait until RAPP catches and corrects its error; the Party itself has already made this change on the literary front. And so that this change should be executed, so that it would be clear to each writer that the Party has turned around and does not subtilize or maneuver, it was decided to liquidate RAPP as a special literary organization and to create a single Union of Soviet Writers.[141]

It is of interest to have an American newspaper man's opinion, written from Moscow in November, 1932, about the dissolution of RAPP:

The day before the decree which ended RAPP's existence, L. Averbach, its most aggressive leader, spoke in public about his organization's plans for the future. He did not expect the blow. Why did it come so suddenly? Why the liberal move which substituted a non-partisan writers' league for the party's literary dog-in-the-manger (if we cannot write proletarian literature we can at least prevent others from writing non-proletarian literature)? I think the new policy was due directly to the disgust in highest quarter with the crude persecutions of the poputchiks by RAPP and with the ugly personal concomitants of such tactics. Literature, and the cinema and theatre too were paralyzed by the reign of RAPP, and more and more complaints began to reach the Big Nine of the Communist Politburo. . . .

But the revolution in the field of Soviet revolutionary literature has a still deeper explanation. There has been, of late, a reaction here against the narrowmindedness of a few Communists who constituted themselves a sort of Soviet Sinai from which they proceed to hand down the laws for all intellectual activities. The privileges granted the intelligentsia in the summer of 1931, and the cessation of intra-party dissensions (Stalin is today the undisputed leader) have been followed by a wave of relative tolerance. It really set in last spring after the bad effects of the "pogrom" against the "Trotskyist contraband" had worn off. There is no guarantee against a relapse. But that the new spirit is more than a mere mood or whim follows from the fact that it has assumed organizational forms. First, the writers' league. . . . The change, of course, bespeaks the increased confidence of Communists in the potency of their ideas. It attests the rapid sovietization of the intelligentsia. But it especially reflects a new air of tolerance in intellectual fields which, if it is not hampered by petty bureaucrats, should quickly enrich Soviet literature, art and science.

Louis Fischer added this prophetic thought:

The poputchiki, and with them most sensible people, welcome these developments. Yet I have reason to believe that any number of non-Communist writers are still wary and suspicious. May they not, some day when the course shifts to the Left again, suffer for their sins of moderation in the period now commencing? [142]

One has only to think of the resolution issued by the Soviet Writers' Union on September 7, 1946, expelling Mikhail Zoshchenko and Anna Akhmatova for "not participating in Socialist construction," [143] to see how right Fischer was.

Zelinski, too, foresaw that the April 23 (1932) Decree did not mean the end of the struggle:

I shall not be mistaken, I think, if I end this review with the prophecy that the struggle will be continued. There are still battles ahead. "Russia bathed in blood" . . . has become . . . U.S.S.R. clothed in metal. But capitalism as a social and economic system is not yet destroyed in the world at large, capitalism is not yet completely rooted out of the consciousness of . . . Soviet writers.[144]

Even Kirpotin realized that "the creation of a single Union of Soviet Writers does not mean that with the spectrum of various shades and characters of which our Union is composed, we shall not have disagreements, shall not have controversies, shall not have fights." [145]

The Fourth Five-Year Plan is not unlike the First in ideology; it is another emergency period of reconstruction, and once more literature must help in the Plan's fulfillment. The writer is again urged to "arm the people ideologically" and to "castigate the remnants of yesterday"; [146] and, "if he knows what is good for him, he lays on ideological material with a trowel." [147] The superiority of Soviet over bourgeois literature is again stridently proclaimed, and art for art's sake is considered "bourgeois hypocrisy and camouflage." [148] As under RAPP, we find the documentary approach and a rampant *partinost*. Critics still "lack principles, political acumen and scholarly objectivity in their appraisal of literary facts" and

THE LIQUIDATION OF RAPP

are often guided in their work, "not by the interests of Soviet literary development, but by personal and group interests." [149] Today, literature must educate the people "in the spirit of the ideas of the Bolshevik party, in the spirit of devotion to the Motherland" [150]—under the First Five-Year Plan, "Socialism in One Country" took the place of "Motherland."

It seems clear that RAPP was dissolved largely because it had served its purpose and had outlived its usefulness. As a Party tool (whether acknowledged as such or not), it had fought against and annihilated ideological deviations in literature and in literary criticism. However, the general artistic standard of performance had declined considerably between 1928 and 1932; and discontented writers, especially Gorky, felt the need for less regimentation and greater freedom of self-expression. "The narrowness of RAPP's creative platform and the erroneousness of a series of slogans told in a negative way on the productions of proletarian writers." [151] Readers, too, showed their dissatisfaction by the fact that Soviet book sales went down and the demand for pre-revolutionary authors, both national and foreign, went up. "The people were tired of the bare bones of propaganda." [152] Stalin had become irritated at the poor results achieved by the Five-Year Plan in literature and probably at the dizziness of RAPP's leaders with their dictatorial successes. RAPP had finished its job, had become too autonomous, and under Averbakh's arrogant leadership was getting more and more out of the Party's control. Times had changed; the wreckers and the kulaks were no longer the threat that they had been; and the class barriers could be relaxed among writers, as among other groups of society. The time had come to clear away all impediments to the entry into a new period, and Comrade Averbakh's RAPP was definitely one of them.

Before the Central Committee's April Decree, declared Kirpotin, Soviet writers would not have spoken as freely nor as extensively about vital questions as they had at this meeting, and there would probably have been fewer writers and more organizational workers present. In the course of the six days of debates an enormous *rapprochement* between different detachments of writers was reached.

"That ideological and spiritual atmosphere has been created without which all codes are nothing but a dead letter and without which it is impossible to carry out daily organizational work." [153] Kirpotin announced that, as a result of the work of the plenum, a single Union of Soviet Writers had been created, "not an apolitical culture-bearing union," but one that stands on the platform of Soviet power and aspires to share in socialist construction.[154]

The Union of Soviet Writers

The aim of the Union was formulated in its statute as,

the creation of works of high artistic significance, saturated with the heroic struggle of the international proletariat, with the grandeur of the victory of Socialism, and reflecting the great wisdom and heroism of the Communist Party . . . the creation of artistic works worthy of the great age of Socialism." [155]

And Gronski demanded: "If you are a writer, then give us literary works of art and not declarations, resolutions, or controversies. . . . We ourselves know very well how to chatter, how to write resolutions and declarations, but literary works of art, we do not know how to write—it is up to you to write them." Henceforth, a writer would be judged by his literary works alone, and not by his declarations or articles.[156]

Kirshon had quoted Stalin's well-known pronouncement on the significance of the writer's work in the U.S.S.R.:

There is a tremendously important work; there are engineers who know how to make a tractor; there are engineers who direct the construction of gigantic industries. You, writers, also are engineers directing the construction of the human soul. This is work no less important than any other work which is performed in our country for the building of socialism and its victory.[157]

In 1934 Zhdanov elaborated upon this theme as follows:

To be an engineer of human souls [by remolding the reader's mentality in the spirit of socialism] means standing with both feet firmly planted on the basis of real life. And this in turn denotes a rupture with romanticism of the old type, which depicted a non-existent life and non-existent heroes, leading the reader away from the antagonisms and oppression of real life into a world of the impossible, into a world of utopian dreams.[158]

"Since our epoch is essentially realist, we, its portrayers, must be so, too," [159] Gorky wrote; and Zhdanov advanced the slogan of socialist realism. "Ours is not the realism which portrays isolated, individual things, cut away from history and the class struggle," explained Kirpotin; "ours is a socialist realism, which shows heroes in their class environment and shows how the activities of individuals contribute to historic changes." [160] Among the works named as examples of the new trend were: *Soil Upturned, Bruski,* and *Time, Forward!* According to Gladkov, socialist realism "demands not general truth, but a specific truth [slanted and sometimes incomplete], our Communist truth," [161] based on the Leninist principle of devotion to the Party.[162]

After 1932 this definite literary method, dictated by Stalin, was imposed on the whole body of writers of the U.S.S.R. One of the conditions of membership in the Writers' Union is acceptance of the method of socialist realism, which obligates the writer to deal in his works only with the socialist realities; the other, is adherence to the political platform of the Soviet government. Authors now enjoy less freedom than the Party's 1925 Resolution gave the fellow-travelers, who were free to write anything except counter-revolutionary literature. If a writer is considered a deviationist and his work is judged incompatible with the spirit of socialist realism, he no longer has a group which will spring to his defense. There is only one monolithic Union directly controlled by the highly centralized Party. A nonconformist does not have a chance.

At the First Soviet Writers' Congress in 1934 the "Bolshevik tendentiousness" of Soviet literature was reaffirmed, Vsevolod Ivanov, a former Serapion Brother, even going so far as to assert that it was a *sine qua non* of the literary equipment of any Soviet writer.[163] "It goes without saying that the revolution and the Party do not exist in order to ensure to all members complete liberty," Karl Radek told the congress.

. . . the proletarian revolution secures freedom to mankind, and it must create an army in which the members are united . . . by the aims of the struggle . . . and must subordinate all individual considerations to this common aim.

The Party of the proletariat is a party of revolution, pursuing its policy on the basis of Marxism-Leninism. It knows whither it is leading the masses. And when a man thinks that he is only upholding some individual shade of opinion against the Party, a political test will always show that he is upholding interests alien to the proletariat. And if a writer finds it hard to give up his most intimate, individual shades of opinion, let him study the experience of the Soviet revolution and he will then see that if he wants to fight against capitalism, against imperialism, if he wants to fight hand in hand with the masses, then he must march in the ranks of these masses. But if he sets his so-called shades of opinion in opposition to the masses, then it will be shown that this is not his individual opinion, but the opinion of some bourgeois group, hostile to the proletariat.[164]

6. CONCLUSION

Results of the First Five-Year Plan

"The results of the Five-Year Plan have shown that the working class is as well able to build something new as it is to destroy the old," reported Stalin to the plenary session of the Central Committee in January, 1933.[1] During this period industrial output as a whole doubled and the Soviet Union was converted into a country "mighty in defense." Industries producing steel, tractors, automobiles, engineering machinery, chemicals, and aircraft were established (for example, the Stalingrad and Kharkov tractor plants, the AMO automobile factory in Moscow, etc.), and unemployment was abolished. New industrial centers were set up in the eastern part of the country with the giant steel works at Magnitogorsk in the Urals and Kuznetsk in Siberia. There was a tremendous expansion of electric power (fulfillment of Lenin's dream of electrification), including the building of the Dnieprostroi Dam. Great advances in transportation were made, among them the construction of the Turk-Sib Railroad uniting Siberia and Central Asia, and the beginning of the Baltic–White Sea Canal. Sixty per cent of the peasant farms were merged into *kolkhozes*.[2]

Panfyorov gave a picture of the contagious enthusiasm which was rampant at the end of 1932 when the success of the "Five-Year-Plan-in-Four" was assured:

Exultantly the country took over enterprise after enterprise. It had already taken over metallurgical works, tractor, motor, chemical works, oil distilleries, cement, armaments and shipbuilding works, giving each its name. And as every new works joined the ranks of active enterprises there was tremendous jubilation: the newspapers wrote about it, the wireless told the world about it, it was called the heritage of the proletariat, everybody was proud of it: in the schools, in the villagers' huts, in the fields, in the workmen's gangs. . . . And before the jubilation over the starting of one factory had died away a new factory was brought into operation, and with even greater enthusiasm the country took over this new enterprise, and was proud of it.[3]

In spite of these remarkable achievements, however, the actual figures fell far short of those so optimistically planned. Little success was met with in reducing economic costs or in reaching the goal which had been set for productivity of labor.[4] The Plan had been based on the premise of a great increase in Soviet exports and, therefore, of imports of foreign machinery, and also on the availability of long-term credits. Party leaders did not foresee the world depression of 1931–32, when the price of exported grain fell much faster than that of imported machinery; Russia received only very expensive short-term credits; the collectivization drive created chaos in the country, cattle being slaughtered and the grain harvest shrinking—these were the factors mainly responsible for the failure to fulfill the almost impossibly high levels demanded by the maximal variant of the Plan.

It was claimed that the cultural *pyatiletka* had been carried out twofold.[5] Universal free elementary education was introduced, and great strides were made in the "liquidation of illiteracy" and in mass politico-educational work (clubs, homes of socialist culture, village reading rooms, city libraries, etc.).

Stalin stated as an "indisputable fact" that the victories of the First Five-Year Plan had mobilized the revolutionary forces of the working class of all countries against capitalism.[6] Finally, these results had shown that "the Party is invincible, *if* it knows its goal, and if it is not afraid of difficulties."[7] By the end of 1932 Stalin was the undisputed and virtually unopposed leader of the Communist party, which had a tighter control of the U.S.S.R. than ever before.

Literature Which Helped the Plan

Did the literary works of this period contribute towards the fulfillment of the Plan and, if so, to what extent? It is very difficult to

CONCLUSION 163

find direct evidence although statements have been made about the propaganda value of some of the novels and plays discussed in Chapter 4. For instance, the "tremendous ideological saturation" of *Energy* was noted,[8] and Stetski spoke of this tendentious novel as both an artistic production and a political handbook: "In art form, the book reveals to every Party worker, to every activist many aspects of the relations between people, or organization and leadership which are indispensable for every Party worker to know in order to lead correctly and conquer in the struggle." [9]

Because Sholokhov had correctly understood the very complex historical process of collectivization, *Soil Upturned* was welcomed as "an event of social significance" which deserved to be made the property of the broadest masses for whom it would be, not only a dynamic picture of the struggle, but also a weapon in it.[10] Mirsky considered the book an invaluable contribution to the practical work of understanding and directing the social forces at work in the U.S.S.R.[11] The reader is given convincing proof that "the direction, regardless of all difficulties, is towards socialism" and that the *kolkhoz* movement "must be victorious over the petty peasant elements and show the peasantry a new road." [12] The kulak (Ostrovnov) is seen coming back to life again and again because the social medium has remained unchanged—"the ocean of petty private households, the petty trading elements which give rise to kulakdom"—and his actions explain "why collectivization necessarily assumed the character of an antikulak movement." [13] Radek asserted that Sholokhov made discontented people in the Soviet Union understand what they had not previously understood because they saw only a small section of life:

Through works like Sholokhov's they came to understand the necessity of those severe, firm, drastic measures which had to be taken in order to build socialism. I have heard with my own ears from intellectuals, from persons who were permeated with humanitarian ideas and who had not grasped what was happening during the period of the First Five-Year Plan, during the period of collectivization when the kulak class was being liquidated, how they declared after reading Sholokhov's book: "He has convinced me that it had to be that way." [14]

An example of fame based on the correct political point of view is *Bruski*, which was praised by everyone in 1930 and then in 1934, condemned by Soviet writers and critics, led by Gorky, as a tendentious, perfunctory work with a slovenly literary technique.[15] Whatever its artistic failings, this *kolkhoz* chronicle was commended by Libedinski in 1931 as an ideological tool:

> When a prominent Party worker is shown making a mistake and when the basic traits of this mistake are uncovered concretely and psychologically, this only helps the Party in its struggle with the Right Deviation. For this we must praise Comrade Panfyorov. His work, *Bruski*, helps the bolshevization of our Party. *Bruski* will help us to make propaganda for our policy in the country.[16]

Even in 1934 Radek had a good word to say for this novel. He told how workers who had escaped from a German concentration camp said that in the camp, where they were flogged by Storm Troopers, they had been given strength by reading *Bruski*. "I felt proud of our literature," he concluded.[17]

Bruski's documentary value has not been questioned. *Skutarevsky*, however, was seriously criticized for a lack of specific concreteness in its scientific material and because "Skutarevsky's discovery has no connection with time and space, and the reader does not know what place it occupies in the history of science."[18] Poor Leonov had not spent enough time studying in a physical science laboratory! He was further attacked for thinking that the building of socialism was trivial, which led to irony, and for having given a picture which was too cold and not enthusiastic enough.[19] *Skutarevsky* was designated a "doubtful work"[20] written with a "crushed perspective"[21] and surely appeared on no recommended reading list in the U.S.S.R.

Propagandizing the Five-Year Plan of national economy was one of the essential missions of literary clubs and Red corners, and calendars of literary work were drawn up to forward various political campaigns.[22] A manual of instructions on how this work should be organized stated that

> the employment of literature in accordance with the aims and tasks of the Party, the highest possible political activity in all literary work of

club and Red corner, the closest connection between literary work and production in the organization of all club work—these are the tasks which now stand before club literary work.[23]

The club librarian and the Circle of Book-lovers organized special Book Evenings and exhibitions, compiled recommended lists of suitable literature, and circulated politically-conscious books among the masses. A 1930 list of suggested reading, chosen for its propaganda value, contained almost no works on contemporary themes because they were then unavailable (the lag of literature behind life). Most of the selections dealt with the NEP period but were considered important for giving a basis of comparison which would show the Five-Year Plan successes in construction.[24] Gladkov's *Cement* and Panfyorov's *Bruski* were listed; also, always the ubiquitous Demyan Bedny's productions. Samuel Harper noted that purely literary journals and books were not prominent on the tables of the club reading rooms, most of the literature being of a political or propagandist character.[25]

During the First Five-Year Plan, with more people becoming literate, there was an enormous demand for books. Ten, twenty, even fifty thousand copies of a first edition of a novel or volume of verse were bought up in a few days.[26] To make books more accessible to the mass of workers and peasants, prices were lowered 25 per cent during 1929–30, the number of bookstands in the factories was increased,[27] and cultvans with newspapers, books, and reviews toured the villages.

Although literary clubs and circles made great efforts to see that the better Five-Year Plan novels were widely read and discussed,[28] plays must have been far more effective propaganda agents, for their message could reach even the illiterate.[29] At the tenth anniversary of the founding of the Vakhtangov Theatre, in 1931, an *udarnik* from Selvinski's Electrofactory, bringing "electrical greetings" from twenty-three thousand workers, testified: "We have seen your plays and liked them, especially *Tempo*. It made us want to work harder for the construction of socialism and the fulfillment of the Five-Year Plan. It made us more enthusiastic." [30] *Bread* and *Fear* were also very popular, both being first produced by the Academic Theatre of

Drama in Leningrad (in 1930 and 1931, respectively) and, the following year, by the Moscow Art Theatre (in 1931 and 1932, respectively). They, too, probably exerted considerable agitational influence.

In 1930 both Meyerhold's Theatre and TRAM (Leningrad Young Workers' Theatre) presented Bezymenski's *The Shot*,[31] the latter with the avowed aim of striking "with all the means of theatrical satire at bureaucratism, conformism, opportunism" and of representing the heroic work of the shock brigades.[32] At the time, this play was considered one of the best Soviet comedies so far produced and a typical example of Soviet self-criticism. It was calculated that "quotations from it, phrases, proverbs, and other features characteristic of working-class life should become so well known as to serve as a source of slogans for the class struggle and socialist construction." [33]

Bezymenski wrote his verses with a view to having them recited to the masses and heard in the streets, over loud speakers, in the theatre. At industrial plants,

> the local artists painted up his verses on huge canvases which were hung up between the houses on either side of the widest avenues. Trams and motor-cars passed under these canvases. His poetical slogans and epigrams (always concrete and to the point) surrounded the machines and benches in the workshops.[34]

In *People of the Stalingrad Tractor Plant* we find the statement that the following verses of Comrade Bezymenski's helped to make tractors:

> No more will I invent;
> I don't want to deceive.
> Once I met a camel who
> Went laughing on his way.
>
> > I was amazed. What was the cause?
> > Why the laughter? Why his joy?
> > He lacked a can of kerosene
> > For the Plant in Stalingrad.
>
> I said to him: "You are so gay,
> But it is time for you to weep;

CONCLUSION

> You cannot hope for mercy here—
> The tractors will replace you.
>
> "The country strengthens year by year,
> And I shall not conceal the truth:
> In bearing fuel to the Plant
> You, brother, carry your own death."
>
> The camel's eyes leered to the left;
> He snorted with his utmost strength.
> Without a trace of bitterness,
> Guffawing now, quoth he:
>
> "Though most unwillingly I'd die,
> Stalingraders won't be the why.
> Ho-ho! With their work such as this
> We'll live a long time yet."
>
> Dzerzhinskyites! You're in a mess,
> So listen well to Moscow's words:
> "You have not been ashamed, yourselves,
> But how ashamed would camels be." [35]

As for the literary *udarniks*, their creative efforts were said to have summarized the revolutionary experience and the industrial achievements of the best workers and to have had "an enormous stirring effect on the masses." [36] Work on the *History of Factories and Works*, in a number of cases, acted as a stimulus to the rise of productive initiative. Socialist competition sprang up among workers for the right to be mentioned in these volumes as one of the best workers. "In this particular, the interweaving of this scientific and artistic work with current life in the Soviet Union is especially apparent." [37]

Conclusions

Fulfill plans, roll up percentages, build, build, build! The six-day plan of production, the monthly plan, the Five-Year Plan. Factories and mines and machines must work two shifts and three shifts. Nobody dare be unemployed. The perpetual motion of continuous twenty-four-hour factories, meetings, drives, campaigns—a dozen of them in progress at the same time, each of them hailed as the most decisive of all.[38]

Endless demands for speed and achievement were constantly and tirelessly directed at every Soviet citizen by the radio, the press, Party and trade-union organizations, schools, the theatre, and, of course, literature. Virtually all the combined resources of the State were single-mindedly concentrated on fulfilling the Five-Year Plan in four years. Under such circumstances, one cannot judge exactly the percentage of the total effort for which the socially-commanded literature of these years was responsible.

Literary works showed the undesirability in the new socialist world of backward human attributes such as laziness, absenteeism, drunkenness, illiteracy, and piety (religion being regarded as the principal obstacle to the training of the new generation in the ideals of socialism [39]); and this presumably helped raise industrial and agricultural tempos. Work, especially in the collective, was depicted as a source of joy and pride as well as a means of remaking the toiler; the great value of technical "know-how" and the importance of time and tempos were stressed; and descriptions of the heroics of labor served to excite the reader's enthusiasm for socialist construction and encouraged him to fight class enemies in the name of the official slogans. Literature strove to rouse in the worker, not only pride in his job and in his plant, but also a sense of responsibility. By being shown how he fitted into the Plan as a whole and given a sense of the dependence of one part of production on another, he was made to feel that the destiny of the country depended on his individual effort. Lastly, the Five-Year Plan literary productions, in general, inspired an optimistic belief in the future and in the inevitability of socialism's eventual victory.

It is a question whether what the professional writers did, assisted in "organizing the consciousness of the masses" more than what they wrote. From the evidence provided by their literary works, it did not, for writers and journalists are almost invariably presented as fools or incompetents who get in everyone's way and understand nothing of what is being done at the enterprise they are visiting. However, their participation in the work of the cultural *pyatiletka* must have been valuable in creating an interest in literature on the part of the workers. The appearance of a well-known author at a

CONCLUSION 169

factory literary circle could not but flatter its members and make them feel their importance, especially if they were asked to criticize something that he had written dealing, perhaps, with them or their plant. Such occasions, apart from the agitational value of the story or the poem read, were bound to be morale builders.

As for the work of the literary *udarniks*, although it was almost never literature, yet it certainly played its part in raising the cultural level of the masses. It is only natural to be more interested in what one has tried to do personally, and the participation of thousands of workers in writing should have given them a greater appreciation of the work of those who could write. The collectively written *History of Factories and Works* and *History of the Civil War* must have demonstrated their educational and propagandist value, for in 1934 work was begun on a new series, *Men of the First and Second Five-Year Plans*, also to be written collectively.[40]

Collective management and socialist competition in Soviet industry and agriculture were recognized as failures by the middle of 1931; and individual management, personal responsibility, and cash incentives were substituted.[41] Unlimited piece work and bonuses proved more effective spurs to greater productivity [42] than the prospect of being pictured as a plane or an express train, instead of as a camel or a crab, in the factory newspaper.[43] By the spring of 1932 socialist competition began to die down on the cultural front also; authors ceased to write in answer to challenges; literary shock brigades were disbanded; and the social command became less explicit.

For propaganda purposes a spectacular quantitative achievement, such as the laying of a huge concrete dam in record time or the opening a year ahead of schedule of a metallurgical giant, or a Magnitostroi of literature, is much more useful than "the slow prosaic processes which make for better quality." [44] However, by the Second Five-Year Plan the general low level of both industrial and literary production was deplored, and a campaign was started to raise it.

Much criticism has been leveled at the vast quantity of plays and novels conforming to a similar standardized pattern which was turned out between 1928 and 1932. The presence of saboteurs ("to judge from the Moscow theatres . . . a regulation part of the equipment on every construction job and in every factory") added to the atmosphere of heroism deliberately fostered around the industrial program. It gave the ordinary worker, engaged in a tedious occupation, the feeling that he was an embattled revolutionary fighting the class enemy and made it easier for him to bear discomforts and deprivations.[45]

The bulk of this so-called literature lacks subtle shading; it contains only "the blackest Whites and the purest Reds." [46] But this is the technique of the advertising poster, and also of the nursery story. A basic propaganda device is the ceaseless repetition of the same simple ideas, especially when directed at an unsophisticated audience.

As a whole, the books called forth by RAPP's social command were excellent documentary sketches reflecting life during the First Five-Year Plan. In almost all cases, the greater their propaganda value, the poorer their literary quality (and vice versa). As literature, these works were very weak; but they played the political role assigned to them by force of sheer numbers. "One can only serve one master . . . either art or . . . social reforms." [47]

NOTES

1. Introductory Material

1. G. Lelevich, whose real name was L. G. Kalmanson, was a Marxist critic and leader of the Left wing of RAPP.
2. R. Waliszewski, *The Romance of an Empress*, New York, 1894, p. 335.
3. John Charpentier, *Napoléon et les hommes de lettres de son temps*, Paris, 1935, p. 13.
4. *Ibid.*, p. 199.
5. William Henry Chamberlin, *Russia's Iron Age*, Boston, 1934, p. 298.
6. Gleb Struve, *25 Years of Soviet Russian Literature (1918–1943)*, new and enlarged ed. of *Soviet Russian Literature*, London, 1946, p. 234.
7. V. I. Lenin, "Partinaya organizatsiya i partinaya literatura," *Sochineniya*, 2d ed., Leningrad, 1935, VIII, 387, reprinted from *Novaya zhizn*, No. 12 (November 26, 1905).
8. "The Proletcult had no dialectic, not even a very small dose of it." (Yuri Libedinski, "Za chto boryutsya napostovtsy" [stenogram report of speech made at meeting of local circles of LAPP, April 25, 1930], *Generalnyie zadachi proletarskoi literatury*, Moscow-Leningrad, 1931, p. 33.)
9. From the unanimously carried resolution proposed by A. Bogdanov at the First All-Russian Conference of Proletarian Cultural-Educational Organizations on September 20, 1918, George Reavey and Marc Slonim, ed. and trans., *Soviet Literature*, New York, 1934, p. 396.
10. In 1934 Gladkov wrote: "Art is an ideological superstructure; it is the consciousness of a class; it is the class war transposed into the language of imagery." ("Soviet Writers about Themselves," M. Apletin, ed., *Literature of the Peoples of the U.S.S.R.*, VOKS Illustrated Almanac, Nos. 7–8 [1934], Fyodor Gladkov, p. 100.)
11. Joseph Freeman, Joshua Kunitz, Louis Lozowick, *Voices of October*, New York, 1930, p. 35.

12. Paul Miliukov, *Outlines of Russian Culture: Part II—Literature*, Michael Karpovich, ed., Valentine Ughet and Eleanor Davis, trans., Philadelphia, 1943, p. 81.
13. Reavey and Slonim, *Soviet Literature*, p. 23.
14. In Leonov's novel, *Skutarevsky*, Osip Benislavitch Struff, who sold second-hand *objets d'art* of questionable provenance and faked old masters, put forward the slogan: "The classics of art for the widest ranks of the people." (Leonid Leonov, *Skutarevsky*, Alec Brown, trans., New York, 1936, p. 248.)
15. Clara Zetkin, *Souvenirs sur Lénine*, Paris, 1926, pp. 15–16.
16. V. I. Lenin, "The Tasks of the Youth Leagues" (speech delivered at the Third All-Russian Congress of the Russian Young Communist League, October 2, 1920), *Selected Works*, Moscow, 1947, II, 664.
17. Leon Trotsky, *Literature and Revolution*, Rose Strunsky, trans., New York, 1925, pp. 185–86.
18. *Ibid.*, p. 201.
19. *Ibid.*, p. 190.
20. *Ibid.*, p. 205.
21. *Ibid.*, p. 194. The critics Voronski and Polonski were accused of thinking, like Trotsky, that proletarian culture was impossible.
22. Vyacheslav Polonski, *Ocherki literaturnovo dvizheniya revolyutsionnoi epokhi*, 2d ed., corrected and enlarged, Moscow-Leningrad, 1929, p. 52.
23. *Ibid.*, p. 53.
24. Vladimir Kirillov, "We," quoted in Alexander Kaun, *Soviet Poets and Poetry*, Berkeley-Los Angeles, 1943, p. 102.
25. Alexei Gastev, "We Grow out of Iron," Babette Deutsch and Avrahm Yarmolinsky, ed. and trans., *Russian Poetry*, new and revised ed., New York, 1930, p. 210.
26. Reavey and Slonim, *Soviet Literature*, p. 21.
27. Vladimir Mayakovsky, "Decree to the Army of Art," Joseph Freeman and Leon Talmy, trans., *The American Quarterly on the Soviet Union*, III, No. 1 (July, 1940), 83.
28. *Ibid.*, p. 84.
29. Struve, *25 Years of Soviet Russian Literature*, p. 83.
30. Polonski, *Ocherki literaturnovo* . . . , p. 227.
31. The name of this group's journal was changed in 1926 from *LEF* to *Novy LEF* (New Left Front), then in 1928 to *REF* (Revolutionary Front of Art), which was discontinued when Mayakovsky joined RAPP in 1930.
32. Mayakovsky and Brik, "Our Literary Work," Reavey and Slonim, *Soviet Literature*, p. 400.

NOTES: INTRODUCTORY MATERIAL

33. Kornely Zelinski, "The 15th Anniversary of Soviet Literature," VOKS, III, Nos. 5–6 (1932), 60.
34. Ibid.
35. This arch-proletarian group was founded on March 15, 1923. ("Dokladnaya zapiska pravleniya MAPP zavagitpropotdelom TsK RKP [b] t. A. Bubnovu," in G. Lelevich, Na literaturnom postu, Moscow, 1924, p. 162.) In 1924 Lelevich spoke of "MAPP, now VAPP." (G. Lelevich, "Vvedeniye," Na literaturnom postu, Moscow, 1924, p. iv.) Kaun says that MAPP arose from the Smithy and subsequently merged with RAPP. (Kaun, Soviet Poets and Poetry, p. 113.)
36. The most fanatical At-the-Postists—Rodov, Lelevich, and Averbakh—were of non-proletarian origin. (Kaun, ibid., p. 156.)
37. Libedinski, "Za chto boryutsya napostovtsy," p. 5.
38. "Editorial Manifesto of the On Guard Group" (appeared in No. 1 of the On Guard review, June, 1923), Reavey and Slonim, Soviet Literature, pp. 403–5.
39. Struve, 25 Years of Soviet Russian Literature, p. 223.
40. Polonski, Ocherki literaturnovo . . . , p. 169.
41. Ibid., p. 171.
42. Smenovekhovstvo, the distinctive ideology of those White émigrés, the "changing-landmarks" group (among them, Alexei Tolstoy), who looked upon NEP as the path to the restoration of capitalist relations and, as a result, proclaimed their allegiance to the Soviet régime.
43. Lelevich, "Vvedeniye."
44. "Dokladnaya zapiska . . . Bubnovu."
45. G. Lelevich, "Tezisy doklada G. Lelevicha o vsesoyuznom syezde proletarskikh pisatelei na 2–oi moskovskoi konferentsii prolet-pisatelei 20 aprelya 1924 g," Na literaturnom postu, Moscow, 1924, p. 164.
46. Polonski, Ocherki literaturnovo . . . , p. 163.
47. A. K. Voronski began his literary career as a vigorous opponent of mysticism and religion. His emphasis on art as knowledge, as contrasted with Bogdanov's theory of art as organization, made Voronski the natural ally of the fellow-travelers. He was attracted by "their superior literary talent and their interest in 'objective' truth" of the life around them, which they wished to describe without accepting the Revolution in a positive way. This tolerant attitude towards the fellow-travelers brought Voronski into sharp conflict with the At-the-Postists.

However, profound differences existed between Voronski and the fellow-travelers, for he was an active revolutionist who fought against the decline of class hatred and the fighting spirit. He warned young writers against Tolstoyan pacifism and egoism, criticized the pessimism and melancholy of certain Soviet poets following the introduction of the NEP, opposed political passivity, and urged young authors to express a clear and active acceptance of the Revolution. (*Voices of October*, pp. 42–43.)

48. Voronski, quoted in Polonski, *Ocherki literaturnovo* . . . , p. 160.

49. Voronski believed that creative art, in its very nature, is individual and (according to the *Literaturnaya entsiklopediya*) that its chief task is not to understand the world in the interest of a class, but to "remove the veils" and discover it.

50. Boris Kushner, writing in *Pravda*, characterized the theory of "direct impressions" as a thoroughly idealistic and wholly incredible theory according to which, "the guiding criterion for the author should be, not reason, not a dialectical analysis of the phenomenon arising before him, but an impression received by him directly from perception of the appearance." The method of direct impressions, he concluded, can easily confuse proletarian writers and lead them astray from the class path. (Boris Kushner, "Prichiny otstavaniya," *Pravda* [October 4, 1930], p. 5.) Kushner, himself, was accused of having "the usual inadequacies of LEF vulgarization and Litfront coloring." ("Kushner, Boris Anisimovich," A. V. Lunacharski, ed., *Literaturnaya entsiklopediya*, Moscow, 1931, V, 774–75.)

51. Kornely Zelinski, "Soviet Criticism," M. Apletin, ed., *Literature of the Peoples of the U.S.S.R.*, VOKS Illustrated Almanac, Nos. 7–8 (1934), p. 32.

52. In the "Young Guard" group was "literature looking to the future," a literature "full of the joy of life and hopeful and energetic in its tone." There was no longer the former abstract approach to the Revolution; the everyday facts of the NEP period were accepted; and interest in small details characterized the proletarian poetry of the second period of the Revolution. (Samuel Northrup Harper, *Civic Training in Soviet Russia*, Chicago, 1929, p. 301.)

53. "Resolution of the First All-Union Conference of Proletarian Writers (Vardin)," quoted in *Voices of October*, p. 47.

54. Reavey and Slonim, *Soviet Literature*, p. 46.

55. Leopold L. Averbakh, *Speech at the Conference of the Literary Department of the Central Committee of the Russian Communist Party*, May 9, 1924 (published in a pamphlet by *Krasnaya nov*, 1924), quoted in Max Eastman, *Artists in Uniform*, New York, 1934, p. 79.

"Printing is an arsenal which must not be put within reach of everyone, but only of those who have the confidence of the government," Napoleon declared to a meeting of his Council of State on December 12, 1809. (Quoted in Charpentier, *Napoléon et les hommes de lettres*, p. 106.)

56. The Constructivists arose as a literary group in 1924 when their

manifesto, *Gosplan literatury*, was published. Zelinski and Selvinski were their theoretician and leading poet, respectively; and among the members were Vera Inber and Evgeni Gabrilovich. "To build, to build at all costs, a plan on the foundation of reason," was their slogan. They held the theory of the subordination of the meaning of work to all its elements. "Constructivism was an original reflection of the mood of the upper strata of highly qualified intelligentsia, apprehending the Revolution through its 'cultural' aspects," wrote Zelinski in 1932. "Subjectively we were heart and soul with the Revolution. Objectively, in actual fact we were often distracted from it by our purely intellectual problems." (Zelinski, "15th Anniversary of Soviet Literature," p. 64.)

57. Kaun, *Soviet Poets and Poetry*, p. 114.
58. *Ibid.*, p. 157.
59. At this time (during the 1923-25 fight), on the side of the At-the-Post group were: P. S. Kogan, Demyan Bedny, P. I. Lebedev-Polyanski, L. L. Averbakh, G. Gorbachyov, A. I. Bezymenski, Yu. Libedinski, G. Lelevich, S. Rodov, V. Pletnev, etc. Against the At-the-Post-ists stood: L. Trotsky, A. K. Voronski, A. V. Lunacharski, N. Bukharin, K. Radek, V. Polonski, and some of the Smithy writers. (Polonski, *Ocherki literaturnovo* . . . , p. 175.)
60. *Voices of October*, p. 48.
61. *Ibid.*, p. 49.
62. *Ibid.*, p. 51.
63. Miliukov, *Outlines of Russian Culture*, p. 95.
64. Struve, *25 Years of Soviet Russian Literature*, p. 224.
65. *Voices of October*, p. 51.
66. "Resolution on Literature Adopted by the Political Bureau of the Communist Party of the U.S.S.R. on July 1, 1924," *ibid.*, p. 59.
67. *Ibid.*, p. 60.
68. *Ibid.*, p. 61.
69. *Ibid.*, p. 62.
70. *Ibid.*, p. 63.
71. *Ibid.*, p. 64.
72. *Ibid.*, p. 65.

"The State Publishing Company must think of the worker when it publishes most of its books and not of the college graduate. Playwrights and novelists speak to a new audience. . . . Authors know that delicate references to distant historical events may pass over the heads of their readers, and foreign words must usually be taboo." (Louis Fischer, *Machines and Men in Russia*, New York, 1932, p. 153.)

73. "K perestroike literaturnykh organizatsi," *Na literaturnom postu*, Nos. 13-14 (May, 1932), p. 2.
74. It is also stated that VOAPP was created in the fall of 1928.

("RAPP," V. M. Friche, ed., *Literaturnaya entsiklopediya*, Moscow, 1935, IX, 520–21.)
75. A. Selivanovski, "RAPP," N. L. Meshcheryakov, ed., *Malaya sovetskaya entsiklopediya*, Moscow, 1930, VII, 175.
76. Libedinski, "Za chto boryutsya napostovtsy," p. 11.
77. *Ibid.*, p. 6. In 1934 Bakhmetyev declared that "only yesterday we were individual snipers in the world of art, today we are a regular army, tomorrow the fighters of the entire world will be in our ranks." ("Soviet Writers about Themselves," V. Bakhmetyev, p. 97.)
78. Polonski, *Ocherki literaturnovo* . . . , p. 286, n. 131.
79. Eastman, *Artists in Uniform*, p. 134.

Averbakh was born in a bourgeois family of Saratov in 1903. From 1917 to 1921 he was engaged in work for the Komsomol and was elected a member of the Central Committee of its First Convocation, then secretary of the Moscow Committee of the R.K.S.M. (Russian Young Communist League) and editor of *Yunosheskoi pravdy* (1920). He was a Party member from 1919. Averbakh worked abroad for the Communist Youth International and on his return edited the magazine *Molodaya gvardiya* and the newspaper *Uralski rabochi*. In 1923 he veered towards the Trotskyite Opposition, but quickly straightened his course. [This was written in 1929.]

From 1922 on, Averbakh was involved in the proletarian literary movement. He was a member of the editorial board of *Na postu* and the editor of *Na literaturnom postu* from its foundation. General secretary of RAPP, he was also one of the founders of VAPP and a board member of VOAPP. Among his most important theoretical and publicist works were his discussions with Voronski over the possibility of the existence of proletarian literature and with Pletnev over the substance of proletarian culture and the Proletcult.

Apart from his journalistic articles devoted directly to literary themes, Averbakh was occupied with problems of the youth movement and of the cultural revolution. Some of his books are: *Bolshevistskaya vesna*, *Za proletarskuyu literaturu*, *Nashi literaturyie raznoglasiya*, *Pisatel bolen* (with Shaginyan), *Za gegemoniyu proletarskoi literatury*, and *Sovremennaya literatura i voprosy kulturnoi revolyutsii*. His most valuable popularized works: *Lenin i yunosheskoye dvizheniye* (with preface by Trotsky) and *Na putyakh kulturnoi revolyutsii*. ("Averbakh, Leopold Leonidovich," V. M. Friche, ed., *Literaturnaya entsiklopediya*, Moscow, 1929, I, 28–29; and "Averbakh, Leopold Leonidovich," N. L. Meshcheryakov, ed., *Malaya sovetskaya entsiklopediya*, 2d ed., Moscow, 1933, I, 52.)
80. Kaun, *Soviet Poets and Poetry*, p. 159.
81. Eastman, *Artists in Uniform*, p. 35.

NOTES: INTRODUCTORY MATERIAL 177

82. In May, 1928, VOKP finally adopted the Bolshevik ideology. "Only the proletarian peasant writers were acknowledged 'authentic peasant writers.' . . . The Fellow Travelers were also repudiated as enemies of social reconstruction, and only the poorer peasants 'capable of accepting fully the proletarian point of view,' were regarded as possible allies." (Miliukov, *Outlines of Russian Culture*, pp. 112–13.)

83. In speaking of VAPP in 1928, Averbakh said: "Our organization is erected on the basis of definite views held on the questions of proletarian art and proletarian literature. . . . Proletarian art is an art which helps the proletariat in the work of building socialism, which organizes our thoughts and feelings towards the building of communism. . . . For us, the proletarian writer is a writer who directs all his creative work to the task of serving the proletariat." (Leopold Averbakh, *Kulturnaya revolyutsiya i voprosy sovremennoi literatury*, Moscow-Leningrad, 1928, p. 64.)

VAPP's work was said to consist of: (1) Problems of creative work—to assist the development of proletarian literature as the result of the collective work of a great many writers. (2) Participation, as an organization, in the class struggle: (a) tasks in connection with the necessity of carrying the Party line into literature (in particular, work with the fellow-travelers and the peasant writers); (b) necessity for responsiveness to all questions of literary discussions; (c) questions connected with proletarian public opinion and the cultural revolution in general (readers, club, participation in social campaigns, etc.). (*Ibid.*, p. 55.)

84. Zelinski, "15th Anniversary of Soviet Literature," p. 63.

85. *Ibid.*, p. 60.

86. The Left Deviation was excluded from the Party in 1927. Zinoviev (G. E. Apfelbaum) was a great demagogue. He worked with Lenin in exile, then helped organize and became leader of the Third International. With Stalin and Kamenev, he controlled the policies of the Soviet Union during Lenin's last illness. He was sentenced to death in 1936.

L. B. Kamenev belonged to a well-to-do bourgeois family of Tiflis (now Tbilisi). He, too, was closely associated with Lenin in Geneva. Kamenev married Trotsky's sister. He became president of the Moscow City Soviet and had a gift for negotiation and compromise. (Sir John Maynard, *Russia in Flux*, S. Haden Guest, ed., New York, 1948, pp. 201–2.)

87. Nikolai Bukharin was a brilliant intellectual who became the leading ideologist of Stalin's ruling group and initiated the attack on the Trotsky Opposition. When Stalin turned to the left in 1928, Bukharin went to the right. In March, 1938, he was sentenced to be shot.

A. I. Rykov was always a man of the right and resigned from the government on the issue of the freedom of the press. He, too, was sentenced to death in March, 1938.

M. P. Tomski was president of the All-Union Central Committee of the Trade Unions for twelve years (1917–29) and was always a champion of trade-union independence. He committed suicide to avoid arrest in July, 1936. (*Ibid.*, pp. 202–3.)

On November 27, 1929, Bukharin was expelled from the Politburo; and Rykov, Tomski, and others were warned that "in the event of the slightest attempt on their part to oppose the line and the decisions of the Central Committee of the Communist Party, the Party would immediately take appropriate measures with them." (Alexander Baykov, *The Development of the Soviet Economic System*, New York, 1947, p. 174.)

88. V.K.P. (*b*) *v resolutsyakh, resheniakh siezdov, konferensii i plenumov Ts.K.*, Chast II (1925–39), 1941, quoted in Baykov, *The Development of the Soviet Economic System*, p. 221.

2. The Literary Five-Year Plan

1. Stuart Chase, "How Russia Charts Her Economic Course," New York *Times* (December 11, 1927), sec. 10, p. 7.
2. William Henry Chamberlin, *Soviet Russia*, rev. ed., Boston, 1931, p. 404.
3. Joseph Stalin, "The Results of the First Five-Year Plan," *Selected Writings*, New York, 1942, p. 245.
4. *Ibid.*, pp. 242–43.
5. *Ibid.*, p. 242.
6. "Resheniya X plenuma IKKI v massy!" *Pravda* (August 29, 1929), p. 1.
7. Stalin, "The Results of the First Five-Year Plan," p. 241.
8. Paul Scheffer in *Berliner Tageblatt* (July 12, 1929), quoted in G. T. Grinko, *The Five-Year Plan of the Soviet Union*, New York, 1930, p. 48.
9. "They are striving to create new habits, new morality, new types of human beings. They are endeavoring to make group loyalties—to the Communist Party, to the Union of Communist Youth, to the Soviet state, to the much vaguer 'working class of the world'—take precedence over personal loyalties to family and friends. While the motive of personal gain is by no means overlooked, indeed is heavily emphasized at the present stage of development, there is an effort, backed by an unrivaled governmental propaganda machine, to dramatize labor achievement, to give to the director or the outstanding workers of a successful

NOTES: THE LITERARY FIVE-YEAR PLAN 179

factory or institution, along with the higher salaries or wages which they can have under the Soviet system, a liberal measure of public and social applause as a substitute for the physical ownership of factory, shop, or land, which of course is rigidly forbidden." (Chamberlin, *Russia's Iron Age*, p. 9.)

10. RAPP journal of 1930, quoted in Reavey and Slonim, *Soviet Literature*, p. 43.

11. B. Ettinhof, "Art in the Five-Year Plan of Cultural Construction," VOKS, II, Nos. 10–12 (1931), 4.

12. *Ibid.*, p. 5.

13. *Ibid.*, p. 7.

14. Joseph Freeman, *The Soviet Worker*, New York, 1932, p. 317. The word "culture," as used in the Soviet Union, means "an observance of the simple rules of good manners and cleanliness and hygiene . . . The unceasing campaign for 'culture' in this sense of the word is an important phase of the general Soviet effort to remake the country by means of propaganda." (Chamberlin, *Russia's Iron Age*, p. 288.)

15. Leopold Averbakh, *Na putyakh kulturnoi revolyutsii*, 3d ed., Moscow, 1929, p. 81.

16. *Ibid.*, p. 135.

17. *Ibid.*, p. 59.

18. *Ibid.*, p. 135.

19. P. Bankov, "Authors from the Factory Bench," *Soviet Culture Review*, Nos. 7–9 (1932), p. 47.

In January, 1923, Lenin wrote: "A cultural revolution is a long drawn out and difficult period of persistent work in all fields, from the alphabet to astronomy, from bath tubs to air fleets, from trade schools to academies of fine arts, from the abolition of the old-fashioned forms of agriculture to the establishment of factories for artificial fertilizers, from top to bottom in all fields, everywhere there must be a seething of constant, uninterrupted toil, not only in cultural institutions, schools and universities, libraries and factories, but throughout the entire country at every worker's bench. Otherwise the work will not be successful. The millions of the population must participate, for the work must be collective in character, and the majority must help under the leadership of the working class. Only such work can bear the proud name of the cultural revolution which is necessary for the attainment of communism." (*Voices of October*, pp. 38–39.)

Trotsky's opinion of the cultural revolution's mission was expressed as follows: "The main task of the proletarian intelligentsia in the immediate future is not the abstract formation of a new culture regardless of the absence of a basis for it, but definite culture-bearing, that is, a systematic, planful and, of course, critical imparting to the backward masses of the essential elements of the culture which already exists." (Trotsky, *Literature and Revolution*, p. 193.)

20. "The psychological value of planning is . . . considerable. It is capable of touching the imagination, not only of administrative workers, but of manual workers as well. It widens their horizons, and gives their work an added dignity and interest as being part of a coherent national plan." (Margaret S. Miller, "The Planning System in Soviet Russia," *The Slavonic [and East European] Review*, IX, No. 26 [December, 1930], 454.)

21. Chamberlin, *Soviet Russia*, p. 405.

The Department of Propaganda and Agitation of the Central Committee of the Communist party is the body that "exercises ultimate powers of initiation and control of policy in the world of art as a whole." (George Reavey, *Soviet Literature Today*, London, 1946, p. 39.)

"Propaganda, as practised today in the Soviet Union, is no longer agitation; it is a method of teaching" and "forms a part of the cultural training of the Soviet peoples." (Kurt London, *The Seven Soviet Arts*, Eric S. Bensinger, trans., London, 1937, p. 199.) Dobb believed that the success of Russia's economic efforts during the First Five-Year Plan depended less on the efficiency of the Party and directing officials than on the Party's ability to stimulate spontaneous activity and initiative among the masses themselves. (Maurice Dobb, "The Significance of the Five-Year Plan," *The Slavonic [and East European] Review*, X, No. 28 [June, 1931], 89.)

During the first year of the First Five-Year Plan the "agit brigades" came into existence. Their purpose was to present "criticism of current problems and to engender enthusiasm for the tasks at hand" (Norris Houghton, *Moscow Rehearsals*, New York, 1936, pp. 29–30); and they staged skits (called "living newspapers") on vital topics of the day, combining music, dancing, and acting. Other propaganda brigades put out "lightning newspapers," which were wall newspapers characterized by the rapidity of their appearance. The "cultvan" was a propaganda van which toured the villages with literature of all sorts for the enlightenment of the peasants. In Gabrilovich's "The Year 1930," we see how "agitvans" were sent to the fields to explain the political nature of the sowing campaign and to agitate for an increase of speed: "*Agitvans* arrived . . . singing popular refrains ('Sow more'), and staging sketches ('Sow more!'). The singers of the Samara civic theatre sang arias ('Sow more!') standing on harrows." (Evgeni Gabrilovich, "The Year 1930," Reavey and Slonim, *Soviet Literature*, p. 252.)

One of the new forms of volunteer participation in the work of the cultural revolution was the "Kultestafeta" (cultural relay race), originated by the Moscow section of the Komsomol and applying "the principle of the regular relay race to the competitions held between collective groups in factories, social organizations, young people's associations and so forth in cultural work among the masses." (S. Afanasiev, "Cultural Movement of the Masses: 'Kulturnaya Estafeta,'" *Soviet Culture Bulletin*, No. 1 [July, 1931], p. 11.)

Chamberlin remarked that "a large part of the huge national propaganda effort is devoted to praising efficient workers and denouncing slackers on 'the labor front.' In line with Stalin's declaration, on one occasion, that 'the country must know its heroes,' feats of scientific and labor achievement are described in the press; and such decorations as the Order of Lenin and the Order of the Red Banner of Labor are awarded to men and women who have especially distinguished themselves. In Moscow's Park of Culture and Rest one . . . can find the faces of *udarniki*—the shock workers—of Moscow factories, commemorated in sculpture by Soviet artists." (Chamberlin, *Russia's Iron Age*, p. 273.)

Propaganda even crept into games and toys. Playing cards were issued by the Society of the Godless; kulak dolls were purged; and a game called "Five-Year Plan" (played on a board each corner of which was occupied by a construction representing a basic national industry, which were pitted against each other) was very popular until *Komsomolskaya Pravda* suddenly discovered that it was a game of "sabotage of our leading industries by each other!" (Eugene Lyons, *Modern Moscow*, London, n.d., pp. 172–76.) To organize the children's consciousness around socialist construction, there was a great increase of industrial subject matter in children's plays and books, which carried such titles as *The Bolshevist Gathering*, *A Savory Factory*, and *A Tale of the Great Plan*. (K. Tikhonova, "Graphic Arts in the U.S.S.R.," *VOKS*, II, Nos. 10–12 [1931], 74.)

22. "How Does the U.S.S.R. Work," *VOKS*, II, No. 1 (January, 1931), 7–8.

Polonski expressed this warlike attitude when he wrote: "Magnitogorsk is one of the decisive sectors of the war now being waged. When the history of our times is written, the Magnitogorsk front will be given a no less prominent place than the description of the battles around Perekop. The fight against the Interventionists and the White armies was really the first act of the campaign. The battle for Magnitogorsk, for Kuznetsk, in Berezniki, on the Dnieper, in Stalingrad, and in other similar places is a continuation of that very same war, only with other weapons.

"The war goes on. We are on the fronts of the Five-Year Plan. Before us lie the trenches from which the working class leads the attack on the new commanding heights." (Vyacheslav Polonski, *Magnitostroi*, Moscow, 1931, p. 7.)

In "A Leninist Song," the same spirit is shown:

Our mills are working day and night—
A ceaseless din and clang and rattle.
For metal and for power we fight—
This is our front of peaceful battle!

(Andrew Alexandrovich, "A Leninist Song," Michael L. Korr, trans., *VOKS*, III, Nos. 3–4 [1932], 81.)

Pilnyak, too, described Moscow as "a military encampment of armies marching into new Russia, into knowledge, equality, socialism." (Boris Pilnyak, *The Volga Falls to the Caspian Sea*, Charles Malamuth, trans., New York, 1931, p. 100.) "Russia marched, gray, made of steel, in crowds of ragged people, the words of command being slogans and placards, in army corps of trade unions, in the infantry of state institutions, the artillery and tanks of the Communist Party, organized the way plants are constructed. And indeed an immense factory was on foot, the workers' army of Russia, welded together, disciplined, well-knit, guided, rectified by tens of thousands of organizations—party, trade-union and state institutions of villages, counties, provinces, by the workers', peasants', and intellectual organizations, by the peoples' commissariats of labor, public health, education, trade, and by hundreds of other organizations which organize man and his work, which subordinate each other, overlap each other, coordinate each other." (*Ibid.*, pp. 301–2.) "Moscow was a single poster, a single slogan at the order of staffs and armies, steel, gray, unconquerable Russia." (*Ibid.*, p. 332.)

23. "How Does the U.S.S.R. Work," p. 10.

24. Benjamin Goriely, *Les Poètes dans la révolution russe*, Paris, 1934, p. 196.

25. Alexei N. Tolstoy (1882–1945) fought with the Whites during the Revolution and then lived in Paris as an émigré. In 1921 he became reconciled to the Bolsheviks and returned to Russia, minus the title of count. (John Cournos, ed. and trans., *Short Stories out of Soviet Russia*, New York, 1929, p. 16.) He was subsequently awarded three Stalin Prizes and in May of 1948 was said to rank second in popularity (after Sholokhov) on the list of contemporary Soviet writers. ("Russians Rank Sholokhov as Leading Writer," New York *Herald Tribune* [May 7, 1948], p. 24.)

26. From a book of a hundred autobiographies of Soviet writers published by "Federatsiya," quoted by L. M. Subotski in *Sovetskaya literatura na novom etape*, Moscow, 1933, Vsevolod Ivanov, p. 40.

27. "Soviet Writers about Themselves," Kornely Zelinski, p. 119.
28. *Ibid.*, Sergei Tretyakov, p. 116.
29. "The Voice of the Soviet Authors," *VOKS*, II, No. 1 (January, 1931), 68.
30. Zelinski, "15th Anniversary of Soviet Literature," p. 67.
31. In 1932 Kirpotin spoke of the great role played by Maxim Gorky, who reared the young cadres of proletarian writers and put out the first collection of works of proletarian writers since the Revolution. Almost all important writers came under his influence in some way because he carried the new word in literature, to which he brought the richness of colors, sounds, and songs. Gorky dethroned Dostoyevsky's hero, a slave who blessed his chains. (*Sov. lit. na novom etape*, Kirpotin, p. 13.)
32. Maxim Gorky, "On Literature and Other Things," *On Guard for the Soviet Union*, New York, 1933, p. 47.
33. *Ibid.*, p. 52.
34. Vladimir Mayakovsky, "Homewards (1925—On the Atlantic Ocean)," Herbert Marshall, trans., in Herbert Marshall, ed., *Mayakovsky and His Poetry*, rev. ed., London, 1945, p. 61.
35. Marshall, *ibid.*, p. 138.
36. Vladimir Mayakovsky, "Good and Bad," Isidor Schneider, trans., *The American Quarterly on the Soviet Union*, III, No. 1 (July, 1940), 79.
37. Marshall, *Mayakovsky and His Poetry*, p. 139. On February 1, 1930, at the Club of the Authors' Federation, an exhibition of twenty years of Mayakovsky's life and work was opened. In the foreword to the catalogue, the poet wrote: "The work of the revolutionary poet does not stop at the book; meetings, speeches, front-line limericks, one-day agit-prop playlets, the living radio-voice and the slogan flashing by on the trams—are all equal and sometimes very valuable examples of poetry." (*Ibid.*, p. 137.)
38. Vladimir Mayakovsky, "Good!" (1927), Isidor Schneider, trans., *The American Quarterly on the Soviet Union*, III, No. 1 (July, 1940), 60.
39. *Ibid.*, p. 61.
40. Marshall, *Mayakovsky and His Poetry*, p. 138. On March 25, 1930, an evening was held at the House of the Komsomols to celebrate Mayakovsky's twenty years of literary activity. It was his last public appearance. In the course of his talk, he explained that "it is very difficult to work, in the way I want to work, trying to establish real contact between the working auditorium and big poetry, poetry genuinely created and without ever lowering its standard and its meaning. . . . Poetry must be made so that without getting rid of the seriousness of your idea, you make your verses necessary to the masses," understand-

able and able to enrich the listener's mind and imagination and to sharpen his will to fight for socialism. (*Ibid.*, pp. 137–39.)

41. *Ibid.*, p. 139.
42. *Ibid.*, p. 140.
43. Vladimir Mayakovsky, "Kak delat stikhi?" *Izbrannoye*, V. A. Katanyana, ed., Moscow, 1948, p. 396.
44. Demyan Bedny (1883–1945), whose real name was Efim Pridvorov, may be called the journalist-laureate of the Revolution if Mayakovsky was its poet. (Kaun, *Soviet Poets and Poetry*, p. 146.) He was "an out-and-out propagandist versifier, without literary pretensions," whose best qualities were "a rough sense for humor and parody and a faculty for adapting quickly popular expressions." (Chamberlin, *Soviet Russia*, p. 293.) During the period of Military Communism he set an example of how poetry can be turned into a weapon of war, his daily poems being regarded as a valuable aid to the morale of the Red Army, and was awarded the Order of the Red Banner. (Zelinski, "15th Anniversary of Soviet Literature," p. 70.) This indefatigable writer on topical themes, whose collected works fill nineteen volumes, after the Civil War devoted his pen to socialist construction and often took part personally in shock-brigade work and socialist competition at plants and factories. However, he avoided active participation in any warring literary groups. (*Voices of October*, p. 44.) Bedny was the most popular modern proletarian revolutionary poet in the U.S.S.R. Every more or less important event in Russian public or political life since 1917 found expression in his works, which, consequently, form a type of chronicle of the Soviets from their beginning up to the end of World War II.

Trotsky wrote that Demyan Bedny was not a poet who had accepted the Revolution, but "a Bolshevik whose weapon is poetry. . . . He grew up in the Party, he lived through the various phases of its development, he learned to think and to feel with his class from day to day and to reproduce this world of thoughts and feelings in concentrated form in the language of verses which have the shrewdness of fables, the sadness of songs, the boldness of couplets, as well as indignation and appeal. . . . Day in and day out, as the events and the Central Committee of the Party demand," he creates, and not just when he is inspired. His verses range from "a great and finished art" to "a daily and second-rate newspaper." No other poet has by his verses "influenced so directly and actively the masses, the working and peasant masses, the Red Army masses, the many-millioned masses, during the greatest of all epochs." His poems are "an invaluable mechanism for the transmission of Bolshevik ideas." "From the point of view of what the proletariat reads, what it needs, what absorbs it, what impels it to action, what elevates its cultural level and so prepares the ground for a new art . . . the work of Demyan Biedny . . . [appears] as proletarian and popular literature, that is, literature vitally needed by an awakened people. If this is not 'true' poetry, it is something more than that." (Trotsky, *Literature and Revolution*, pp. 212–14.)

45. Vladimir Mayakovsky, "How One Writes a Poem," trans. from *Europe*, *The Living Age*, CCCXLV, No. 4405 (October, 1933), 153.

46. *Ibid.*

47. Vladimir Mayakovsky, "Domoi," quoted in L. I. Timofeyev, *Sovremennaya literatura*, 2d ed., corrected and enlarged, Moscow, 1947, p. 289.

48. Chamberlin, *Russia's Iron Age*, p. 299.

49. G. Lelevich, "Aleksandr Bezymenski," *No literaturnom postu*, Moscow, 1924, p. 80.

50. Alexander Bezymenski, Speech in XVI *syezd vsesoyuznoi kommunisticheskoi partii* (*b*), 2d ed., Moscow-Leningrad, 1931, p. 394.

51. *Ibid.*

52. *Ibid.*, p. 395.

53. The Serapion Brothers existed as a group of individualists in Leningrad from February 1, 1921, to May, 1923. Evgeni Zamyatin was their teacher. They did not recognize a link between art and society and would not write for propaganda. Literature, the Brothers felt, need not reflect its period. (See William Edgerton, "The Serapion Brothers," *The American Slavic and East European Review*, VIII, No. 1 [February, 1949], 47–64.)

54. Vyacheslav Polonski, "The Social Command" (1929), Reavey and Slonim, *Soviet Literature*, p. 423.

55. Lenin, quoted in London, *The Seven Soviet Arts*, p. 84.

56. Trotsky, *Literature and Revolution*, p. 218.

57. "Resolution on Literature . . . July 1, 1924," p. 64.

58. Ettinhof, "Art in the Five-Year Plan of Cultural Construction," p. 5.

59. "Mesto sovetskovo pisatelya," *Literaturnaya gazeta*, No. 25 (October 7, 1929), p. 1.

60. Averbakh, *Kulturnaya revolyutsiya i voprosy sovremennoi literatury*, p. 64.

61. *Ibid.*

62. *Ibid.*, p. 91.

63. Maxim Gorky, "O deistvitelnosti" (1929), *O literature*, N. F. Belchikov, ed., 3d ed., enlarged, Moscow, 1937, p. 337.

64. "Urals and Siberia in Soviet Art," *Soviet Culture Review*, No. 5 (1932), p. 28.

65. Vladimir Lidin, "Soviet Literature," VOKS, II, No. 6 (1931), 69.
66. Yuri Libedinski, "O razreshenii generalnykh zadach proletarskoi literatury" (report given at second general plenum of the directors of RAPP, September, 1929), Generalnyie zadachi proletarskoi literatury, Moscow-Leningrad, 1931, p. 40.
67. Ibid., p. 41.
68. Ibid., p. 76.
69. Chamberlin, Russia's Iron Age, p. 295.
70. Vladimir Kirshon, Speech in XVI syezd vsesoyuznoi kommunisticheskoi partii (b), p. 280.
71. "Resolution on Literature . . . July 1, 1924," p. 61.
72. Kirshon, Speech, p. 280.
73. Ibid.
74. Ibid.
75. Ibid., p. 281.
76. Reavey and Slonim, Soviet Literature, p. 43.
77. Kushner, "Prichiny otstavaniya."
"The work of our writers is a difficult and complicated work," said Gorky. "It is not made up of criticism of the old reality, of the unmasking of its defects. The task of our young writers is to study, to formulate, to depict, and, at the same time, to affirm the new reality. One must study to see how the light of the future flares up and begins to burn in the smoky decay of the old rot. The young writers must tell about the new joys of life, about the variegated flowering of creative forces in the country. They must search for inspiration and subject matter in the wide and tempestuous flow of work which is creating new forms of life. They ought to live as close as possible to the creative will of our epoch, which is embodied in the working class." (Gorky, "O deistvitelnosti," p. 343.)
78. Antoni Slonimski was a pro-Soviet Polish lyric poet who went on a visit to Russia in 1932. (Z. St. Klingsland, "Un Poète polonais au pays des réalités soviétiques," Pologne littéraire, No. 73 [October 15, 1932], p. 4.)
79. Fischer, Machines and Men in Russia, p. 234.
80. Libedinski, "Za chto boryutsya napostovtsy," p. 25.
81. Gorky, "On Literature . . . ," p. 43.
"With all the tremendous development of Soviet literature and the extraordinary many-sidedness of Soviet writers there are still few among them who can, by their creative perspicacity, forecast in artistic imagery the outlines of the new socialist society as the leaders of the Soviet government do in their political, ideological and organizational creative work." (S. Ludkevich, "Soviet Literature as the Forepost of World

NOTES: DEMANDS MADE OF THE "SKETCHERS"

Literature," M. Apletin, ed., *Literature of the Peoples of the U.S.S.R.*, VOKS Illustrated Almanac, Nos. 7–8 [1934], p. 22.)

82. Letter written by Gorky to a literary circle early in 1928, Harper, *Civic Training in Soviet Russia*, p. 307.
83. Averbakh, *Kulturnaya revolyutsiya* . . . , p. 61.
84. Libedinski, "O razreshenii . . . ," pp. 40–41.
85. Fischer, *Machines and Men in Russia*, p. 240.

3. Demands Made of the "Sketchers"

1. Karl Marx and Friedrich Engels, *The German Ideology*, Part II, MEGA, Part I, V, 372–73, *Literature and Art*, New York, 1947, p. 76.
"Whether an individual . . . develops his talent depends entirely upon the demand which in turn depends upon the division of labor and the cultural relations of people arising from this." (*Ibid.*, p. 75.)
2. "Shock Workers in Literature," VOKS, II, No. 4 (1931), 26.
3. N. Putnikova, "Woman in Literature," VOKS, II, No. 2 (February, 1931), 18.
4. Kushner, "Prichiny otstavaniya."
5. "Chronicle of Culture: Literature," *Soviet Culture Bulletin*, No. 3 (July, 1931), p. 14.
6. Zelinski, "15th Anniversary of Soviet Literature," p. 68.
7. Kirshon, Speech in *XVI syezd vsesoyuznoi kommunisticheskoi partii (b)*, pp. 281–82.
8. Leopold Averbakh, ed., *Belomor*, Amabel Williams-Ellis, ed., New York, 1935, p. 230.
9. Vladimir Mayakovsky, "Brother Writers," Reavey and Slonim, *Soviet Literature*, pp. 363–64.
10. "Soviet Writers about Themselves," Marietta Shaginyan, p. 114.
11. Medicinal baths of carbonic mineral water, named from the Narzan Spring at Kislovodsk (a Russian watering-place in the Caucasus).
12. Marietta Shaginyan, "The Armenian Woman and the October Revolution," *Soviet Transcaucasus: Armenia*, VOKS, III, Nos. 3–4 (1932), 150–51.
13. Struve, *25 Years of Soviet Russian Literature* (1918–1943), p. 91.
14. "Soviet Writers about Themselves," Gladkov, pp. 99–100.
15. A literary evening, held at the club of the Komsomols, is described in Ehrenburg's *The Second Day*. An actor from Novosibirsk read poems by Nekrasov and Mayakovsky (including "Left, March!") and stories by Zoshchenko, after which two Komsomol members read their own poems. "One of them vowed that Kuznetsk would never be

second to Magnitogorsk. The other wrote lyrics, and exclaimed about 'Your phisicultural lips!' Both were loudly applauded." (Ilya Ehrenburg, *Out of Chaos* [*The Second Day*], Alexander Bakshy, trans., New York, 1934, p. 47.) There was a "Mayakovsky Brigade, whose members recited the poems of their favorite poet at 'evenings.'" (*Ibid.*, p. 52.) At the Kuznetsk theatre, "plays by Shakespeare and Kirshon were produced." (*Ibid.*, p. 53.)

16. Marshall, *Mayakovsky and His Poetry*, p. 2.

17. Vladimir Mayakovsky, "Miracles," Isidor Schneider, trans., *The American Quarterly on the Soviet Union*, III, No. 1 (July, 1940), 73.

18. Every industrial enterprise and state or collective farm had a workers' club or "Red Corner" (developed as part of the cultural work of the trade unions) where cultural activities were carried on. Here the literary circles organized creative study, work on the factory and wall newspapers, and the readings of artistic works. In 1930 there were fourteen hundred such circles, composed of twenty-eight thousand novice worker and peasant writers (Freeman, *The Soviet Worker*, p. 322) who contributed poems, stories, sketches, and articles to their local newssheets, and issued literary pages. The subject matter dealt mostly with production and the new factory life and was provided by the circle members' own observations, as well as by the notes sent to the editors by worker correspondents. (A. Zhuchkov, "Factory Literary Circles," M. Apletin, ed., *Literature of the Peoples of the U.S.S.R.*, VOKS Illustrated Almanac, Nos. 7–8 [1934], p. 91.)

In club circles the principle of collectivism was always emphasized. Literary circles were not intended to serve the needs of the individual member who wished to perfect himself in a particular line, for their work was supposed to be exclusively of a mass character. (Harper, *Civic Training in Soviet Russia*, p. 159.) The manual, *Litrabota v klube i v krasnom ugolke*, suggested the collective writing of slogans as a project and added that "a rhymed slogan is easier to remember." (N. S. Vertinski, *Litrabota v klube i v krasnom ugolke*, Moscow, 1930, p. 13.) It was also recommended that circles hold competitions for: (1) the best literary layout of a wall newspaper (as to the political impact of its contents); (2) reader-activists; (3) the best sketch, story, etc. (*Ibid.*, p. 41.) Socialist competition agreements should be entered into between clubs and circles. Agree, for instance, during a given period to increase membership and discipline of the literary circles, to widen literary activity, to create closer ties with all the other organizations in the enterprise, to give not less than a certain number of literary evenings propagandizing the Five-Year Plan, to organize literary competition between local wall newspapers, and not to slacken during the summer. (*Ibid.*, pp. 44–46.)

NOTES: DEMANDS MADE OF THE "SKETCHERS" 189

The mass literary movement was supposed to raise the general cultural level, to develop and advance talented worker-writers, and to mobilize their efforts towards higher tempos and quality of work in the struggle for the Plan. "The literary circle brings up cadres of young, new writers—workers and collective farmers—and teaches them from the very beginning to aid with their work in the building of socialism. Such is the work of the literary circle." (Zhuchkov, "Factory Literary Circles," p. 90.)

19. Fischer, *Machines and Men in Russia*, p. 266.
20. *Ibid.*
21. "There are many varieties of patronage societies. The underlying principle of all of them is that a group which is better organized, economically stronger, and politically more conscious assumes with respect to a group which is less well organized, economically weaker, and politically backward the special responsibility of material and moral assistance. The first and the largest field for patronage activity is that of the relations between the proletariat and the peasantry." (Harper, *Civic Training in Soviet Russia*, p. 67.)
22. "Resolution Passed by the Workers and Employees of the Electrofactory after the Reading of Ilya Selvinski's Poem: 'The Electrofactory Newspaper,' " quoted in Ilya Selvinski, "How I Worked at the Electrofactory," *VOKS*, II, No. 6 (1931), 64–65. Needless to say, this is a very poor translation.
23. The young Communist writer Poshekhonov protested against those who demanded that all writers should go to the factories: "It is bad for a writer to see everything as it is and have no power to say what is good and what is ugly." (Struve, *25 Years of Soviet Russian Literature*, p. 242.)
24. Leonov, *Skutarevsky*, p. 245.
25. *Ibid.*, p. 313.
26. *Ibid.*, p. 441.
27. Fyodor Panfyorov, *And Then the Harvest*, Stephen Garry, trans., London, 1939, p. 331.
28. S. M., "Collectivization and the Countryside in Contemporary Fiction," *VOKS*, Nos. 8–10 (1930), 25.
29. Libedinski, "O razreshenii generalnykh zadach proletarskoi literaturny," p. 44.
30. Sergei Tretyakov, "Writers, to the Collective Farms!" *VOKS*, II, No. 1 (January, 1931), 86.
31. *Ibid.*, p. 85.
32. Ilya Ilf and Evgeni Petrov, *The Little Golden Calf*, Charles Malamuth, trans., New York, 1932, p. 281. Ostap Bender is the resourceful hero of these adventures.

33. "Pervaya brigada pisatelei konchila svoyu rabotu," *Literaturnaya gazeta*, No. 25 (October 7, 1929), p. 3.
34. "Literature of the Peoples of the U.S.S.R.," *VOKS*, II, No. 5 (1931), 65.
35. See also p. 63.
36. P. Pavlenko, "Notes on the Spring," A *Journey to Turkmenistan*, VOKS, III, Nos. 3–4 (1932), 52.
37. Fischer, *Machines and Men in Russia*, p. 246.
38. Ilya Selvinski, "Puteshestviye po Kamchatke" (1932), *Lirika*, Moscow, 1937, p. 186.
39. Polonski, *Magnitostroi*, p. 32.
40. See p. 65.
41. "New Soviet Literature," *VOKS*, Nos. 6–7 (April, 1930), p. 41.
42. G. A., "The U.S.S.R. in the Arctic," *VOKS*, Nos. 8–10 (1930), p. 78.
43. Kushner, "Prichiny otstavaniya."
44. Ehrenburg, *Out of Chaos*, p. 29. A "Cowper's" is a hot-blast stove, used for pre-heating the air blown into the blast-furnace.
45. Valentin Katayev, *Time, Forward!*, Charles Malamuth, trans., New York, 1933, p. 118.
46. V. P. Ilyenkov, *Driving Axle*, New York, 1933, p. 267.
47. Marshall, *Mayakovsky and His Poetry*, p. 139.
48. The official post-RAPP point of view (1934) about this question was as follows: The fact that the writer must become an active participant in the process going on in the U.S.S.R. "did not at all mean, as some Soviet writers thought several years ago when socialist construction was just beginning to acquire its real and palpable contours, that it was necessary to throw aside the creative pen and go to a plant or *kolkhoz* as a worker or farmer. According to these writers, only direct participation in the collective production process at the plant or *kolkhoz* could give them the possibility correctly to clarify for themselves what is taking place in the consciousness of the Soviet workers.

"No, the activity of the Soviet writer consists in *taking a direct part* in the process of breaking away from the old life and the building of a new one in any field to which *his own creative interests* attract him." (Ludkevich, "Soviet Literature as the Forepost of World Literature," p. 21.)

49. Maxim Gorky, "La Mission des écrivains soviétiques," Z. Lvovsky, trans., *La Revue hebdomadaire*, No. 42 (October 21, 1933), pp. 310–11.
50. A *subbotnik* is a gathering to perform volunteer collective labor (contributed without pay to the Soviet state) at a socially useful task. This form of socialist work was carried out for the first time by the

workers of the Moscow-Kazan Railroad in Moscow on May 10, 1919. *Subbotniks*, as the name implies, were originally held on Saturdays but, subsequently, on free evenings or rest days.

51. "Shock Workers in Literature," p. 26.
52. V. Katayev, *Time, Forward!*, p. 265.
53. "New Soviet Literature," VOKS, II, No. 1 (January, 1931), 95.
54. Fischer, *Machines and Men in Russia*, p. 248.
55. Marietta Shaginyan's parents were Armenian intellectuals, and she started her literary activity as a music critic and a symbolist poet. She was one of the first representatives of the older generation of writers, "who sincerely took the side of the October Revolution and who grasped its world-historic importance." ("Preface" [1930], Marietta Shaginyan, *Soviet Transcaucasus*, VOKS, III, Nos. 3–4 [1932], 140.) Tirelessly studying the new world of socialism at various constructions, she participated actively in its life.

The success of *Hydrocentral* (1931) was attributed to the correctness of her method of work, and the novel has been described as "a sort of 'art construction job.'" (Kornely Zelinski, "Hydrocentral by Marietta Shaginyan," M. Apletin, ed., *Literature of the Peoples of the U.S.S.R.*, VOKS Illustrated Almanac, Nos. 7–8 [1934], p. 161.) The book, socialist in content and national in material, is a "highly artistic literary summary of dispatches from the front of socialist construction, enlivened by a narrative dealing with the fate and psychology of the fighters for a new and better life of the human race." ("Preface . . . Transcaucasus.") It reflects correctly the "irreconcilable, unceasing mass struggle in every field . . . of life" (Putnikova, "Woman in Literature," p. 19) and demonstrates and expounds the social philosophy behind the Soviet industrialization and electrification program. (Samuel H. Cross, "Russian Literature since 1918," *The Harvard Advocate*, CXXIX, No. 4 [Spring-Summer, 1943], 14.)

56. Zelinski, "15th Anniversary of Soviet Literature," p. 67.
57. Putnikova, "Woman in Literature," p. 19.
58. D. S. Mirsky, "Russia," *Tendencies of the Modern Novel*, London, 1934, p. 116.
59. Zelinski, "Hydrocentral . . . ," p. 164.
60. Selvinski, the son of a very wealthy merchant, was brought up in bourgeois traditions, but as a young student he enlisted in the Red Guards. (M. Mir, "Ilya Selvinski and His Poetry," VOKS, II, No. 6 [1931], 65.) He said that "my biography is rather varied and restless: I used to be a ship-mate, a model, a coach, a Red Guard fighter, a lecturer in political economy, a wrestling teacher, a water-pumper in a hotel, a worker in preserved food factory, the paid companion of a lunatic, a reporter, an actor, the chief of a rags department, a fur-trade agent

in Kirghizia, etc. All this was complicated by the fact that I had to graduate as a student of law and to become the leader of the literary school of constructivism." (Selvinski, "How I Worked . . . ," p. 61.)

During the NEP he wrote about his generation of the intelligentsia in "Our Biography," confessing that "with the breath of the masses my soul goes wild," (Ilya Selvinski, "Our Biography," Vera Sandomersky, trans., *New Directions in Prose and Poetry 1941*, Norfolk, Conn., 1941, p. 562) and

> That because of our age, our heart, our ideology,
> And, what's more—our social fate,
> We couldn't now escape the proletarian class.
> Comrade! You there! In the docks!
> You there! Making locomotives wail!
> Consider us, switch our nerves onto your circuit,
> Tune us in, like any of your plants.

(*Ibid.*, p. 564.) In 1927 Selvinski published *Pushtorg*, a novel in verse which tells the story of a Soviet fur trust and, with its diagrams, figures, and specifications, makes one feel that the poet must have studied the fur business. (Vladimir Pozner, "Ilia Selvinski et le constructivisme," *Les Nouvelles littéraires, artistiques et scientifiques*, No. 460 [August 8, 1931], p. 6.)

After the publication of his *Elektrozavodskaya gazeta* by the Federation of Soviet Writers in 1931, this former fellow-traveler was considered to have "definitely entered into the ranks of the poets who are 'allies' of the proletariat" (Mir, "Ilya Selvinski . . . ," p. 66), and he became leader of the Moscow Brigade of Writers No. 1. In a long poem, "A Poet's Declaration of Rights," Selvinski spoke of his unreserved moral and intellectual bond with the proletariat, apart from which any art of ideal or aesthetic meaning would be unthinkable. ("Voice of Soviet Authors," p. 67.) The poet prized, above all, the new régime's spirit of order and organization; and he emphasized this side of communism to the belittlement of other aspects. (Pozner, "Ilia Selvinski. . . .")

61. Selvinski, "How I Worked . . . ," p. 61.
62. *Ibid.*, pp. 62–63.
63. *Ibid.*, p. 63.
64. *Ibid.*, p. 65.
65. "Soviet Writers about Themselves," Tretyakov, p. 116.
66. Tretyakov, "Writers, to Collective Farms!" p. 86.
67. *Ibid.*, pp. 86–87.
68. *Ibid.*, p. 87.
69. "New Soviet Literature" (January, 1931), p. 95.

70. "A Proletarian Writer, Vsevolod Vishnevski," *VOKS*, II, No. 3 (1931), 72.

71. Chamberlin, *Russia's Iron Age*, p. 194.

In *An Optimistic Tragedy*, a chorus leader reminds the audience that "as long as he can lift a hand—even his left hand—a Communist fighter keeps on fighting. . . . Should you die, as the axe falls on your neck, give your last thought to the Revolution. Remember that even death can be Party work." (Vsevolod Vishnevski, *An Optimistic Tragedy*, H. G. Scott and Robert S. Carr, trans., Ben Blake, ed., *Four Soviet Plays*, London, 1937, p. 165.)

Vishnevski's plays, which had great popular success, were characteristic of the First Five-Year Plan period because of their "extraordinarily dynamic nature, the complete transfer of their center of gravity to action, the absence of psychologism." This dramatist considered all psychology a symptom of decay and introduced it only when representing negative, decadent types. His positive types are always in action.

The Last Decisive was severely criticized by LOKAF, VOAPP, and the Communist Academy. Vishnevski is too fascinated by the fighting process itself, too much of a "battle-painter." The play could take place elsewhere than under the socialist Revolution, the critics said; and the battle scenes lack the particular spirit which the Red Army has in reality. The front in Vishnevski's works is self-sufficing; it is isolated from the masses. A fight between two countries, and not between two worlds, is depicted. Man is reduced to a mere figure. ("Proletarian Writer . . . ," p. 72.)

72. Socialist competition was a basic method in Soviet economy at this time and involved a "contest between groups of workers in an enterprise, or departments in an enterprise, or between factories or groups of factories within an industry, or between two industries, or between 'shock brigades.'" (Freeman, *The Soviet Worker*, p. 129.) The workers of one group would sign a pledge to achieve definite results in the way of increased output, reduced costs, diminished absenteeism, etc. Then they would send a challenge to other units to match or exceed their record. The object of the contest was to raise production, the standard of measurement being the schedule set by the industrial-financial plan (the "promfinplan," or annual plan based on the Control Figures and assigned to the individual enterprise by the higher planning bodies).

73. *Voices of October*, pp. 51–52.

74. In *Head Thus*, Lavrenyov described the *voenkor:* "in the newspaper work, on board his ship and in the general naval press, the Red sailor becomes an active journalist with a sharp eye-sight and the abil-

ity to draw conclusions from his observations. In his press the Red sailor learns the technique of newspaper work, which knowledge he carries with him to the factory and to the village and can organize there an active press fight for the Party line, for collectivization, against the class enemy, and will always be on guard." (B. Lavrenyov, "Men," last chapter of *Head Thus*, VOKS, III, Nos. 3–4 [1932], 94.)

75. B. Persov, "The Soviet Press," VOKS, II, Nos. 7–9 (1931), 116.
76. *Voices of October*, p. 26.
77. Harper, *Civic Training in Soviet Russia*, p. 99.
78. *Voices of October*, pp. 25–26.

As an instrument of propaganda and agitation, the Soviet press is considered more effective than book or pamphlet; and the Party's Central Committee itself appoints the newspaper editorial staffs, which see to it that all news is passed "through a Communist prism" before being printed. (Harper, *Civic Training in Soviet Russia*, p. 107.) The Soviet press is looked upon as a "lever of the cultural revolution," not as merely descriptive and informative. It serves as an instrument for the exchange of experience between large human collectives and must, therefore, chronicle the daily progress of socialist construction. It "leads a relentless and open struggle against all deviations and perversions of the victorious proletariat's ideology and tactics, a struggle against all remains of capitalist elements within the country and all attempts to hinder socialist construction from the outside." (Persov, "The Soviet Press," p. 116.) When necessary, the newspaper rouses public opinion for or against something; it criticizes concrete defects and irregularities in the execution of the construction plan, from the point of view of the construction's interest (self-criticism); it describes as socialist victories the opening of every big new factory and the progress of every sowing and harvesting campaign; and it gives much space to accounts of the creators of the Five-Year Plan: shock workers, inventors, and active workers in various fields. "The pens of the best Soviet authors, feuilleton-writers, *rabkor* brigades draw the pictures of the men of socialist labour, they write their biographies, they describe their experience in production, the rising of their cultural level." (*Ibid.*, p. 120.)

At the end of 1931 there were 1,409 newspapers in the U.S.S.R., 1,200 factory and 460 *kolkhoz* and *sovkhoz* ones (*ibid.*, pp. 113–14); about 600 were published in 64 languages in the national districts. (*Ibid.*, p. 119.) Soviet mass newspapers appear in a great variety of forms. A factory has its general printed paper whose worker correspondents form a network of signalizers. There are, in addition, shop-papers, brigade-papers, and often many specialized papers dealing with individual fields or problems. The sections of almost all enterprises issue wall newspapers, chronicles of the daily life of the workers and peasants created by themselves, written by hand or typewritten and appearing in all sizes and degrees of proficiency.

References to wall newspapers are frequently met with in First Five-Year Plan literature. Nalbandov, of *Time, Forward!*, speaks of "the gawky wall-newspapers—yard-wide rolls of wall-paper—with their semi-literate remarks and clamorous, insistent, exhorting slogans." (V. Katayev, p. 229.) And in the same novel the hotel's kitchen wall newspaper exposes the outrage committed by "our Comrade Zhukov," a Young Communist who, in the course of a quarrel with Citizen Molyavina, "threw the innards of some game . . . into her eyes." (*Ibid.*, p. 103.) The wall newspaper in *The Volga Falls to the Caspian Sea* runs pictures of "model malingerers." (Pilnyak, p. 34.)

Wall newspapers and bulletins are put out by *kolkhoz* brigades, often right where they are working. Besides this, during various campaigns special propaganda railroad cars with traveling editorial departments go out to the fields to publish sowing or reaping campaign newspapers, with the help of the local correspondents' brigades. The first wall newspapers appeared in the Red Army barracks at the battlefront in 1920. By 1930 there were thousands of district, regiment, and squadron ("Ilyichevka") newspapers served by *voenkors*.

79. Persov, "The Soviet Press," p. 117.
80. *Belomor*, p. 221.
81. In *Bread*, for instance, the editor of the regional newspaper, Perevozhnikov, keeps constantly muttering, "Just fancy . . ." and is so incompetent that Mikhailov finally has to write his article for him. (Vladimir Kirshon, *Bread*, Sonia Volochova, trans., Eugene Lyons, ed., *Six Soviet Plays*, Boston-New York, 1934, p. 242.) Bach, editor of the local newspaper in Volume IV of *Bruski*, is called "a twaddler" and reminds everyone of "a very cheeky little dog: the kind that must go running everywhere, sniffing at everything and cocking its leg against every post." (Panfyorov, *And Then the Harvest*, p. 65.) Besides being a coward, he turns out to be a Trotskyite.
82. V. Katayev, *Time, Forward!*, p. 33.
83. *Ibid.*, pp. 112–13.
84. *Ibid.*, p. 308.
85. Maxim Gorky, "Udarniki v literature" (1931), *O literature*, N. F. Belchikov, ed., 3d ed., enlarged, Moscow, 1937, p. 65.
86. Persov, "The Soviet Press," p. 118.
87. Gorky, "La Mission . . . ," p. 314.
88. Goriely, *Les Poètes dans la révolution russe*, p. 193.

"Thousands of them [*udarniks*] are invading literature and occupying the front line trenches of the cultural revolution," said Gorky. (Gorky, "On Literature and Other Things," p. 52.)

89. "Shock Workers in Literature," p. 26.
90. Kushner, "Prichiny otstavaniya."
91. Persov, "The Soviet Press," p. 118.
In October of 1930, the single worker correspondent prevailed in the Electrofactory's press. A new form of collective work, the *rabkor* brigade, was inaugurated by the newspaper, *The Electrofactory*, which then began to organize worker correspondents' factory raids. An effort was made to get all of the shock workers of the industrial brigades to participate. Eighty per cent of the members of the punching section of the transformer department systematically took part in these raids, and a woman worker declared: "We did the polishing and never knew what was going on next to us. And now we went with the raid and know what is the joiners' section and what are its defects. You can call for us, when you need us; we shall come willingly." This feature of collective labor is credited with helping the Electrofactory to finish its Five-Year Plan in two and a half years. (N. Butomo, "The Worker Correspondents Take the Five-Year Plan by Storm," VOKS, II, No. 6 [1931], 60.)

92. Persov, "The Soviet Press," p. 118.
93. "Shock Workers in Literature," pp. 27–28.
94. Persov, "The Soviet Press," p. 118.
95. Extract from a decision of the secretariat of the Council of Syndicates, quoted in Goriely, *Les Poètes dans la révolution russe*, p. 194.
96. Bankov, "Authors from the Factory Bench," p. 46. The best *rabkor* book was Zhiga's *The Diary of a Rabkor*, which told "the thoughts of the workers, their worries, their affairs." (Goriely, *Les Poètes dans la révolution russe*, p. 196.)
97. "RAPP," *Lit. entsik.*, p. 522.
98. Zelinski, "15th Anniversary of Soviet Literature," p. 70.
99. Fischer, *Machines and Men in Russia*, pp. 253–54.
100. "Shock Workers in Literature," p. 28.
101. Bankov, "Authors from the Factory Bench," p. 46.
102. Stalin, quoted in *ibid*.
103. *Ibid*.
104. N. Mikhailov, "The Fight for the Metal," VOKS, II, No. 4 (1931), 31.
105. I. Berman, "Amo," VOKS, II, No. 4 (1931), 38.
106. Vassili Semyakin, "Industrial 1931," Michael L. Korr, trans., VOKS, II, No. 4 (1931), 29–30.

A camp poet at Belomorstroi, formerly a forger and thief, produced these verses:

> I had a pen and a bunch of fine keys,
> And I often went to the pen;

But I always looked with envy
At the life of the working men.
(*Belomor*, p. 220.)

107. In order to raise the political and literary qualifications of these young authors and to help them master the writer's technique, many Soviet publishing houses set up literary consultation bureaus where the beginner could get the advice of a specialist (a trained writer or poet) or special literature to help him. Various courses, seminars, literary evenings, and group consultations were organized, also stationary and traveling exhibitions to show the worker-author how to draw up the plan of his book, how to gather material, how to work out a theme, etc. (Bankov, "Authors from the Factory Bench," pp. 46–47.)

108. Goriely, *Les Poètes dans la révolution russe*, p. 195.

109. Kushner, "Prichiny otstavaniya."

110. The magazine, *Writers to the Shock Brigades*, published by the Federation of Associations of Soviet Writers, was composed of sketch-type literature devoted to the struggle for the industrial and economic Plan. Bezymenski, Veresayev, Gladkov, Utkin, Lyasho, Zhiga, Vera Inber, Ivan Katayev, Bakhmetyev, and others contributed tales, sketches, poems, and selections from longer works dealing with the themes of the day—shock brigades, socialist competition, etc.

111. Maxim Gorky, "O literature" (1931), *O literature*, N. F. Belchikov, ed., 3d ed., enlarged, Moscow, 1937, p. 58.

112. Gleb Alekseyev's *Deeds and People of Competition* contains sketches of miners of the Donets Basin and of workers in a glass factory.

113. Gorky, "O literature," p. 58.

114. *Ibid.*, pp. 59 and 62. The attitude that anyone can write sketches is shown by Olga, Mikhailov's pretty, blonde, bored wife when she is looking for an excuse to accompany Rayevsky to the country: "Journalists are needed in the country. I'll write sketches. I'm going with Rayevsky tomorrow!" (Kirshon, *Bread*, p. 245.)

115. See p. 45.

116. G. Sannikov, "The Struggle for Cotton Independence," *VOKS*, III, Nos. 3–4 (1932), 57–58.

117. *Ibid.*, p. 62.

118. Venyamin Kaverin was one of the Serapion Brothers.

119. Venyamin Kaverin, "The Return of the Kirghiz," sketch from *The Prologue* (1931), Reavey and Slonim, *Soviet Literature*, p. 261.

120. Ivan Katayev, "The Conquerors," *Front*, I, No. 4 (June, 1931), 387–88.

121. Gabrilovich, "The Year 1930," p. 235.

122. *Ibid.*, p. 254.

123. Marietta Shaginyan, "The School of Dzorages," *Soviet Transcaucasus: Armenia,* VOKS, III, Nos. 3–4 (1932), 159.
124. *Ibid.,* p. 155.
125. Marietta Shaginyan, "Chiatura," *Soviet Transcaucasus: Georgia,* VOKS, III, Nos. 3–4 (1932), 178.
126. *Ibid.,* p. 184.
127. See p. 46.
128. Polonski, *Magnitostroi,* p. 12.
129. *Ibid.,* p. 8.
130. *Ibid.,* p. 78.
131. *Ibid.,* p. 43.
132. *Ibid.,* p. 75.
133. *Ibid.,* p. 78.
134. *Ibid.,* p. 50.
135. Only the foreign specialists at the construction had a good dining room, and this was very bad for the workers' morale. (*Ibid.,* p. 47.)
136. *Ibid.,* p. 60.
137. *Ibid.,* p. 78.
138. "Theatre Season 1931/32 (Moscow-Leningrad)," VOKS, II, Nos. 10–12 (1931), 24.
The workers at the building of the White Sea–Baltic Canal had a book of poems, marches, slogans, and songs, written by the collective. It contained "descriptions of all the hard struggles we have had in the workings, at the dams, and at the locks; and answers to the commander's orders about reforging people." "In these songs we don't try to recall the past, but to stir ourselves up to new battle and new life." (*Belomor,* p. 281.)
139. Shock Workers, "The First Cruise," Anthony Wixley, trans., *International Literature,* No. 1 (1932), p. 3.
140. Eastman, *Artists in Uniform,* pp. 4–5.
141. Gorky, "On Literature . . . ," p. 52.
142. The *History of the Civil War,* according to Gorky, "should tell how the workers and peasants of tsarist Russia conducted an armed struggle for the power of the Soviets, for their rights to rebuild their society on a socialist system, for the right to create a free country out of an enslaved one, for a proletarian government." (N. Myamlin, "A Literary Monument to the Civil War," M. Apletin, ed., *Literature of the Peoples of the U.S.S.R.,* VOKS Illustrated Almanac, Nos. 7–8 [1934], p. 87.) "The role of the working class and its vanguard, the Communist Party, the role of the great leaders of the proletariat—Lenin and Stalin —in the organization of the great victory, will be reflected in the pages of the *History of the Civil War.*" (*Ibid.*) It was to sum up and trans-

NOTES: DEMANDS MADE OF THE "SKETCHERS" 199

mit the experience of this period to new generations of toilers of the U.S.S.R.

The work was planned in fifteen volumes, which would cover all the most important events of the Civil War from the February Revolution of 1917 down to the suppression of the last uprisings against the Soviet government in 1922. Although the description and exposition of the armed struggle against the background of economic and political events was to be strictly scientific, these volumes were to be written in a popular style intelligible to the broadest masses of readers.

The *History of the Civil War* was to be not only an outstanding production of science, history and art literature, but also a specimen of collective authorship. (I. Danilov, "How the History of Civil War Is Being Written," *Soviet Culture Review*, Nos. 7–9 [1932], p. 52.) Those who had participated in the events related, from the masses to the most important figures of the Communist party, were drawn into the writing of this history; and prominent historians and the greatest writers were asked to bring it into literary shape. Among the editors were: Gorky, Demyan Bedny, Fadeyev, Vs. Ivanov, Leonov, Kirshon, Fedin, and Panfyorov. ("Cultural News: 'History of the Civil War' Going To Be Published," *Soviet Culture Bulletin*, No. 5 [September, 1931], p. 13.)

143. V. Katayev, *Time, Forward!*, p. 340.

144. Gorky also appealed to the participants in the Civil War to write up all they knew of the events which they had witnessed. "It is necessary for everyone who took direct part in this war: members of the Red Guard, partisans, Red Army men, commanders and military commissars of those years, as well as the people that suffered from robbery and violence on the part of the White armies, the contingents of interventionists, robber bands, etc. to take an active part in the compilation of this data." (Myamlin, "A Literary Monument to the Civil War," p. 88.)

The appeal met with an enthusiastic response; and in the center, as well as in the provinces and in large plants, societies were formed of those who had taken part in the armed struggle of 1917–21. Members collected and put into shape a wealth of material on the events that they had lived through, thus sharing in the collective composition of the *History of the Civil War*.

145. P. Novliansky, "The Workers Are Writing the History of Their Factories and Works," *Soviet Culture Review*, Nos. 7–9 (1932), p. 48.

The mass movement for the creation of the *History of Factories and Works* spread quickly to mines, railroads, etc. and assumed diverse forms. The work was assisted by historians, writers, economists, engineers, journalists, and artists. Archives were examined, materials in museums and in the pre-revolutionary press were studied, and Old Bolsheviks were interviewed. Some factories held exhibitions of historical documents, diaries, letters, and photographs; mass excursions were organized to places where "militant gatherings of workers took place in the pre-October period"; the Moscow "Sickle and Hammer" even arranged a special "Victorina" (an "Information-Please" kind of game in which participants have to answer a series of questions, in this case, about the history of the "Sickle and Hammer"). (*Ibid.*) By these methods interest in Soviet history was still further aroused and used to educate the masses.

146. *Ibid.*, p. 49.

147. *Ibid.*

"The task of the *History of Factories* is that of recreating the pictures of the great road the workers of tsarist Russia and the Soviet Union have travelled since the beginning of the struggle for liberation and ending with the fulfilment of the First Five-Year Plan and the transition to the building of classless society.

"The *History of Factories* is called upon to portray in a vivid complex the comparative techno-economic history of the enterprises up to October and after, the history of the revolutionary struggle at the plant, the stories of the lives of the individual participants and heroes of the plants, their manners and culture. The *History of Factories* is supposed to show the living people who made the revolution, reconstructed the national economy, fought for the fulfilment of the plan, learning the technique of their work; to show the Bolsheviks who guided all these processes." (M. Simkhovich, "The History of Factories," M. Apletin, ed., *Literature of the Peoples of the U.S.S.R.*, VOKS Illustrated Almanac, Nos. 7–8 [1934], p. 84.)

148. *Ibid.*

149. *Ibid.*, p. 85.

Mirsky said that the Soviet attitude towards imaginative work as a form of knowledge "finds expression in a tendency to break down the boundaries separating imaginative literature from other forms of knowledge, especially from social science and history. In this connection a highly symptomatic development is the *History of the Factories* . . . [which] aims at being a scientific history of the individual plants which together form the vast army of Soviet industry. Without surrendering a tittle of scientific rigour, it aspires at producing at the same time genuine art, 'the great epic of the Soviet proletariat,' as Averbakh puts it, and thus bringing together these two essentially cognate forms of knowledge." (Mirsky, *Tendencies of the Modern Novel*, p. 118.)

150. "The *History of Izhorsk Plant* (the first volume published embraces the period from the foundation of the enterprise up to the Feb-

ruary Revolution) gives a complete picture, based on a tremendous amount of documentary data, of the slavelike work and life, first under the conditions of serfdom, and then under capitalism in Russia. It shows, on the basis of official data about a government-owned plant, the technico-economic backwardness of Russia, the forms of the revolutionary struggle of the workers from elemental upsurges to conscious struggles organized by the Bolshevik Party." (Simkhovich, "The History of Factories," p. 86.)

151. *Ibid.*, p. 85.
152. Yakov Ilin, ed., *Lyudi stalingradskovo traktornovo zavoda imeni Feliksa Dzerzhinskovo*, volume of *Istoriya zavodov*, Moscow, 1933.
153. Yakov Ilin and B. Galin, "Vstupleniye," *Lyudi stalingradskovo . . . zavoda*, p. 12.
154. Maxim Gorky, "V knige mnogo prostoi, bolshevistskoi pravdy," *Lyudi stalingradskovo . . . zavoda*, p. 3.
155. Ilin and Galin, "Vstupleniye."
156. Gorky, "V knige . . . ," p. 2.
157. Leopold Averbakh, "Literaturnyie zametki," *Lyudi stalingradskovo . . . zavoda*, p. 461.
158. *Ibid.*, p. 433.
159. *Ibid.*, p. 455.
160. *Ibid.*, p. 446.
161. *Lyudi stalingradskovo . . . zavoda*, p. 17.
162. Yakov Ilin, "Chitatelyu" (May, 1932), *Bolshoi konveiyer*, Moscow, 1934, p. 7.
163. Yakov Ilin, *Bolshoi konveiyer*.
164. Ilin, "Chitatelyu," p. 8.
165. Publisher's blurb in front of book, Ilin, *Bolshoi konveiyer*, p. 2.
166. "Predisloviye" (by a group of comrades), Ilin, *Bolshoi konveiyer*, p. 5.
167. Mirsky, *Tendencies of the Modern Novel*, pp. 118–19.
168. *Belomor*, p. vi.
169. *Ibid.*, p. 117.
170. *Ibid.*, p. 37.
171. *Ibid.*, p. 122.
172. The Captain, in Pogodin's *Aristocrats* (1935), puts it very well: "The Chekists aren't magicians. Before every man they simply set a ladder and say—'Climb it.' The higher you climb, the better life becomes. One rung gives you better boots and clothes, another—better food. Then there is the shock-brigade rung: when you get on that you forget you're in a prison camp and you're allowed to send for your wife. But

there is still a higher rung, when your entire ten-year sentence is cancelled and vanishes like a nightmare after a spree. But . . . the Chekists do not wait until you make up your mind yourself to climb the ladder. They know our characters too well: some of us have to be shown how to start, others need a boost, some a good shove, while others . . . have to be given two or three hard knocks and then they're off up the ladder." (Nikolai Pogodin, *Aristocrats*, Anthony Wixley and Robert S. Carr, trans., Ben Blake, ed., *Four Soviet Plays*, London, 1937, p. 260.)
173. *Belomor*, p. 301.

4. Some Literary Works of the First Five-Year Plan Period

1. Gorky, "On Literature and Other Things," p. 51.
2. Averbakh, *Na putyakh kulturnoi revolyutsii*, p. 189.
3. Marietta Shaginyan, "Literature and Plan," *Soviet Culture Review*, No. 5 (1932), p. 24.
4. Karl Radek, "Contemporary World Literature and the Tasks of Proletarian Art," H. G. Scott, ed., *Problems of Soviet Literature*, New York, 1935, p. 140. Radek was a brilliant Polish Jew, at one time Trotsky's close political friend, then principal editor of *Izvestiya*.
5. Ilin, "Chitatelyu," *Bolshoi konveiyer*, p. 7.
6. Fischer, *Machines and Men in Russia*, p. 265.
7. Kushner, "Prichiny otstavaniya." The specific gravity of journalism in the literature of a given period is directly proportionate to the degree of its revolutionism, asserted Kushner. The saturation of all literary genres with journalism is characteristic of the reconstruction period. (*Ibid.*)
8. Mirsky, "Russia," *Tendencies of the Modern Novel*, p. 106.
9. In 1923 Libedinski wrote an article, "Subjects That Await Their Authors," about the subjects which interest proletarian writers. In 1928 the leaders of VAPP said in their respective articles on thematic problems that Libedinski's three groups remained the same, in spite of the change of subject. These groups of literary themes, as given in 1923, are as follows: "*First Group*: The activity of the working class in the development of the social economy; struggle against ruin; NEP; construction of electric stations, scientific expeditions, construction of the air fleet, etc. *Second Group*: The working class in the extra-economic struggle (political struggle in the narrow sense of the word) against the bourgeoisie; the world revolution; October; Civil War; Cheka and its work. *Third Group*: Decomposition of the old forms of life and appearance of new forms; creation of institutes of social provisionment and of industrial education; destruction of the old forms of the family; change of the forms of leisure (transformation of beer parlors and

churches into workers' clubs); change of attitude towards woman and her liberation; new forms of marriage; Party life and its influence on the masses; the life of the youth of the factories, of the Party, and of the schools; the life of the middle strata of the Party; the bourgeoising of a part of the workers under the influence of the NEP; the intellectual and the bourgeois; the kulak, the co-operatives, the poor peasants; the children of the revolutionary epoch." (Goriely, Les Poètes dans la révolution russe, pp. 169–71.)

10. Another example of new form was Mikitenko's play, Point of Honor, written in a very original form of dramatic oratorio and dealing with the heroic fight of the Donbas miners for the fulfillment of the coal industry's industrial and financial plan. ("Theatre Season 1931/32," p. 22.)

11. Mayakovsky, "How One Writes a Poem," p. 152.

12. Alexei Tolstoy, "Trends in Soviet Literature," Science and Society, VII, No. 3 (Summer, 1943), 244.

First Five-Year Plan literature abounded in titles such as The Birth of a Hero (Libedinski's novel), On the Hero's Trail (Dmitri Lavrukhin, January, 1930), The Hunt for the Hero, The Successors of the Heroes, etc., which indicated that it was still searching for its hero. (N. Gnedina, "On the Hero's Trail," VOKS, II, No. 2 [February, 1931], 79.)

According to Polonski, the new Soviet hero is characterized chiefly by revolutionary activity. "He runs the lathe, he carries a rifle, he directs the government, he does big deeds and engages in a work that may remain unnoticed. He builds plants and collectives, railways and blast furnaces. He destroys illiteracy, eradicates religion, banishes the dirt of ages, and uproots the advocates of private property. He loves work. He hates phrases. He is a soldier of the revolution. . . . He identifies himself with society. His aim is to understand the world in order to remould it. His personal responses are secondary. Social interests dominate over the egoistic. Indeed, his social and individual interests coincide. His life is broad and embraces a universe. . . .

"The hero of our day . . . does not know sentimentality. He is a bit dry, somewhat hard, likes to stick to concrete facts. He is a realist. The unearthly, the unmaterial does not exist for him. He abhors idealism, mysticism and religion. He prefers dialectic materialism to metaphysics. He thirsts for knowledge so that he may destroy and create efficiently. And, of course, he lives a full, healthy personal life just because it is not the core and end of his existence." (Fischer, Machines and Men in Russia, pp. 262–63.)

13. Ibid., p. 264.

14. The late A. A. Zhdanov explained in 1934 that Soviet literature

"is optimistic in essence, because it is the literature of the rising class of the proletariat, the only progressive and advanced class. Our Soviet literature is strong by virtue of the fact that it is serving a new cause—the cause of socialist construction." (A. A. Zhdanov, "Soviet Literature—the Richest in Ideas; the Most Advanced Literature," H. G. Scott, ed., *Problems of Soviet Literature*, New York, 1935, p. 20.)

15. Mirsky, *Tendencies of the Modern Novel*, p. 110.

16. State Planning Commission of the Council of People's Commissars of the U.S.S.R., *Summary of the Fulfilment of the First Five-Year Plan for the Development of the National Economy of the U.S.S.R.*, Moscow, 1933, p. 14.

17. The motives which had caused the Party to push for industrialization were: (1) to increase the relative strength of the proletariat, as politically desirable; (2) to prepare a material basis for the evolution of socialism into communism (a great abundance of goods are needed for the stage when the state can wither away); (3) to compete successfully with capitalism (socialism can only justify itself as a system if it raises productivity of labor above that under capitalism); and (4) to increase the defense capacity of the country. (Abram Bergson, "Structure of Soviet Economy," Russian Institute course given at Columbia University.)

18. Eugene Lyons, "Introduction" to *Tempo, Six Soviet Plays*, Boston–New York, 1934, p. 157.

19. Chamberlin, *Russia's Iron Age*, p. 134.

20. "Soviet Writers about Themselves," Gladkov, p. 99.

21. Fyodor Gladkov, "Granite" (from *Energy*), *Literature of the Peoples of the U.S.S.R.*, VOKS Illustrated Almanac, Nos. 7–8 (1934), p. 155.

22. Fyodor Gladkov, "The Ragged Brigade" (from *Energy*), Reavey and Slonim, *Soviet Literature*, p. 293.

23. *Ibid.*, p. 295.
24. *Ibid.*, p. 298.
25. *Ibid.*, p. 290.
26. Pilnyak, *The Volga Falls to the Caspian Sea*, p. 36.
27. *Ibid.*, p. 249.
28. *Ibid.*, p. 309.
29. *Ibid.*, p. 113.
30. *Ibid.*, pp. 162–63.
31. *Ibid.*, p. 159.
32. *Ibid.*, p. 21.
33. *Ibid.*, p. 45.
34. *Ibid.*, p. 30.

NOTES: SOME LITERARY WORKS 205

35. Pilnyak believes in "doubles," that "men have always two lives: the life given by the brain, by the feeling of duty, of honor, by the open blinds of consciousness; and a second life given by the subconscious element in man, by instinct, by blood, by the sun." (*Ibid.*, p. 185.)
36. *Ibid.*, p. 51.
37. *Ibid.*, pp. 87–88.
38. *Ibid.*, p. 75.
39. *Ibid.*, p. 33.
40. *Ibid.*, p. 294.
41. *Ibid.*, p. 349. Poletika's plan is not unlike the present Soviet scheme to prevent soil erosion.
42. Leonid Leonov, *Soviet River* [*Sot*], Ivor Montagu and Sergei Nolbandov, trans., New York, 1932, p. 63.
43. *Ibid.*, p. 252.
44. *Ibid.*, p. 50.
45. *Ibid.*, p. 161.
46. *Ibid.*, p. 350.
47. *Ibid.*, p. 238.
48. *Ibid.*, p. 119.
49. *Ibid.*, p. 159.
50. *Ibid.*, p. 165.
51. *Ibid.*, p. 161.
52. *Ibid.*, p. 287.
53. See Section (1) of note 17 (Chapter 4), p. 204.
54. Leonov, *Soviet River*, p. 383.
55. Gorky considered Leonov "one of the most prominent of the group of modern Soviet authors who are continuing the task of Russian classical literature." (Maxim Gorky, "Foreword," Leonov, *Soviet River*, p. v.) "L. Leonov wrote the book *Sot*, taking as material for it, current reality," stated Gorky in 1931. "And imagine the result! An 'original creation,' a remarkable thing, written in the most savory, strong, clear Russian language—Leonov's words positively sparkle. And he knows reality as if he himself had made it." (Gorky, "O literature," p. 56.)
56. Ehrenburg, *Out of Chaos*, p. 12.
57. *Ibid.*, p. 39.
58. *Ibid.*, p. 37.
59. *Ibid.*, p. 11.
60. *Ibid.*, p. 98.
61. *Ibid.*, p. 97.
62. *Ibid.*, p. 159.
63. *Ibid.*, p. 167.

64. Pechorin is the hero of Lermontov's novel, A Hero of Our Times (1840), and was one of the first of the "superfluous men" in nineteenth-century Russian literature.

65. Ehrenburg, Out of Chaos, p. 312.

66. Ibid., p. 264. Volodia influences Tolia to become a wrecker and break the lever in the same subtle way that Ivan Karamazov suggests murder to Smerdyakov. He, too, feels himself an accomplice in the crime and comes to a bad end (he hangs himself).

67. This thought is reminiscent of Zamyatin's statement, made in the first years of the Revolution, that, in his opinion, Soviet Russia would not produce a real literature because "real literature can exist only where it is produced, not by painstaking and well-intentioned officials, but by madmen, hermits, heretics, dreamers, rebels and sceptics." (Struve, 25 Years of Soviet Russian Literature [1918–1943], p. 22.)

68. Ehrenburg, Out of Chaos, p. 219.

69. Ibid., pp. 353–54.

70. Ibid., p. 382.

71. Nikolai Pogodin, "Autobiography," International Literature, No. 3 (July, 1933), p. 134.

72. Ibid.

73. Nikolai Pogodin, Tempo, Irving Talmadg, trans., Eugene Lyons, ed., Six Soviet Plays, Boston–New York, 1934, p. 204.

74. See p. 18.

75. Pogodin, Tempo, p. 176.

76. Ibid., p. 204.

77. Oblomov, the apathetic hero of I. A. Goncharov's novel of the same name (1858), became a symbol of laziness, lack of energy, indecision, and do-nothingness. In 1929 Averbakh exclaimed: "Oblomovishness—to the wall! The hydra of Oblomovishness is very much alive." (Averbakh, Na putyakh . . . , p. 171.) He continued: "Socialist industry's tempo of development depends in great measure on how quickly we can pry out of the factories and enterprises the Oblomov type of workman." (Ibid., p. 174.)

78. Pogodin, Tempo, p. 224.

79. V. Katayev, Time, Forward!, pp. 11–12.

80. "Recent Soviet Literature," International Literature, No. 2 (1933), p. 148.

81. Concrete-mixers are imported machines; they have a maximal productive capacity which can be attained only by rational organization of work, with a minimum of unproductive waste of time and motion. And so their productivity depends on the organization of the supply of raw materials, of the loading and emptying of the mixers. This requires skill, adroitness, keenness of observation, and organizational tal-

ent. "Therefore, the fight for records with concrete-mixers has great significance, not only because it raises production: it is a fight for cadres; for a rise in qualification; for the exercise of experience; for the performance of the most efficient, quickest, and most skillful workers. The fight for records is the school of intensive and conscious work." (Polonski, *Magnitostroi*, p. 73.)

82. V. Katayev, *Time, Forward!*, p. 337.
There actually was a fight for the highest productivity in cement-mixing between Magnitogorsk, Kuznetsk, and the Kharkov Tractor Plant. The competition began on May 29 when Kuznetsk set a record with 324 mixtures in 10 hours of work. "Sagadeyev's shock brigade at Magnitogorsk exceeded this figure: in 7 hours and 50 minutes, the brigade made 429 mixtures. But this world record, too, was beaten . . . by the Kharkovites." At the Kharkov Tractor Plant, on the night of July 10, Zozuli's brigade, consisting of 37 men, turned out 501 concrete mixtures in 7 hours and 35 minutes of work—a world record at that time. (Polonski, *Magnitostroi*, pp. 73–74.) In *Time, Forward!* Ishchenko's shift pours the 429 mixtures to beat both Kharkov and Kuznetsk. But, as Katayev says, "Statistics could not keep up with life! Time left behind rows of dead figures." (V. Katayev, p. 155.)

83. Vladimir Mayakovsky, "Our March" (1918), Joseph Freeman, trans., quoted in *Voices of October*, p. 78.

84. V. Shklovski, *Literaturnaya gazeta*, No. 37 (1932), quoted in "Recent Soviet Literature," p. 148.

85. V. Katayev, *Time, Forward!*, p. 62.

86. *Ibid.*, p. 154.

87. *Ibid.*, p. 328.

88. *Ibid.*, pp. 138–39.

89. See p. 26.

90. Ilyenkov, *Driving Axle*, p. 150.

91. *Ibid.*, p. 443.

92. *Ibid.*, p. 130.

93. *Ibid.*, p. 283.

94. This state of affairs lasted until 1934 when the manager's full and exclusive power within his plant was recognized in the "Model Statutes for Plants in Heavy Industry." (Gregory Bienstock, Solomon M. Schwarz, and Aaron Yugow, *Management in Russian Industry and Agriculture*, Arthur Feiler and Jacob Marschak, ed., London–New York–Toronto, 1944, p. 12.)

95. Ilyenkov, *Driving Axle*, p. 449.

96. *Ibid.*, p. 191.

97. *Ibid.*, p. 406.

98. *Ibid.*, pp. 388–89.

99. *Ibid.*, p. 433.
100. *Ibid.*, p. 446.
101. Gladkov, "Ragged Brigade," p. 288.
102. Alexander Avdeyenko, *I Love*, Anthony Wixley, trans., New York, n.d., p. 36.
103. *Ibid.*, p. 243.
104. The worker Zaytsev in *Driving Axle* was also fascinated by machines. "They seemed to him living beings, endowed with a thinking mind and a complicated inner life." He had "an inner consciousness of machinery" and evaluated people according to their attitude towards it. (Ilyenkov, pp. 26–27.)
105. Avdeyenko, *I Love*, p. 271.
106. *Ibid.*, p. 223.
107. *Ibid.*, p. 281.
108. Anatol Lunacharski, "Introduction," Ilf and Petrov, *The Little Golden Calf*, p. xviii.
109. Ilf and Petrov, *The Little Golden Calf*, p. 26.
110. *Ibid.*, pp. 386–87.
111. Lunacharski, "Introduction," p. xvi.
112. Ilf and Petrov, *The Little Golden Calf*, p. 195.
113. In 1920 Lenin had said that, because of the shortage of personnel for administrative and construction jobs, "we are obliged to use bureaucrats in the old way, and we shall end up by having a bureaucracy. I despise bureaucracy. Not individual bureaucrats. . . . But I despise the system. It paralyzes and corrupts from top to bottom. The main factor in overcoming and definitively suppressing the bureaucratic régime is education and popular instruction, distributed as widely as possible." (Zetkin, *Souvenirs sur Lénine*, p. 19.)
114. Petrov (Evgeni Petrovich Katayev) was the brother of Valentin Petrovich Katayev.
115. Ilf and Petrov, *The Little Golden Calf*, pp. 172–73.
116. *Ibid.*, p. 226.
117. *Ibid.*, p. 190.
118. The Turk-Sib Railroad, one of the great attainments of Soviet enterprise, was officially opened on May 1, 1930, a year ahead of time. Its purpose was to connect the vast cotton-growing territory of Turkestan with the vast grain-growing and mineral territory of Siberia.
119. Ilf and Petrov, *The Little Golden Calf*, p. 327.
120. Lunacharski, "Introduction," p. xviii.
121. Chamberlin, *Soviet Russia*, p. 184.
122. *Summary of the Fulfilment of the First Five-Year Plan*, p. 19.
123. "The object of the Five-Year Plan in the sphere of agriculture was to unite the scattered and small individual peasant farms, which

lacked the opportunity of utilizing tractors and modern agricultural machinery, into large collective farms, equipped with all the modern implements of highly developed agriculture, and to cover unoccupied land with model state farms. . . . [also] to convert the U.S.S.R. from a small-peasant and backward country into a large-scale agriculture organized on the basis of collective labor and providing the maximum output for the market." (Stalin, "Results of the First Five-Year Plan," pp. 253–54.)

124. J. Stalin, *Leninism*, p. 298, quoted in Baykov, *The Development of the Soviet Economic System*, p. 192.

125. The purpose of the drive for all-out collectivization and liquidation of the kulaks as a class was: (1) to get more grain for the cities by (*a*) the creation of large-scale mechanized farms which would increase the amount of marketed grain, and (*b*) elimination of "the scissors" (higher prices of retail manufactured goods as compared to agricultural products) and prices as deciding factors in the amount of grain sold; and (2) to pay for imports of machinery needed for industrialization, by grain exports. (Here an international "scissors" set in, however.)

126. Ilyenkov, *Driving Axle*, p. 454.

127. Zelinski, "15th Anniversary of Soviet Literature," p. 66.

128. Mikhail Sholokhov, *Seeds of Tomorrow* [*Soil Upturned*], Stephen Garry, trans., New York, 1935, p. 28.

129. *Ibid.*, p. 259.

130. *Ibid.*, p. 170.

131. Stalin, "Results of the First Five-Year Plan," p. 266.

132. Sholokhov, *Seeds of Tomorrow*, p. 22.

133. *Ibid.*, p. 165.

Nikita Morgunok, peasant hero of Tvardovski's *Muravia Land*, is also very attached to his horse. His passion for ownership leads him to seek an alternative to the *kolkhoz*, and he sets out in quest of:

> Muravia the ancient, Muravia Land.
> Far and wide, from side to side,
> The land is your own, all round.
> Plant, if you will, just one seed—
> But then, it's your own.

(Kaun, *Soviet Poets and Poetry*, p. 177.)

134. Struve, *25 Years of Soviet Russian Literature*, p. 126.

135. Sholokhov, *Seeds of Tomorrow*, p. 400.

136. *Ibid.*, p. 404. A second volume of *Soil Upturned* was planned.

137. Fyodor Panfyorov, *Bruski*, Z. Mitrov and J. Tabrisky, trans., London, 1930, p. 63.

138. *Ibid.*, p. 294.

139. *Ibid.*, p. 104.

140. *Ibid.*, p. 139.
141. Panfyorov, *And Then the Harvest*, p. 29.
142. See note 133 (Chapter 4), p. 209.
143. Panfyorov, *And Then the Harvest*, p. 395.
144. Eugene Lyons, "Introduction" to *Bread, Six Soviet Plays*, Boston–New York, 1934, p. 227.
145. Chamberlin, *Russia's Iron Age*, pp. 299–300.
146. Kirshon, *Bread*, p. 237.
147. *Ibid.*, p. 236.
148. *Ibid.*, p. 245.
149. *Ibid.*, pp. 288–89.
150. *Ibid.*, p. 229.
151. *Ibid.*, p. 236.
152. *Ibid.*, p. 287.
153. *Ibid.*, p. 240.
In Pogodin's play, *My Friend* (1932), the Economic Director similarly threatens Guy, a factory manager who has come to request some money for badly needed machines: "And if Comrade Guy—a respected comrade of ours, a good comrade though he is—doesn't start the works according to plan, we'll cancel his Party membership card and kick him out of the Party." (Nikolai Pogodin, "My Friend" [Episode 5], Anthony Wixley, trans., *International Literature*, No. 3 [July, 1933], p. 35.)
154. To Shor, the Old Bolshevik director at the Kuznetsk construction works, "the Party was not a state, a policy, a means to constructive work, but something supremely intimate, so that leaving the Party was like leaving life itself." (Ehrenburg, *Out of Chaos*, p. 131.)
The attitude of Nagulnov, the deviationist in *Soil Upturned*, is similar to Rayevsky's: "Where am I to go outside the Party? . . . No. I won't give up my Party card. . . . My life's got no point now, so expel me from that, too." (Sholokhov, *Seeds of Tomorrow*, p. 310.)
155. Kirshon, *Bread*, p. 242.
156. *Ibid.*, p. 243.
157. *Ibid.*
158. Mikhailov gives the Party-line answer: "Such a thing as a united peasant mass doesn't exist. Country and city—those are but geographical and poetical labels—they have no sociological meaning." (*Ibid.*, p. 272.)
159. *Ibid.*, p. 282.
160. *Ibid.*, p. 260.
161. *Ibid.*, p. 261.
162. *Ibid.*, p. 310.

163. Alexander Afinogenov, *Fear*, Charles Malamuth, trans., Eugene Lyons, ed., *Six Soviet Plays*, Boston–New York, 1934, p. 433.
164. *Ibid.*, pp. 468–69.
165. A *vydveezhenets* (plural, *vydveezhentsy*) is "a worker or peasant who is advanced by the Soviet shop or Party organization to higher duties in the fields of research or public administration." (*Ibid.*, p. 393.)
166. *Ibid.*, pp. 405–6.
167. *Ibid.*, pp. 399–400.
168. *Ibid.*, p. 406.
169. *Ibid.*, p. 451.
170. Leonov, *Skutarevsky*, p. 417.
171. *Ibid.*, p. 302.
172. *Ibid.*, p. 314.
173. *Ibid.*, p. 50.
174. *Ibid.*, p. 345.
175. *Ibid.*, p. 221.
176. About Arseny's dissolute and degenerate friends, Leonov says: "They every one suffered from some organic defect, something wrong with the mouth or nose or ears, and their faces definitely reminded one of lifeless waxwork faces." (*Ibid.*, p. 74.) One might call it an outward and visible sign of an inward and spiritual vacuum.

In "Taman" (*A Hero of Our Times*) Pechorin acknowledges that "I have a strong prejudice against all who are blind, crooked, deaf, dumb, footless, handless, humpbacked, etc. I have noticed that there is always a certain strange connection between the physical appearance of a man and his inner soul as if, with the loss of a part of the body, the soul loses some of its senses." (M. Yu. Lermontov, "Taman," *Izbrannyie proizvedeniya*, Leningrad, 1946, p. 277.)

177. Leonov, *Skutarevsky*, p. 79.
178. *Ibid.*, p. 329.
179. Nikolai Bukharin, "Poetry, Poetics and the Problems of Poetry in the U.S.S.R.," H. G. Scott, ed., *Problems of Soviet Literature*, New York, 1935, pp. 196–97.
180. *Ibid.*, p. 223.
181. *Ibid.*, p. 225.
182. Chamberlin, *Soviet Russia*, p. 334.

Bezymenski's popularity reached its height during the First Five-Year Plan and declined after the abolition of RAPP. Trotsky said about him: "He did not need to 'accept' the Revolution because it had itself accepted him on the day of his spiritual birth, named and commanded him to be its poet. . . . He grasps the Revolution completely because it is the spiritual planet on which he was born and intends to live. Of all our poets who write about and for the Revolution, Bezymenski is the one who approaches it most organically because he is its offspring, a son of the Revolution, an Octobrist." (Quoted in Lelevich, "Aleksandr Bezymenski," p. 81.)

183. M. Mir, "Alexander Bezymenski," *VOKS*, II, No. 2 (February, 1931), 78.

184. Alexander Zharov, "Our Songs," Dan Levin, trans., *New Directions in Prose and Poetry 1941*, Norfolk, Conn., 1941, p. 648.

185. Semyon Kirsanov, "Pyatiletka," *Krasnaya nov*, No. 11 (November, 1930), p. 83.

186. Andrew Alexandrovich, "The Whistles Shrill . . . ," Michael L. Korr, trans., *VOKS*, III, Nos. 3-4 (1932), 81. Alexandrovich is called the "proletarian poet of White Russia," and his poems are "proletarian in content and national in form." (M. Mir, "Andrew Alexandrovich," *VOKS*, III, Nos. 3-4 [1932], pp. 79-80.)

187. Selvinski's lyrical play, *Pao-Pao*, tells the story of an ape, symbol of the low animal instincts and of bourgeois culture. (Reavey and Slonim, *Soviet Literature*, p. 370.)

188. Ilya Selvinski, *Pao-Pao* (1932), *ibid.*, pp. 370-71.

189. Aseyev, "Dnieprostroi," quoted in Goriely, *Les Poètes dans la révolution russe*, p. 197. Dnieprostroi, the biggest dam in the world, was ready for operation on July 1, 1932.

190. Vera Inber, "Bonne Année!" M. Mir, trans. into French, *Front*, I, No. 1 (December, 1930), p. 96.

191. Robert de Saint Jean, "Préface," Maxim Gorky, "La Mission des écrivains soviétiques," p. 309.

192. Lidin, "Soviet Literature," p. 67.

193. V. Yermilov, "RAPP dolzhen byt bolshevistskim avangardom sovetskoi literatury," *Literaturnaya gazeta*, No. 25 (October 7, 1929), p. 2.

194. Friedrich Engels, "Letter to Mehring" (July 14, 1893), Karl Marx and Friedrich Engels, *Correspondence, 1846-1895*, London, 1934, p. 512.

195. Tolstoy, "Trends in Soviet Literature," p. 237.

196. *Ibid.*, p. 245.

197. Ivan Thorgevsky, *De Gorki à nos jours*, Paris, 1945, pp. 115-16.

In a letter to Minna Kautsky about the characters in a novel, Engels wrote: "Each person is a type, but at the same time a completely defined personality. . . . That is as it should be." (Friedrich Engels, "Letter to Minna Kautsky" [November 26, 1885], in Karl Marx and Friedrich Engels, *Briefe an A. Bebel, W. Liebknecht, K. Kautsky und Andere*, pp. 413-16, *Literature and Art*, p. 44.)

Some years before, Marx had complained to Lassalle: "I do not find any characteristic traits in your characters. . . . [They are] drawn too abstractly." (Karl Marx, "Letter to Ferdinand Lassalle" [April 19, 1859], in Gustav Mayer, ed., *Ferdinand Lassalle, Nachgelassene Briefe und Schriften*, III, 172–75, Marx and Engels, *Literature and Art*, p. 48.)

198. Leonid Leonov, "Appeal to Courage," quoted in Struve, *25 Years of Soviet Russian Literature*, p. 242.

From Leonov's description of the standardized, colorless, First Five-Year Plan literature, one might imagine that its authors had availed themselves of Ostap Bender's trouble-saving "Complete Celebrator." This "indispensable manual for the composition of articles for gala occasions, feuilletons for state holidays, odes, hymns, and also poems for parades" is made up of Part I, a glossary, and Part II, the creative section. Samples of an editorial, an artistic sketch-feuilleton, and literary verse are given—all composed exclusively of words from Part I. "With the aid of materials in Part I following the methods in Part II may be composed also: novels, tales, poems in prose, stories, local color sketches, literary reporting, chronicles, epics, plays, political reviews, radio orations, etc." This boon to incompetent writers Bender sold to the "editorial worker of the trade union organ" who had been completely at a loss as to how to write his newspaper dispatch on the opening of the Turk–Sib Railroad. (Ilf and Petrov, *The Little Golden Calf*, pp. 319–22.)

199. Tolstoy, "Trends in Soviet Literature," p. 235.
200. Gorky, "On Literature . . . ," p. 51.
201. Tolstoy, "Trends in Soviet Literature," p. 235.
202. Lidin, "Soviet Literature," p. 69.
203. Gorky, "On Literature . . . ," p. 50.
204. Gorky, "O literature," p. 55.
205. Radek, "Contemporary World Literature . . . ," p. 130.
206. Sergei Tretyakov, "Words Become Deeds," *International Literature*, No. 3 (1933), p. 56.
207. *Sovetskaya literatura na novom etape*, Kulik, p. 62.

5. The Liquidation of RAPP

1. Zelinski, "15th Anniversary of Soviet Literature," p. 63.
2. *Sovetskaya literatura na novom etape*, Subotski, p. 45.
3. It is interesting to recall Article 14 of the Party's 1924 Resolution: "It is out of the question that there should be a decree or Party declaration legalizing the monopoly by any group or literary organization of literary publication." ("Resolution on Literature . . . July 1, 1924," p. 63.)

4. P. M. Kerzhentzev, a "stalwart upholder of pure proletarian canons in art," quoted in Chamberlin, *Soviet Russia*, p. 300.

5. "RAPP," *Lit. entsik.*, p. 522.

6. Zelinski, "Soviet Criticism," pp. 33–34.

The Litfront was a new leftist tendency which developed in the midst of the At-Lit-Post group. The views of these Literary Front critics were essentially the continuation under conditions of the reconstruction period of the theoretical errors of LEF ("Art is the opium of the people"—*Left Front*, p. 31). To the Litfrontists literature had no conceptual side; they saw in it chiefly the structural factor. "Hence the mechanical emphasis on publicism which they considered the core of proletarian literature [and] their underestimation of the value of literary craftsmanship." (Zelinski, "Soviet Criticism," p. 34.)

Kirpotin said that the Litfront, "with greater or lesser frankness, proceeded from the idea that individuality should be painted apsychologically. This, of course, is wrong. It is impossible to give a lifelike, actual figure in the form of some sort of automatic or mechanical man." (*Sov. lit. na novom etape*, Kirpotin, p. 29.)

7. Miliukov, *Outlines of Russian Culture: Part II—Literature*, p. 98.

V. F. Pereverzev's group, "the vulgar sociologists," was attacked by Lunacharski, Polonski, Averbakh, and Libedinski during 1928–30 for the belief that a writer could not change his class (and come over to the Revolution). In an article written in 1929, Pereverzev called the social command theoretically and practically harmful.

According to Zelinski, Professor Pereverzev and his critical group "reduced the entire literary process to two of its elements: style and image. Both of these elements Pereversev inferred directly, mechanically, from the vital style and social type of a definite class group. Pereversev argued that the writer lives in a world of determinate images. If he (the writer) cannot get out of this circle of conception in literature, there can be no progress in it, the class struggle falls by the wayside. Pereversev brought menshevism into criticism, brought in a vulgar, mechanistic approach to events. And the discussion which the critics from *Na Literaturnom Postu* developed around Pereversev's theories exposed their erroneousness and their harmfulness." (Zelinski, "Soviet Criticism," p. 34.)

8. Libedinski, "Za chto boryutsya napostovtsy," p. 23.

9. Kaun, *Soviet Poets and Poetry*, p. 160.

10. Struve, *25 Years of Soviet Russian Literature* (1918–1943), p. 227.

11. In *The Bath*, which was first produced in Leningrad on January 30, 1930, Mayakovsky fiercely attacked government bureaucracy, ignorance, and stupidity. An inventor produces a time-machine which

will enable the tempo of Soviet life to be increased and which will bring people in contact with the coming period of communism—in the year 2030. By means of the time-machine a Woman of the Future, a "delegate from the year 2030," comes to select those who are to be transferred to the future. "Those who are chosen as passengers on the time-machine come singing their vigorous 'March of Time' with its refrain of 'Time, forward!' 'Forward, time!' This was the same slogan that was taken up two years later by Katayev in his well-known novel and play called 'Time, Forward!'"

"The Future will accept all in whom is found any trait akin to the collective commune," announces the Woman of the Future. The others (bureaucrats, etc.) will be thrown off as ballast by time, as it flies, because they are not necessary to communism. (H. W. L. Dana, "Mayakovsky's Plays," *The American Quarterly on the Soviet Union*, III, No. 1 [July, 1940], 54–55.) Thus did Mayakovsky give the bureaucrats a "hot bath." His poem, "Lost in Conference," also made fun of bureaucrats and their conferences.

12. Miliukov, *Outlines of Russian Culture*, pp. 115–16.
13. Selivanovski, "RAPP."
14. Libedinski, "Za chto boryutsya napostovtsy," p. 35.
15. Vladimir Mayakovsky, "At the Top of My Voice" (1930), Herbert Marshall, trans., *Mayakovsky and His Poetry*, p. 144.
16. *Ibid.*, p. 148.
17. Goriely, *Les Poètes dans la révolution russe*, p. 183. Averbakh, too, was of bourgeois origin.
18. Alexander Bezymenski, "Poem about Love," Reavey and Slonim, *Soviet Literature*, p. 375.
19. *Ibid.*
20. Zelinski, "15th Anniversary of Soviet Literature," p. 67.
21. "This Carthage, this Voronski, must be destroyed!" proclaimed Averbakh. Voronski was expelled from the Party in 1928 and sent to Siberia. His strong group, the Pereval ("Defile"), was mentioned with the Smithy by Gronski as an example of one of the other groups, besides RAPP. It "is not dissolved and is not overcome," continued Gronski. "The circumstance, that on this tribune the Perevaltsy did not appear but sent to the presidium only a formal statement, shows that the leaders of this group do not wish to enter into the general work of overcoming clannishness. We can very well understand that. Pereval is the most rightist group of Soviet literature and the smallest; it occupied the attention of our literary organizations less than the others. I am asked in notes: can one criticize the Pereval as the Right flank of our Soviet literature? Of course one can; more than that, it is indispensable; but this criticism should not carry with it any administrative measures

on the part of the Orgcommittee." (*Sov. lit. na novom etape*, Gronski, p. 257.)
22. Formalism wanted to establish a scientific study of literature. During 1929–30 it was eliminated as a trend, being attacked by Gorbachyov and purged by Averbakh.
23. *Sov. lit. na novom etape*, Kirpotin, p. 18.
24. *Ibid.*, Gronski, p. 7.
25. "Na uroven novykh zadach," *Pravda* (May 9, 1932), reprinted in *Na literaturnom postu*, No. 12 (April, 1932), p. 4. (These dates seem chronologically wrong, but I have verified them.)
26. Charpentier, *Napoléon et les hommes de lettres de son temps*, p. 33.
27. *Ibid.*, p. 226.
28. Ferdinand Brunetière, "La Littérature française sous le premier Empire," *Études critiques sur l'histoire de la littérature française*, new ed., Paris, 1888, p. 258.
29. The memoirs of M. de Fontanes, Napoleon's Grand Maître de l'Université, as told by Elias L. Tartak.
30. At about this time a group of Communist playwrights and novelists, including Libedinski and Kirshon, went to see Stalin. They expected praise for writing class-consciously; but instead, Stalin asked them who would look at their works ten years hence and suggested that it would be better for them to take two or three years to do one job of more permanent value, rather than to turn out two or three plays or novels a year. Kalinin, president of the U.S.S.R., expressed similar sentiments at a public meeting of writers. (Fischer, *Machines and Men in Russia*, p. 233.)
31. Gorky, "On Literature and Other Things," p. 52.
32. Reavey and Slonim, *Soviet Literature*, p. 45.
33. RAPM stands for Russian Association of Proletarian Musicians.
34. "O perestroike literaturno-khudozhestvennykh organizatsi" (decree of the Central Committee of the All-Union Communist Party [bolshevik] of April 23, 1932), *Na literaturnom postu*, No. 12 (April, 1932), p. 1.
35. *Ibid.*
36. *Sov. lit. na novom etape*, Bruno Yasenski, p. 216.
37. "K perestroike literaturnykh organizatsi," p. 1.
38. *Sov. lit. na novom etape*, Simmen, p. 94.
39. *Ibid.*, Gronski, p. 8.
40. Hugh McLean, Jr., seminar report for Russian 310, "Voronski's Philosophy of Art and the VAPP Orthodoxy," April 12, 1948, given at the Russian Institute of Columbia University.

41. Louis Fischer, "A Revolution in Revolutionary History," *New York Herald Tribune Books* (November 27, 1932), p. 10.
42. *Sov. lit. na novom etape*, Subotski, p. 42.
43. Dinamov, editor of the *"Litgazeta"* (see p. 31) was attacked by Bruno Yasenski as follows: "Shortly before the liquidation of RAPP, Comrade Dinamov in critical conferences came forward violently with his leftist excesses. After the historic decree of the Central Committee, Comrade Dinamov nowhere bothered to disavow his RAPPist mistakes, did not utter a word about them although he had a whole newspaper at his disposal in which to do this. Neither did we hear a self-critical speech by Comrade Dinamov from this tribune from which the majority of RAPP's members criticized its errors. And this is not by chance. Comrade Dinamov up to now has not realized his RAPPist mistakes, has not overcome them. He only turns his old errors inside out. Comrade Dinamov's activity in the *Litgazeta* bears witness to this clearly enough. Having preserved untouched all the worst methods of the RAPP vulgarizers, he continues to use them in the old way only in another direction: formerly he used them against RAPP's adversaries; now he uses them against his companions-in-arms of the former RAPP leadership." (*Ibid.*, Bruno Yasenski, p. 216.)
44. *Ibid.*, Subotski, p. 44.
45. *Ibid.*, Bakhmetyev, p. 191.
46. "The Congress of Soviet Writers," *Soviet Culture Review*, Nos. 10–12 (1932), p. 54.
47. *Sov. lit. na novom etape*, Bruno Yasenski, p. 215.
48. *Ibid.*, Gronski, p. 12.
49. *Ibid.*, Fadeyev, pp. 124–25.
The critics from *Na literaturnom postu* revealed their own weakness in the struggle with the Litfront although they won. "The principal theoretical mistake they made (Averbakh) was the contrasting of proletarian and socialist culture. They also made a number of other political and theoretical mistakes. These can be formulated concisely thus: they themselves descended to the level of purely publicistic polemics in which the artistic side of a work is entirely ignored, and then they made of criticism a weapon of the group interests of a small clique of writers." (Zelinski, "Soviet Criticism," p. 34.)
50. Maxim Gorky, "Literaturnyie zabavy, I" (1934), *O literature*, N. F. Belchikov, ed., 3d ed., enlarged, Moscow, 1937, p. 357.
Although Maxim Gorky was honorary chairman of the Orgcommittee, he was not present at its first plenum. However, some of his opinions about RAPP, written during the period of its dictatorship or shortly after its liquidation, have been included in this chapter.

51. *Sov. lit. na novom etape*, Averbakh, p. 120.
52. Gorky, "O literature," p. 60.
53. *Sov. lit. na novom etape*, Gronski, p. 8.
54. Fischer, "A Revolution. . . ."
Louis Fischer was Moscow correspondent for the *Nation* and the *Baltimore Sun*.
55. *Sov. lit. na novom etape*, Chumandrin, p. 88.
RAPP's promotion of young writers was especially outstanding in the theatre. (*Ibid*., Gorodetski, p. 132.)
56. *Ibid*., Fadeyev, p. 125.
57. *Ibid*., Kirshon, p. 195.
58. *Ibid*., Fadeyev, p. 125.
59. *Ibid*., Kozakov, p. 109.
60. This circle situation was ridiculed by Ilf and Petrov in their account of "the mutual and many-sided fraud which had unnoticeably become a part of HERCULES [an enterprise supposedly trading in lumber materials] and for some reason was called 'Civic Obligations.'" (Ilf and Petrov, *The Little Golden Calf*, p. 210.) "Yegor [Skumbrievich] delivered the correct speeches about Soviet civic life, about cultural work, about vocational guidance, about various active circles. But behind all these passionate words there was—nothing. Fifteen circles, political, musical, dramatic, had been working out their respective plans for two years. Nuclei of voluntary societies, aiming to help the development of aviation, chemical knowledge, automobiling, horse-racing, road building, contact with the village, prisoners of capital, as well as the most rapid eradications of illiteracy, homelessness, religion, drunkenness, and godalmighty chauvinism, existed only in the swollen imaginations of the members of the respective local committees. . . . Of all this volcanic ring of civic activities with which Skumbrievich surrounded HERCULES, there were actually in operation only two smoldering cones: the wall newspaper, 'The Chairman's Voice,' . . . and a veneered board with the inscription: 'We stop drinking and challenge others to follow our example,' under which, however, there was not a single name." (*Ibid*., pp. 211–12.) Skumbrievich was also so busy organizing "a very powerful circle of harmonica players" that he had no time to acquaint the newly arrived German specialist with his duties. (*Ibid*., p. 216.)
61. *Sov. lit. na novom etape*, Subotski, pp. 50–52.
62. *Ibid*., Zamoiski, p. 238.
63. The Ukrainian author, Ostap Vishnya, complained: "They [VAPP, RAPP, and VUSPP] fenced me off with a wall. Being interested in questions of literature, I had to peek through some little hole to see just what was being done in this literature and why I was not al-

lowed there. They shoved me aside and never said in what lay my sin, did not say concretely whom in literature I had 'killed' or 'murdered.' I suffered for myself, for my comrades, and for literature because in the group of writers who had withdrawn from literary activity there were comrades who had, and could still have accomplished much. It is a pity that during the past two and a half years my contemporaries, who were beyond enrollment age but still could have done something, as it was, had to waste time in emotional clashes and other nonsense." (*Ibid.*, Ostap Vishnya, p. 139.)

64. On January 28, 1930, which was immediately after the Moscow trial of the wreckers and almost two years before the adoption of the resolution by the Fourth Plenum of RAPP, Kuibyshev made a speech entitled, "He Who Is Not with Us Is against Us," before an assembly of engineering-technical workers in Leningrad. This speech, perfectly correct and fully expressing the Party line towards the technical intelligentsia at that particular time, was used as a basis for the formulation of the slogan, "Ally or Enemy," which was launched by RAPP in a later and altered situation. Moreover, what Kuibyshev actually said was that the working class stretched out its hand and shook the hand of the engineers, saying to them: "Let us together proclaim—'He who is not with us is against us.'" (*Ibid.*, Subotski, pp. 46–47.)

65. *Ibid.*, pp. 47–48.

66. B. Kor, "Ne poputchik, a soyuznik ili vrag," *Na literaturnom postu*, No. 2 (January, 1931), p. 40.

67. M. Luzgin, "Bolshe samokritiki" (stenogram report of speech delivered at plenum of RAPP in February, 1931), *Na literaturnom postu*, No. 11 (April, 1931), p. 24.

68. "Rezolyutsii 4-vo plenuma pravleniya RAPP o poputnichestve i soyuznichestve," *Literaturnaya gazeta*, No. 50 (September 15, 1931), p. 3.

69. Leopold Averbakh, *Iz rappovskovo dnevnika*, 1931.

70. "Na uroven . . . ," p. 4.

71. *Ibid.*, pp. 3–4.

In an article entitled, "Na vysshuyu stupen," printed in the final number of *Na literaturnom postu*, the editors wrote as follows: "The new stage in the development of Soviet literature is a new examination (and the deepest), a new verification which history presents to proletarian writer-cadres. With ally and fellow-traveler writers in a single Union of Soviet Writers, proletarian writers should be the foremost creative detachment, in its creative works expressing best and most artistically the vital truth of socialist construction, the class struggle, and socialist heroic deeds. The greater its successes in this respect, the stronger ideologically creative will be this detachment (which will be increased by new cadres, first from shock workers entering literature from factories and *kolkhozes*, and from fellow-traveler writers closest to the socialist proletariat) and the quicker, easier, and surer will the process of ideologically creative reconstruction of the wide masses of writers take place." ("Na vysshuyu stupen," *Na literaturnom postu*, Nos. 13–14 [May, 1932], p. 11.)

72. *Sov. lit. na novom etape*, Subotski, p. 49.
73. *Ibid.*, Kulik, p. 61.
74. *Ibid.*, Utkin, p. 232.
75. *Ibid.*
76. Gorky, "On Literature . . . ," pp. 49–50.
77. *Sov. lit. na novom etape*, Chumandrin, p. 87.
78. As recently as 1947 we find Fadeyev upbraiding Soviet critics for forgetting "that they should correct mistakes, teach and educate, and not beat the writer over the head, especially when it is a young writer. Some critics think that when it comes to evaluating literature there are only two colors—black and white. But literature appears in such variety that critics should know how to use all the colors of the spectrum. The beat-over-the-head type of criticism must be done away with and only that type of criticism which teaches and educates should be applied." (Alexander A. Fadeyev, "The Tasks of Literary Criticism," *Oktyabr*, No. 7 [July, 1947], Zina Voynow, trans., *The American Review on the Soviet Union*, IX, No. 1 [March, 1948], 55.)

79. Tolstoy, "Trends in Soviet Literature," p. 239.

"The dominating clique of RAPP . . . was later revealed as a group of Trotskyites, headed by . . . Averbakh, associated with the counter-revolutionary network. One of the favorite methods of these conspirators for disorganizing Soviet work was to demand impossible standards under pretense of zealousness." (Marshall, *Mayakovsky and His Poetry*, p. 6.)

80. *Sov. lit. na novom etape*, Vera Inber, p. 156.
81. The opposition within RAPP represented the trend of a certain romanticism and the preponderance of the publicist element in art. (Zelinski, "15th Anniversary of Soviet Literature," p. 69.)
82. From a resolution passed by the last plenum of the board of directors of VAPP, quoted by Averbakh, *Kulturnaya revolyutsiya i voprosy sovremennoi literatury*, p. 60.
83. Libedinski's report to a VAPP conference, quoted in Libedinski, "Za chto boryutsya napostovtsy," p. 10.
84. Zelinski, "15th Anniversary of Soviet Literature," p. 69.
85. "According to Kushner's testimony the method of psychological realism 'holds a large part of our proletarian writers prisoners, by replacing the problem of creating a new man with an analysis of psycho-

NOTES: THE LIQUIDATION OF RAPP 221

logical experiences. . . . The socialist construction . . . is reduced, after all, to a subordinate part of the background, against which is unfolded the personal drama of the characters, while mass psychology is ignored.'" (Miliukov, *Outlines of Russian Culture*, p. 114.)

86. "Theoretical inventions about individual psychology . . . basically contradict the methodological aims of Lenin and inevitably lead to loss of contact with the actual problems of socialist construction and the class struggle. This is excellently demonstrated . . . in *The Birth of a Hero*." ("Na uroven . . . ," p. 3.)

87. *Sov. lit. na novom etape*, Yermilov, p. 184.

88. *The Shot* was a poem of social drama, written in an elevated romantic and abstract tone. In 1930, after its appearance, Bezymenski became the leader of the Left wing of RAPP. "For a time it seemed as if Bezymenski, who took up arms against every public evil, would become the official party poet." (Reavey and Slonim, *Soviet Literature*, p. 274.) Kirpotin spoke of Bezymenski as a revolutionary romantic and said that in the idealization to which he subjected his heroes there was still much rhetoric and schematization. (*Sov. lit. na novom etape*, Kirpotin, p. 33.)

89. The official attitude towards Zamyatin is that, as a bourgeois intellectual, he could not understand the "world-wide historic meaning of the proletarian revolution," and that he did not believe in or accept it because he did not want it, since it doomed his class to destruction. Zamyatin was for universal, not socialist, revolution and is quoted in the *Bolshaya sovetskaya entsiklopediya* thus: "The social revolution is only one of an innumerable number; the law of revolution is not a social law, but an immeasurably greater cosmic universal one." He is also said to have remarked: "I fear that Russian literature has only one future—its past." ("Zamyatin," *Bolshaya sovetskaya entsiklopediya*, Moscow, 1933, XXVI, 154; and "Zamyatin," *Literaturnaya entsiklopediya*, Moscow, 1930, IV, 309.)

90. *Sov. lit. na novom etape*, Tarasov-Rodionov, pp. 176–77.

91. *Ibid.*, Marietta Shaginyan, p. 241.

92. *Ibid.*, p. 242.

93. Tolstoy, "Trends in Soviet Literature," p. 244.

94. *Sov. lit. na novom etape*, Mikitenko, pp. 170–71.

95. "Chronicle of Culture."

96. "RAPP," *Lit. entsik.*, p. 525.

97. *Sov. lit. na novom etape*, Utkin, p. 233.

98. It was the Libedinski group in RAPP which urged a war against schematization and mechanicalness (Libedinski, "Za chto boryutsya napostovtsy," p. 9) and which tried to replace the "stamp" (stereotype) in literature by "an attempt to picture the social revolution in its

everyday concreteness as revealed in the activities of living man" and to give a more profound psychological analysis, based on "the exposition of man's inner nature as formed and developed under the influence of his social surroundings." The more radical minority of RAPP attacked these theories, believing that the "living man" would overshadow the "class man" and that psychology led to "probing into the problems of family life, and thus diverted the people from fighting at various political fronts." The latter "demanded that the offensive novels in which the living man was depicted against the background of a non-class family life be replaced by literary reports from different sections of the Communist front." (Miliukov, *Outlines of Russian Culture*, p. 99.)

In 1930, Boris Kushner wrote in *Pravda* that the completely erroneous slogan, "living man," in teaching proletarian writers to show the many-sidedness of the psychology of their characters, teaches them how "to find the good in evil, to reveal the stabs of conscience in the deserter, to find flashes of remorse in the traitor." He accused this slogan of turning the proletarian writer into an objective observer and an impartial judge, of blunting his class consciousness, and of weakening "his orientation in relation to the most important of the problems of the reconstruction period—the problem of the class struggle and of the extirpation of the roots of capitalism." (Kushner, "Prichiny otstavaniya.")

An article appearing in *Pravda* in May of 1932 mentioned as one of RAPP's mistakes the development of the idealistic theory of living man, which was most fully formulated in the thesis: "The world, this is man." ("Na uroven . . . ," p. 3.)

Berezovski, in his speech, said that Yermilov and the others who stood up for living harmonious man did not present a novel theory, but one that originated before Averbakh and Yermilov were born. He claimed that it was put forward by the critic N. K. Mikhailovski, theorist of the *narodnik* movement, and that before the 1905 Revolution and up to the October Revolution this theory was an important "philosophical trump card" in the Social-Revolutionary arguments against the Marxists. (*Sov. lit. na novom etape*, Berezovski, p. 140.)

99. See note 50 (Chapter 1), p. 174.
The slogan of "spontaneous impressions" substituted an "inner analysis of the soul" for the "truthful portrayal of the real processes of the new actuality and the appraisal of people by their share in this actuality." ("RAPP," *Lit. entsik.*, p. 524.)
100. Kushner, "Prichiny otstavaniya."
101. Eastman, *Artists in Uniform*, p. 15.
102. *Sov. lit. na novom etape*, Kirpotin, p. 22.
103. *Ibid.*, pp. 22–23.

104. A *raznochinets* (plural, *raznochintsy*) was a liberal member of the intelligentsia in Russia during the sixties of the nineteenth century. He did not belong to the nobility, but was a member of the clergy, officialdom, the petty bourgeoisie, or the peasantry. Among the *raznochintsy* writers were Dobrolyubov and Chernyshevski.
105. *Sov. lit. na novom etape*, Yermilov, p. 182.
106. *Ibid.*, Kirpotin, pp. 22–23.
107. Gorky, "On Literature . . . ," p. 48.
108. *Sov. lit. na novom etape*, Averbakh, p. 119.
109. Alexander Fadeyev, "Staroye i novoye voprosy khudozhestvennovo tvorchestva," *Literaturnaya gazeta*, No. 49 (October 29, 1932), p. 3.
110. *Sov. lit. na novom etape*, Kirshon, p. 198.
111. Gorky, "On Literature . . . ," p. 50.
112. Gorky, "O literature," p. 60.
113. Gorky, "On Literature . . . ," p. 49.
114. Fischer, "A Revolution. . . ."
115. *Sov. lit. na novom etape*, Kirpotin, p. 30.
116. *Ibid.*, Gronski, p. 257.
117. *Ibid.*, Bakhmetyev, pp. 191–92.
118. *Ibid.*, Serafimovich, p. 138.
119. *Ibid.*, Averbakh, p. 118.
120. *Ibid.*
121. *Ibid.*, pp. 118 and 122.
122. *Ibid.*, Chariyev, p. 124.
123. *Ibid.*, Berezovski, p. 140.
124. *Ibid.*, Buachidze, p. 229.
125. *Ibid.*, Mikitenko, p. 171.
126. *Ibid.*, Klychkov, p. 160.
127. *Ibid.*, Tarasov-Rodionov, p. 178.
128. *Ibid.*, Vishnevski, p. 247.
129. *Ibid.*, Libedinski, p. 167.
130. *Ibid.*, pp. 167–68.
131. *Ibid.*, Kirpotin, p. 251.
132. The *Malaya sovetskaya entsiklopediya* says that Averbakh's inadequate understanding of Lenin's doctrines led him often to base himself upon the erroneous positions of Plekhanov, Deborin, and Bukharin in his statements on literary questions and in his criticisms of Voronski, Pereverzev, and the creative purposes of the Litfront. ("Averbakh," *Mal. entsik.*)
133. *Sov. lit. na novom etape*, Kirpotin, p. 253.
134. *Ibid.*, p. 254.
135. Averbakh was an unpleasant little man whose sister was the

wife of Yagoda, chief of the OGPU. After RAPP's dissolution, Averbakh edited a newspaper in the Urals. He was shot as a result of the public trial in March, 1938, of the "Bloc of Rightists and Trotskyites" which included Bukharin, Rykov, and Yagoda (who was accused of having poisoned Gorky in 1936). (Joshua Kunitz.)

136. *Sov. lit. na novom etape*, Averbakh, p. 117.
137. *Ibid.*, Yermilov, p. 182.
138. *Ibid.*, Fadeyev, pp. 125–26.
139. *Ibid.*, Subotski, p. 37.
140. *Ibid.*, Berezovski, p. 140.
141. *Ibid.*, Gronski, p. 7.
142. Fischer, "A Revolution. . . ."
143. Reavey, *Soviet Literature Today*, p. 179.
144. Zelinski, "15th Anniversary of Soviet Literature," p. 71.
145. *Sov. lit. na novom etape*, Kirpotin, p. 250.
146. Fadeyev, "The Tasks . . . ," pp. 32–33.
147. Drew Middleton, "Soviet Arts Trace Political Patter," *New York Times* (February 10, 1948), p. 12.
148. Fadeyev, "The Tasks . . . ," p. 31.
149. A. M. Egolin (corresponding member of the Academy of Sciences of the U.S.S.R.), *The Ideological Content of Soviet Literature* (stenographic report of a public lecture delivered in Moscow in 1946), Mary Kriger, trans., Washington, D.C., 1948, p. 8.
150. *Ibid.*, p. 9.
151. "RAPP," *Lit. entsik.*, p. 525.

RAPP contributed nothing new towards the working out of the principles of proletarian aesthetics. One of its first creative slogans was that of the "living man"; another was the one about the tearing away of each and every mask. These slogans exhausted RAPP's artistic platform and its understanding of realism. (*Ibid.*, pp. 523–24.)

152. Mrs. Cecil Chesterton, *Sickle or Swastika?*, London, 1935, p. 178.
153. *Sov. lit. na novom etape*, Kirpotin, p. 247.
154. *Ibid.*, p. 248.
155. Statute of the Soviet Writers' Union, quoted in Struve, *25 Years of Soviet Russian Literature*, p. 238.
156. *Sov. lit. na novom etape*, Gronski, pp. 10–11.
157. *Ibid.*, Kirshon, p. 194.
158. Zhdanov, "Soviet Literature—the Richest in Ideas; the Most Advanced Literature," p. 21.
159. Gorky, "La Mission des écrivains soviétiques," p. 313.
160. V. Ya. Kirpotin, "The Socialist Realism of Soviet Literature," M. Apletin, ed., *Literature of the Peoples of the U.S.S.R.*, VOKS Illustrated Almanac, Nos. 7–8 (1934), p. 9.

161. Struve, *25 Years of Soviet Russian Literature*, p. 258.
162. Fyodor Gladkov, "Soviet Literature in a New Upsurge," *Kultura i zhizn* (August 21, 1949), p. 1, summarized in *Current Digest of the Soviet Press*, I, No. 36 (October 4, 1949), 61.
163. Struve, *25 Years of Soviet Russian Literature*, p. 235.
164. Radek, "Contemporary World Literature and the Tasks of Proletarian Art," p. 142.
Trotsky (who was exiled to Alma-Ata in 1928 and deported to Turkey in 1929) has given his conception of how literature under socialism should be handled: "Our [class] standard is, clearly, political, imperative and intolerant. . . . we ought to have a watchful revolutionary censorship, and a broad and flexible policy in the field of art, free from petty partisan maliciousness." (Trotsky, *Literature and Revolution*, p. 221.)

6. Conclusion

1. Joseph Stalin, "Results of the First Five-Year Plan," quoted in Kirpotin, "The Socialist Realism of Soviet Literature," p. 7.
2. Stalin, "Results of the First Five-Year Plan," p. 254.
3. Panfyorov, *And Then the Harvest*, p. 167.
4. Bergson, "Structure of Soviet Economy."
5. A. Bubnov, "On the Rise of Culture in the U.S.S.R. during the First Pyatiletka" (speech delivered at the Third Session of the Central Executive Committee of the U.S.S.R., January 28, 1933), *VOKS*, IV, Nos. 1–2 (1933), 27.
6. Stalin, "Results of the First Five-Year Plan," p. 241.
7. *Ibid.*, p. 270.
8. "Recent Soviet Literature," p. 149.
9. A. Stetski, "About Gladkov's 'Energy,'" *International Literature*, No. 2 (1934), p. 136.
10. Karl Radek, "The Epic of Collectivization," M. Apletin, ed., *Literature of the Peoples of the U.S.S.R.*, VOKS Illustrated Almanac, Nos. 7–8 (1934), p. 142.
11. Mirsky, "Russia," *Tendencies of the Modern Novel*, p. 115.
12. Radek, "Epic . . . ," p. 142.
13. V. Dorofeyev, *Soviet Literature of the 1930's*, Moscow, 1947, pp. 6–7.
14. Radek, "Contemporary World Literature and the Tasks of Proletarian Art," p. 124.
15. Gleb Struve, "The Pan-Soviet Literary Congress," *The Slavonic and East European Review*, XIII, No. 39 (April, 1935), 641.
16. Libedinski, "O razreshenii generalnykh zadach proletarskoi literatury," p. 61.

17. Radek, "Contemporary World Literature . . . ," p. 160.
18. Venyamin Kaverin, "Literature and Science," M. Apletin, ed., *Literature of the Peoples of the U.S.S.R.*, VOKS Illustrated Almanac, Nos. 7–8 (1934), p. 40.
19. Kirpotin's criticism in 1933, quoted in Kenneth E. Harper, seminar report for Russian 310, "Socialist Realism in the Nineteen-Thirties," April 30, 1948, given at the Russian Institute of Columbia University.
20. Kaverin, "Literature and Science," p. 39.
21. I. Anisimov, quoted in "Recent Soviet Literature," p. 148.
22. "The most important aspects of construction, which must be stressed by the literary groups in their propaganda, are: (1) the difficulties of socialist construction, (2) the setting-up of the agricultural sector of the Five-Year Plan, and (3) questions of cultural construction and of living conditions during the reconstruction period." (Vertinski, *Litrabota v klube i v krasnom ugolke*, p. 52.)
23. Vertinski, "Vvedeniye," *ibid.*, p. 5.
24. Vertinski, *Litrabota* . . . , p. 52.
25. Harper, *Civic Training in Soviet Russia*, p. 157.
26. Zelinski, "15th Anniversary of Soviet Literature," pp. 69–70.
27. Freeman, *The Soviet Worker*, p. 322.
28. *Soil Upturned* was discussed at a literary evening at the "Serp i Molot" factory and praised for its clarity, realism, and correct understanding of the class struggle in the village. In preparation for this discussion, questionnaires about the novel were passed out to workers who had read it. Readers wrote essays and held preliminary discussions in the shops. It was read aloud during the lunch hour. The factory was urged to apply what had been learned from *Soil Upturned* to the farm of which it was the patron. This method of mass literary education is a Soviet propaganda technique. (Ernest J. Simmons, lecture for Russian 311, October 11, 1948, given at the Russian Institute of Columbia University.)
29. Communists regard and use the theatre as a weapon, "as a tool of the all-powerful and all-pervading State: an implement for disseminating the tenets of the Communist philosophy, for the graphic presentation of simple object lessons to an audience just emerged from illiteracy, and, in a more general sense, for the bringing to the masses of that 'culture' which is regarded as one of the essential perquisites of the citizen of a Socialist State." (Elmer Rice, "Preface," Eugene Lyons, ed., *Six Soviet Plays*, Boston–New York, 1934, p. v.)
Norris Houghton says that during the First Five-Year Plan the theatre ceased to be agitational (satirizing and condemning the old) and

turned propagandist (depicting the new). (Houghton, *Moscow Rehearsals*, p. 195.)
  30. Lyons, *Modern Moscow*, p. 243.
  31. See note 88 (Chapter 5), p. 221.
  32. "The Leningrad Young Workers' Theatre (TRAM)," *VOKS*, Nos. 11–12 (1930), p. 36.
  33. "New Meyerhold Productions," *VOKS*, Nos. 1–3 (January-February, 1930), p. 106.
  34. A. Selivanovski, "The Poetry of Socialism," M. Apletin, ed., *Literature of the Peoples of the U.S.S.R.*, VOKS Illustrated Almanac, Nos. 7–8 (1934), p. 51.
  35. Bezymenski, quoted in Iosif Borisovich Lapidus, "Pervy god," *Lyudi stalingradskovo traktornovo zavoda*, pp. 89–90.
  36. Bankov, "Authors from the Factory Bench," p. 46.
  37. Simkhovich, "The History of Factories," p. 85.
  38. Lyons, *Modern Moscow*, p. 26.
  39. Bernard Pares, *A History of Russia*, 4th ed., rev., New York, 1946, p. 507.
  40. "Foreword," M. Apletin, ed., *Literature of the Peoples of the U.S.S.R.*, VOKS Illustrated Almanac, Nos. 7–8 (1934), pp. 5–6.
  41. Lyons, *Modern Moscow*, p. 161.
  42. Aaron Yugow, "The Five-Year Plan," B. Sacharoff, trans., *The American Socialist Quarterly*, I, No. 3 (Summer, 1932), 16.
  43. Chamberlin, *Russia's Iron Age*, p. 273.
  In *Time, Forward!* Shura paints a new Henri Rousseau-ish picture of the three brigadiers every ten days, after considering and comparing the work indicators of their respective shifts. "At first, when Khanumov had been proudly speeding along on the motorcycle, and Yermakov had been cavorting on the horse, Ishchenko had stayed on the snail or at best in the peasant cart." (V. Katayev, p. 130.) Then, Khanumov sat on the tortoise, Yermakov sat backwards on the nag, and Ishchenko rode the bicycle. (*Ibid.*, p. 26.) But after Ishchenko's shift breaks the concrete-pouring record, he appears in a six-winged airplane. (*Ibid.*, p. 318.)
  44. Chamberlin, *Soviet Russia*, p. 413.
  45. Lyons, *Modern Moscow*, p. 246.
  46. *Ibid.*, p. 245.
  47. Leonov, himself, perhaps agreed with this subversive thought, expressed by the wrecker Petrygin's decadent bourgeois father-in-law. (*Skutarevsky*, p. 236.)

RUSSIAN TRANSLITERATION TABLE

(Approved by the Department of Slavic Languages, Columbia University)

1. Russian Christian names (Петр, Александр, etc.) that have common English equivalents (Peter, Alexander, etc.) retain their English form, except when they appear in the titles of books or articles.
2. The family names of a few Russian authors that have acquired fixed spellings in English (Gorky, etc.) retain their popular English spellings, except when they appear in the titles of books or articles.

А	A		Н	N
Б	B		О	O
В	V		П	P
Г	G (in the genitive endings его and ого, г equals v)		Р	R
			С	S
Д	D		Т	T
Е	E (when initial and after ъ, ь and all vowels, except ы, е = ye; after ы, е = ie)		У	U
			Ф	F
			Х	Kh
			Ц	Ts
Ё	Yo (after ж and ш, ё = o)		Ч	Ch
Ж	Zh		Ш	Sh
З	Z		Щ	Shch
И	I (after ь, и = yi)		ъ	(omitted)
Й	I (the combinations ий = i, and ый = y)		ы	y
			ь	(omitted)
К	K		Э	E
Л	L		Ю	Yu (after ы, ю = iu)
М	M		Я	Ya (after ы, я = ia)

BIBLIOGRAPHY

General Works

Baykov, Alexander. The Development of the Soviet Economic System: an Essay on the Experience of Planning in the U.S.S.R. New York, Macmillan Company, 1947.

Bienstock, Gregory, Solomon M. Schwarz, and Aaron Yugow. Management in Russian Industry and Agriculture. Arthur Feiler and Jacob Marschak, ed. London–New York–Toronto, Oxford University Press, 1944.

Brunetière, Ferdinand. "La Littérature française sous le premier Empire," Études critiques sur l'histoire de la littérature française. New ed. Paris, Librairie Hachette et Cie, 1888.

Chamberlin, William Henry. Russia's Iron Age. Boston, Little Brown and Company, 1934.

—— Soviet Russia: a Living Record and a History. Rev. ed. Boston, Little Brown and Company, 1931.

Charpentier, John. Napoléon et les hommes de lettres de son temps. Paris, Mercure de France, 1935.

Chase, Stuart. "How Russia Charts Her Economic Course," New York Times (December 11, 1927), sec. 10, p. 7.

Chesterton, Mrs. Cecil. Sickle or Swastika? London, Stanley Paul & Co., Ltd., 1935.

Dobb, Maurice. "The Significance of the Five-Year Plan," The Slavonic (and East European) Review, X, No. 28 (June, 1931), 80–89.

Fischer, Louis. Machines and Men in Russia. New York, Harrison Smith, 1932.

Freeman, Joseph. The Soviet Worker: an Account of the Economic, Social and Cultural Status of Labor in the U.S.S.R. New York, Liveright, Inc., 1932.

G., A. "The U.S.S.R. in the Arctic," VOKS, Nos. 8–10 (1930), pp. 73–78.

Grinko, G. T. (Vice-chairman, State Planning Commission of U.S.S.R.). The Five-Year Plan of the Soviet Union: a Political Interpretation. New York, International Publishers, 1930.

Harper, Samuel Northrup. Civic Training in Soviet Russia. Chicago, University of Chicago Press, 1929.
Houghton, Norris. Moscow Rehearsals: an Account of Methods of Production in the Soviet Theatre. New York, Harcourt Brace and Company, 1936.
"How Does the U.S.S.R. Work," VOKS, II, No. 1 (January, 1931), 5–12.
Lenin, V. I. "The Tasks of the Youth Leagues" (speech delivered at Third All-Russian Congress of Russian Young Communist League, October 2, 1920), Selected Works. Moscow, Foreign Languages Publishing House, 1947, II, 661–74.
Lermontov, M. Yu. "Taman" (Geroi nashevo vremeni), Izbrannyie proizvedeniya. Leningrad, Ogiz, 1946, pp. 276–81.
London, Kurt. The Seven Soviet Arts. Eric S. Bensinger, trans. London, Faber and Faber, Ltd., 1937.
Lyons, Eugene. Modern Moscow. London, Hurst & Blackett, Ltd., n.d.
Maynard, Sir John. Russia in Flux. S. Haden Guest, ed., from Russia in Flux and The Russian Peasant and Other Studies. New York, Macmillan Company, 1948.
Miller, Margaret S. "The Planning System in Soviet Russia," The Slavonic (and East European) Review, IX, No. 26 (December, 1930), 449–56.
Pares, Bernard. A History of Russia. 4th ed., rev. New York, Alfred A. Knopf, 1946.
"Resheniya X plenuma IKKI v massy!" Pravda (August 29, 1929), p. 1.
Stalin, Joseph. "The Results of the First Five-Year Plan" (report delivered at plenary session of Central Committee and Central Control Commission of Communist Party of Soviet Union, January 7, 1933), Selected Writings. New York, International Publishers, 1942, pp. 234–70.
State Planning Commission of the Council of People's Commissars of the U.S.S.R. (Gosplan). The Soviet Union Looks Ahead: the Five-Year Plan for Economic Construction. New York, Horace Liveright, 1929.
—— Summary of the Fulfilment of the First Five-Year Plan for the Development of the National Economy of the U.S.S.R. Moscow, State Planning Commission, 1933.
Tikhonova, K. "Graphic Arts in the U.S.S.R.," VOKS, II, Nos. 10–12 (1931), 70–78.
"Urals and Siberia in Soviet Art," Soviet Culture Review, No. 5 (1932), p. 28.
Waliszewski, R. The Romance of an Empress: Catherine II of Russia. Trans. from the French. New York, D. Appleton & Co., 1894.

Yugow, Aaron. "The Five-Year Plan," B. Sacharoff, trans., *The American Socialist Quarterly*, I, No. 3 (Summer, 1932), 10–21.
Zetkin, Clara. Souvenirs sur Lénine. Paris, Bureau d'Éditions de Diffusion et de Publicité, 1926.

Literature and Literary Organizations

Brodski, N. L., ed. Literaturnyie manifesty (ot simvolizma k Oktyabryu): sbornik materialov. Moscow, Izdatelstvo "Federatsiya," 1929.
"Chronicle of Culture: Literature," *Soviet Culture Bulletin*, No. 3 (July, 1931), p. 14.
"Congress of Soviet Writers, The," *Soviet Culture Review*, Nos. 10–12 (1932), pp. 54–56.
Cross, Samuel H. "Russian Literature since 1918," *The Harvard Advocate*, CXXIX, No. 4 (Spring–Summer, 1943), 11–15.
Dorofeyev, V. Soviet Literature of the 1930's. Moscow, U.S.S.R. Society for Cultural Relations with Foreign Countries, 1947.
Eastman, Max. Artists in Uniform: a Study of Literature and Bureaucratism. New York, Alfred A. Knopf, 1934.
Edgerton, William. "The Serapion Brothers: an Early Soviet Controversy," *The American Slavic and East European Review*, VIII, No. 1 (February, 1949), 47–64.
Fischer, Louis. "A Revolution in Revolutionary History," *New York Herald Tribune Books* (November 27, 1932), p. 10.
Freeman, Joseph, Joshua Kunitz, and Louis Lozowick. Voices of October: Art and Literature in Soviet Russia. New York, Vanguard Press, 1930.
Goriely, Benjamin. Les Poètes dans la révolution russe. Paris, Gallimard, 1934.
Kaun, Alexander. Soviet Poets and Poetry. Berkeley–Los Angeles, University of California Press, 1943.
Klingsland, Z. St. "Un Poète polonais au pays des réalités soviétiques," *Pologne littéraire*, No. 73 (October 15, 1932), p. 4.
"K perestroike literaturnykh organizatsi," *Na literaturnom postu*, Nos. 13–14 (May, 1932), pp. 1–2.
Kunitz, Joshua, ed. Russian Literature since the Revolution. New York, Boni and Gaer, 1948.
Lavrin, Janko. An Introduction to the Russian Novel. New York, Whittlesey House, McGraw-Hill Book Company, Inc., 1947.
"Leningrad Young Workers' Theatre, The (TRAM)," *VOKS*, Nos. 11–12 (1930), pp. 36–37.
"Literature of the Peoples of the U.S.S.R.," *VOKS*, II, No. 5 (1931), 63–69.

Markov, P. "The Results of the Moscow Theatre Season 1930/31," *VOKS*, II, Nos. 10–12 (1931), 15–21.
Middleton, Drew. "Soviet Arts Trace Political Patter," *New York Times* (February 10, 1948), p. 12.
Miliukov, Paul. *Outlines of Russian Culture: Part II—Literature.* Michael Karpovich, ed., Valentine Ughet and Eleanor Davis, trans. Philadelphia, University of Pennsylvania Press, 1943.
Mirsky, D. S. "Russia," *Tendencies of the Modern Novel.* London, George Allen & Unwin, Ltd., 1934, pp. 101–19.
"New Meyerhold Productions," *VOKS*, Nos. 1–3 (January–February, 1930), p. 106.
"New Soviet Literature," *VOKS*, Nos. 6–7 (April, 1930), pp. 39–48.
"New Soviet Literature," *VOKS*, II, No. 1 (January, 1931), 93–98.
"O perestroike literaturno-khudożhestvennykh organizatsi" (April 23, 1932, Decree of Central Committee of All-Union Communist Party [bolshevik]), *Na literaturnom postu*, No. 12 (April, 1932), p. 1.
Putnikova, N. "Women in Literature," *VOKS*, II, No. 2 (February, 1931), 18–22.
"RAPP," V. M. Friche, ed., *Literaturnaya entsiklopediya.* Moscow, Ogiz R.S.F.S.R., 1935, IX, 519–26.
Reavey, George. *Soviet Literature Today.* London, Lindsay Drummond, 1946.
—— and Marc Slonim, ed. and trans. *Soviet Literature: an Anthology.* New York, Covici Friede, 1934.
"Recent Soviet Literature," *International Literature*, No. 2 (1933), pp. 146–52.
Rice, Elmer. "Preface," Eugene Lyons, ed., *Six Soviet Plays.* Boston–New York, Houghton Mifflin Company, 1934, pp. v–vi.
S., M. "Collectivization and the Countryside in Contemporary Fiction," *VOKS*, Nos. 8–10 (1930), pp. 25–28.
Selivanovski, A. "RAPP," N. L. Meshcheryakov, ed., *Malaya sovetskaya entsiklopediya.* Moscow, Aktsionernoye obshchestvo "Sovetskaya entsiklopediya," 1930, VII, 175.
Simmons, Ernest J. *An Outline of Modern Russian Literature (1880–1940).* Ithaca, N.Y., Cornell University Press, 1944.
"Sozdan orgkomitet soyuza sovetskikh pisatelei," *Na literaturnom postu*, Nos. 13–14 (May, 1932), pp. 1–2.
Struve, Gleb. "The Pan-Soviet Literary Congress," *The Slavonic and East European Review*, XIII, No. 39 (April, 1935), 641–43.
—— *25 Years of Soviet Russian Literature (1918–1943).* New and enlarged ed. of *Soviet Russian Literature.* London, George Routledge & Sons, Ltd., 1946.

"Theatre Season 1931/32 (Moscow-Leningrad)," *VOKS*, II, Nos. 10–12 (1931), 21–26.
Thorgevsky, Ivan. De Gorki à nos jours: la nouvelle littérature russe. Paris, Éditions La Renaissance, 1945.
Tolstoy, Alexei N. "Trends in Soviet Literature," *Science and Society*, VII, No. 3 (Summer, 1943), 233–50.
"Voice of the Soviet Authors, The," *VOKS*, II, No. 1 (January, 1931), 66–68.
Yermilov, V. "RAPP dolzhen byt bolshevistskim avangardom sovetskoi literatury," *Literaturnaya gazeta*, No. 25 (October 7, 1929), p. 2.

Literary Theory and Criticism

Bezymenski, Alexander I. Speech in XVI syezd vsesoyznoi kommunisticheskoi partii (b): stenograficheski otchyot. 2d ed. Moscow-Leningrad, Ogiz-Moskovski rabochi, 1931, pp. 393–96.
Egolin, A. M. (corresponding member of Academy of Sciences of U.S.S.R.). The Ideological Content of Soviet Literature (stenographic report of public lecture delivered in Moscow in 1946), Mary Kriger, trans. Washington, D.C., Public Affairs Press, 1948.
Engels, Friedrich. Letter to Mehring (London, July 14, 1893), Karl Marx and Friedrich Engels, Correspondence, 1846–1895: a Selection with Commentary and Notes. London, Martin Lawrence, Ltd., 1934, pp. 510–12.
Fadeyev, Alexander A. "Staroye i novoye voprosy khudozhestvennovo tvorchestva," *Literaturnaya gazeta*, No. 49 (October 29, 1932), p. 3.
—— "The Tasks of Literary Criticism," *Oktyabr*, No. 7 (July, 1947), Zina Voynow, trans., *The American Review on the Soviet Union*, IX, No. 1 (March, 1948), 30–59.
Gladkov, Fyodor V. "Soviet Literature in a New Upsurge," *Kultura i zhizn* (August 21, 1949), p. 1, summarized in *Current Digest of the Soviet Press*, I, No. 36 (October 4, 1949), 61.
Gnedina, N. "On the Hero's Trail," *VOKS*, II, No. 2 (February, 1931), 79–80.
Gorky, Maxim. "Literaturnyie zabavy, I" (1934), O literature: stati i rechi 1928–1936. N. F. Belchikov, ed. 3d ed., enlarged. Moscow, Sovetski pisatel, 1937, pp. 351–61.
—— "La Mission des écrivains soviétiques," Z. Lvovsky, trans., *La Revue hebdomadaire*, No. 42 (October 21, 1933), pp. 307–15.
—— "O deistvitelnosti" (1929), O literature: stati i rechi 1928–1936. N. F. Belchikov, ed. 3d ed., enlarged. Moscow, Sovetski pisatel, 1937, pp. 337–42.

BIBLIOGRAPHY

Gorky, Maxim. "O literature" (1931), O literature: stati i rechi 1928–1936. N. F. Belchikov, ed. 3d ed., enlarged. Moscow, Sovetski pisatel, 1937, pp. 51–62.
—— "On Literature and Other Things," On Guard for the Soviet Union. New York, International Publishers, 1933, pp. 42–53.
Kaverin, Venyamin. "Literature and Science," M. Apletin, ed., *Literature of the Peoples of the U.S.S.R.*, VOKS Illustrated Almanac, Nos. 7–8 (1934), pp. 35–40.
Kirpotin, V. Ya. "The Socialist Realism of Soviet Literature," M. Apletin, ed., *Literature of the Peoples of the U.S.S.R.*, VOKS Illustrated Almanac, Nos. 7–8 (1934), pp. 7–11.
Kirshon, Vladimir. Speech in XVI syezd vsesoyuznoi kommunisticheskoi partii (b): stenograficheski otchyot. 2d ed. Moscow-Leningrad, Ogiz-Moskovski rabochi, 1931, pp. 277–82.
Kor, B. "Ne poputchik, a soyuznik ili vrag," *Na literaturnom postu*, No. 2 (January, 1931), pp. 39–40.
Kushner, Boris A. "Prichiny otstavaniya," *Pravda* (October 4, 1930), p. 5.
Lelevich, G. Na literaturnom postu (stati i zametki). Moscow, Partizdat "Oktyabr," 1924.
Lenin, V. I. "Partinaya organizatsiya i partinaya literatura," Sochineniya. 2d ed. Leningrad, Partizdat TsK VKP (b), 1935, VIII, 386–90, reprinted from *Novaya zhizn*, No. 12 (November 26, 1905).
Libedinski, Yuri. Generalnyie zadachi proletarskoi literatury. Moscow-Leningrad, Ogiz (LAPP), 1931.
Lidin, Vladimir. "Soviet Literature," *VOKS*, II, No. 6 (1931), 67–69.
Ludkevich, S. "Soviet Literature as the Forepost of World Literature," M. Apletin, ed., *Literature of the Peoples of the U.S.S.R.*, VOKS Illustrated Almanac, Nos. 7–8 (1934), pp. 20–26.
Luzgin, M. "Bolshe samokritiki" (stenogram report of speech delivered at plenum of RAPP in February, 1931), *Na literaturnom postu*, No. 11 (April, 1931), pp. 21–26.
Marx, Karl, and Friedrich Engels. Correspondence, 1846–1895: a Selection with Commentary and Notes. New York, International Publishers, n.d.
—— Literature and Art: Selections from Their Writings. New York, International Publishers, 1947.
Mayakovsky, Vladimir V. "How One Writes a Poem" (1926), trans. from *Europe*, The Living Age, CCCXLV, No. 4405 (October, 1933), 148–55.
—— "Kak delat stikhi?" Izbrannoye. V. A. Katanyana, ed. Moscow, Ogiz, 1948, pp. 390–426.

"Mesto sovetskovo pisatelya," *Literaturnaya gazeta*, No. 25 (October 7, 1929), p. 1.
"Na uroven novykh zadach," *Pravda* (May 9, 1932), reprinted in *Na literaturnom postu*, No. 12 (April, 1932), pp. 2–5. (These dates seem chronologically wrong, but I have verified them.)
"Na vysshuyu stupen," *Na literaturnom postu*, Nos. 13–14 (May, 1932), pp. 3–11.
Polonski, Vyacheslav. Ocherki literaturnovo dvizheniya revolyutsionnoi epokhi. 2d ed., corrected and enlarged. Moscow-Leningrad, Gosizdat, 1929.
Resolution Passed by the Workers and Employees of the Electrofactory after the Reading of Ilya Selvinski's Poem: "The Electrofactory Newspaper," quoted in Ilya Selvinski, "How I Worked at the Electrofactory," *VOKS*, II, No. 6 (1931), 64–65.
"Rezolyutsii 4-vo plenuma pravleniya RAPP o poputnichestve i soyuznichestve: rezolyutsiya po dokladu A. Selivanovskovo," *Literaturnaya gazeta*, No. 50 (September 15, 1931), p. 3.
Scott, H. G., ed. Problems of Soviet Literature: Reports and Speeches at the First Soviet Writers' Congress. New York, International Publishers, 1935.
Selivanovski, A. "The Poetry of Socialism," M. Apletin, ed., *Literature of the Peoples of the U.S.S.R.*, VOKS Illustrated Almanac, Nos. 7–8 (1934), pp. 41–53.
Shaginyan, Marietta. "Literature and Plan," *Soviet Culture Review*, No. 5 (1932), pp. 23–24.
Sovetskaya literatura na novom etape: stenogramma pervovo plenuma orgkomiteta soyuza sovetskikh pisatelei (29 oktyabrya–3 noyabrya 1932). Moscow, Sovetskaya Literatura, 1933.
Tretyakov, Sergei. "Words Become Deeds," *International Literature*, No. 3 (1933), pp. 54–56.
Trotsky, Leon. Literature and Revolution. Rose Strunsky, trans. New York, International Publishers, 1925.
Zelinski, Kornely. "The 15th Anniversary of Soviet Literature," *VOKS*, III, Nos. 5–6 (1932), 51–71.
—— "Soviet Criticism," M. Apletin, ed., *Literature of the Peoples of the U.S.S.R.*, VOKS Illustrated Almanac, Nos. 7–8 (1934), pp. 27–35.

Shock Workers and the Cultural Revolution

Afanasiev, S. "Cultural Movement of the Masses: 'Kulturnaya Estafeta' (Cultural Relay Race)," *Soviet Culture Bulletin*, No. 1 (July, 1931), pp. 11–14.

Averbakh, Leopold L. Kulturnaya revolyutsiya i voprosy sovremennoi literatury. Moscow-Leningrad, Gosizdat, 1928.
—— Na putyakh kulturnoi revolyutsii. 3d ed. Moscow, Moskovski rabochi, 1929.
Bankov, P. "Authors from the Factory Bench," *Soviet Culture Review*, Nos. 7–9 (1932), pp. 45–47.
Bubnov, A. (People's Commissar for Education of R.S.F.S.R.). "On the Rise of Culture in the U.S.S.R. during the First Pyatiletka" (speech delivered at Third Session of Central Executive Committee of U.S.S.R., January 28, 1933), *VOKS*, IV, Nos. 1–2 (1933), 26–31.
Butomo, N. "The Worker Correspondents Take the Five-Year Plan by Storm," *VOKS*, II, No. 6 (1931), 57–60.
Ettinhof, B. "Art in the Five-Year Plan of Cultural Construction," *VOKS*, II, Nos. 10–12 (1931), 3–10.
Gorky, Maxim. "Udarniki v literature" (1931), O literature: stati i rechi 1928–1936. N. F. Belchikov, ed. 3d ed., enlarged. Moscow, Sovetski pisatel, 1937, pp. 63–66.
Persov, B. "The Soviet Press," *VOKS*, II, No. 7–9 (1931), 113–21.
"Pervaya brigada pisatelei konchila svoyu rabotu," *Literaturnaya gazeta*, No. 25 (October 7, 1929), p. 3.
Rodionov. "Cultural Work in the Red Army," *VOKS*, Nos. 1–3 (January–February, 1930), pp. 34–36.
Shock Workers. "The First Cruise," Anthony Wixley, trans., *International Literature*, No. 1 (1932), pp. 3–15.
"Shock Workers in Literature," *VOKS*, II, No. 4 (1931), 26–29.
Vertinski, N. S. Litrabota v klube i v krasnom ugolke. Moscow, Teakino-pechat, 1930.
Zhuchkov, A. "Factory Literary Circles," M. Apletin, ed., *Literature of the Peoples of the U.S.S.R.*, VOKS Illustrated Almanac, Nos. 7–8 (1934), pp. 89–93.

Individual Writers and Critics

"Averbakh, Leopold Leonidovich," N. L. Meshcheryakov, ed., Malaya sovetskaya entsiklopediya. 2d ed. Moscow, Ogiz R.S.F.S.R., 1933, I, 52.
"Averbakh, Leopold Leonidovich," V. M. Friche, ed., Literaturnaya entsiklopediya. Moscow, Izdatelstvo Kommunisticheskoi Akademii, 1929, I, 28–29.
Kaun, Alexander. "Vladimir Mayakovsky 1894–1930," *The American Quarterly on the Soviet Union*, III, No. 1 (July, 1940), 21–43.
"Kushner, Boris Anisimovich," A. V. Lunacharski, ed., Literaturnaya

entsiklopediya. Moscow, Izdatelstvo Kommunisticheskoi Akademii, 1931, V, 774-75.
Marshall, Herbert, ed. Mayakovsky and His Poetry. Rev. ed. London, Pilot Press, 1945.
Mir, M. "Alexander Bezymenski: the Tenth Anniversary of His Poetic Work," VOKS, II, No. 2 (February, 1931), 77-78.
—— "Alexander Zharov and His Poetry," VOKS, II, Nos. 10-12 (1931), 157-58.
—— "Andrew Alexandrovich, Proletarian Poet of the White Russia," VOKS, III, Nos. 3-4 (1932), 79-80.
—— "Demyan Bedny: Proletarian and National Poet of the U.S.S.R.," *Soviet Culture Bulletin*, No. 5 (September, 1931), pp. 7-8.
—— "Ilya Selvinski and His Poetry," VOKS, II, No. 6 (1931), 65-66.
Mstislavsky, S. (Vice-president of All-Russian Union of Soviet Writers). "Vladimir Mayakovsky," VOKS, Nos. 6-7 (April, 1930), pp. 19-25.
Nusinov, Prof. I. "Gorky and Soviet Literature," M. Apletin, ed., *Literature of the Peoples of the U.S.S.R.*, VOKS Illustrated Almanac, Nos. 7-8 (1934), pp. 11-19.
Pogodin, Nikolai. "Autobiography," *International Literature*, No. 3 (July, 1933), pp. 133-34.
Pozner, Vladimir. "Ilia Selvinski et le constructivisme," *Les Nouvelles littéraires, artistiques et scientifiques*, No. 460 (August 8, 1931), p. 6.
"Proletarian Writer, A, Vsevolod Vishnevski," VOKS, II, No. 3 (1931), 71-73.
"Russians Rank Sholokhov as Leading Writer," New York *Herald Tribune* (May 7, 1948), p. 24.
Schneider, Isidor. "Mayakovsky, Poet of the Revolution," *The American Quarterly on the Soviet Union*, III, No. 1 (July, 1940), 13-20.
Selvinski, Ilya. "How I Worked at the Electrofactory," VOKS, II, No. 6 (1931), 61-65.
"Soviet Writers about Themselves," M. Apletin, ed., *Literature of the Peoples of the U.S.S.R.*, VOKS Illustrated Almanac, Nos. 7-8 (1934), pp. 94-119.
Tretyakov, Sergei. "Report," *Front*, I, No. 1 (December, 1930), 45-52.
—— "Writers, to the Collective Farms!" VOKS, II, No. 1 (January, 1931), 85-87.
"Zamyatin," Bolshaya sovetskaya entsiklopediya. Moscow, Ogiz R.S.F.-S.R., 1933, XXVI, 154-55.
"Zamyatin," V. M. Friche, ed., Literaturnaya entsiklopediya. Moscow, Izdatelstvo Kommunisticheskoi Akademii, 1930, IV, 302-9.

Concerning Individual Works

Averbakh, Leopold L. "Literaturnyie zametki," Yakov Ilin, ed., *Lyudi stalingradskovo traktornovo zavoda*. Moscow, Ogiz, 1933, pp. 431–61.

Brainin, W. "Avdeyenko's Novel 'I Love,'" M. Apletin, ed., *Literature of the Peoples of the U.S.S.R.*, VOKS Illustrated Almanac, Nos. 7–8 (1934), pp. 173–76.

"Cultural News: 'History of the Civil War' Going To Be Published," *Soviet Culture Bulletin*, No. 5 (September, 1931), p. 13.

Dana, H. W. L. "Mayakovsky's Plays," *The American Quarterly on the Soviet Union*, III, No. 1 (July, 1940), 44–55.

Danilov, I. "How the History of Civil War Is Being Written," *Soviet Culture Review*, Nos. 7–9 (1932), pp. 50–52.

Gorky, Maxim. "Foreword," Leonid Leonov, *Soviet River*, Ivor Montagu and Sergei Nolbandov, trans. New York, Dial Press, Inc., 1932, pp. v–vi.

Lunacharski, Anatol V. "Introduction," Ilya Ilf and Evgeni Petrov, *The Little Golden Calf: a Satiric Novel*. Charles Malamuth, trans. New York, Farrar & Rinehart, Inc., 1932, pp. xi–xix.

Myamlin, N. "A Literary Monument to the Civil War," M. Apletin, ed., *Literature of the Peoples of the U.S.S.R.*, VOKS Illustrated Almanac, Nos. 7–8 (1934), pp. 87–89.

Novliansky, P. "The Workers Are Writing the History of Their Factories and Works," *Soviet Culture Review*, Nos. 7–9 (1932), pp. 47–50.

Radek, Karl. "The Epic of Collectivization," M. Apletin, ed., *Literature of the Peoples of the U.S.S.R.*, VOKS Illustrated Almanac, Nos. 7–8 (1934), pp. 138–42.

Simkhovich, M. "The History of Factories," M. Apletin, ed., *Literature of the Peoples of the U.S.S.R.*, VOKS Illustrated Almanac, Nos. 7–8 (1934), pp. 84–87.

Stetski, A. "About Gladkov's 'Energy,'" *International Literature*, No. 2 (1934), pp. 135–36.

Struve, Gleb. "Current Russian Literature: Leonid Leonov and his 'Skutarevsky,'" *The Slavonic and East European Review*, XII, No. 34 (July, 1933), 190–95.

Zelinski, Kornely. "Hydrocentral by Marietta Shaginyan," M. Apletin, ed., *Literature of the Peoples of the U.S.S.R.*, VOKS Illustrated Almanac, Nos. 7–8 (1934), pp. 160–64.

Novels

Ehrenburg, Ilya. Out of Chaos [The Second Day]. Alexander Bakshy, trans. New York, Henry Holt and Company, 1934.
Gladkov, Fyodor V. "Granite" (from Energy), *Literature of the Peoples of the U.S.S.R.*, VOKS Illustrated Almanac, Nos. 7–8 (1934), pp. 155–59.
——— "The Ragged Brigade" (from Energy), George Reavey and Marc Slonim, ed. and trans., Soviet Literature: an Anthology. New York, Covici Friede, 1934, pp. 279–98.
Ilf, Ilya, and Evgeni Petrov. The Little Golden Calf: a Satiric Novel. Charles Malamuth, trans. New York, Farrar & Rinehart, Inc., 1932.
Ilyenkov, V. P. Driving Axle: a Novel of Socialist Construction. New York, International Publishers, 1933.
Katayev, Valentin P. Time, Forward! Charles Malamuth, trans. New York, Farrar & Rinehart, Inc., 1933.
Leonov, Leonid. Skutarevsky. Alec Brown, trans. New York, Harcourt Brace and Company, 1936.
——— Soviet River [Sot]. Ivor Montagu and Sergei Nolbandov, trans. New York, Dial Press, Inc., 1932.
Panfyorov, Fyodor. Bruski: a Story of Peasant Life in Soviet Russia. Z. Mitrov and J. Tabrisky, trans. London, Martin Lawrence, Ltd., 1930.
——— And Then the Harvest. Stephen Garry, trans. London, Putnam, 1939. [This is Volume IV of Bruski.]
Pilnyak, Boris. The Volga Falls to the Caspian Sea. Charles Malamuth, trans. New York, Farrar & Rinehart, Inc., 1931.
Shaginyan, Marietta. "Heard in the Train" (from Hydrocentral), *Literature of the Peoples of the U.S.S.R.*, VOKS Illustrated Almanac, Nos. 7–8 (1934), pp. 165–68.
Sholokhov, Mikhail A. Seeds of Tomorrow [Soil Upturned]. Stephen Garry, trans. New York, Alfred A. Knopf, 1935.

Plays

Afinogenov, Alexander. Fear: a Play in Four Acts and Nine Scenes. Charles Malamuth, trans., Eugene Lyons, ed., Six Soviet Plays. Boston–New York, Houghton Mifflin Company, 1934.
Kirshon, Vladimir. Bread: a Play in Five Acts and Nine Scenes. Sonia Volochova, trans., Eugene Lyons, ed., Six Soviet Plays. Boston–New York, Houghton Mifflin Company, 1934.

Pogodin, Nikolai. Aristocrats: a Comedy in Four Acts. Anthony Wixley and Robert S. Carr, trans., Ben Blake, ed., Four Soviet Plays. London, Lawrence & Wishart, Ltd., 1937.
—— "My Friend" (Selected Episodes from a New Soviet Play), Anthony Wixley, trans., International Literature, No. 3 (July, 1933), pp. 35–41.
—— Tempo: a Play in Four Acts and Nine Scenes. Irving Talmadg, trans., Eugene Lyons, ed., Six Soviet Plays. Boston–New York, Houghton Mifflin Company, 1934.
Vishnevski, Vsevolod. An Optimistic Tragedy: a Play in Three Acts. H. G. Scott and Robert S. Carr, trans., Ben Blake, ed., Four Soviet Plays. London, Lawrence & Wishart, Ltd., 1937.

Poetry

Alexandrovich, Andrew. "A Leninist Song," Michael L. Korr, trans., VOKS, III, Nos. 3–4 (1932), 80–81.
—— "The Whistles Shrill . . . ," Michael L. Korr, trans., VOKS, III, Nos. 3–4 (1932), 81.
Bezymenski, Alexander I. Tragedinaya noch. Moscow, Gosizdat "Khudozhestvennaya Literatura," 1935.
Deutsch, Babette, and Avrahm Yarmolinsky, ed. and trans. Russian Poetry: an Anthology. New and rev. ed. New York, International Publishers, 1930.
Inber, Vera. "Bonne Année!" M. Mir, trans. into French, Front, I, No. 1 (December, 1930), 96.
Kirsanov, Semyon. "Pyatiletka," Krasnaya nov, No. 11 (November, 1930), pp. 71–83.
Mayakovsky, Vladimir V. "At the Top of My Voice," Herbert Marshall, trans., The Anglo-Soviet Journal, X, No. 2 (April, 1940), 106–12.
—— "Decree to the Army of Art," Joseph Freeman and Leon Talmy, trans., The American Quarterly on the Soviet Union, III, No. 1 (July, 1940), 83–84.
—— "Domoi," quoted in L. I. Timofeyev, Sovremennaya literatura. 2d ed., corrected and enlarged. Moscow, Uchpedgiz, 1947, p. 289.
—— "Good!" Isidor Schneider, trans., The American Quarterly on the Soviet Union, III, No. 1 (July, 1940), 60–63.
—— "Good and Bad," Isidor Schneider, trans., The American Quarterly on the Soviet Union, III, No. 1 (July, 1940), 78–79.
—— "Miracles," Isidor Schneider, trans., The American Quarterly on the Soviet Union, III, No. 1 (July, 1940), 73–74.
—— "Tale of the Kuznetsky Construction," Isidor Schneider, trans.,

The American Quarterly on the Soviet Union, III, No. 1 (July, 1940), 70–71.
Selvinski, Ilya. Lirika. Moscow, Gosizdat "Khudozhestvennaya Literatura," 1937.
——— "Our Biography," Vera Sandomersky, trans., New Directions in Prose and Poetry 1941. Norfolk, Conn., New Directions, 1941, pp. 562–64.
Semyakin, Vassili. "Industrial 1931," Michael L. Korr, trans., VOKS, II, No. 4 (1931), 29–30.
Zharov, Alexander. "Our Songs," Dan Levin, trans., New Directions in Prose and Poetry 1941. Norfolk, Conn., New Directions, 1941, pp. 647–48.

Sketches and Stories

Avdeyenko, Alexander. I Love. Anthony Wixley, trans. New York, International Publishers, n.d.
Averbakh, Leopold L., ed. Belomor: an Account of the Construction of the New Canal between the White Sea and the Baltic Sea. Amabel Williams-Ellis, ed. New York, Harrison Smith and Robert Haas, 1935.
Berman, I. "Amo," VOKS, II, No. 4 (1931), 38–39.
Cournos, John, ed. and trans. Short Stories out of Soviet Russia. New York, E. P. Dutton & Co., Inc., 1929.
Gabrilovich, Evgeni. "The Year 1930" (August, 1931), George Reavey and Marc Slonim, ed. and trans., Soviet Literature: an Anthology. New York, Covici Friede, 1934, pp. 233–54.
Ilin, Yakov. Bolshoi konveiyer. Moscow, Ogiz-Molodaya Gvardiya, 1934.
———, ed. Lyudi stalingradskovo traktornovo zavoda imeni Feliksa Dzerzhinskovo, volume of Istoriya zavodov. Moscow, Ogiz, 1933.
Katayev, Ivan. "The Conquerors," *Front,* I, No. 4 (June, 1931), 385–90.
Kaverin, Venyamin. "The Return of the Kirghiz" (sketch from The Prologue [1931]), George Reavey and Marc Slonim, ed. and trans., Soviet Literature: an Anthology. New York, Covici Friede, 1934, pp. 255–63.
Lavrenyov, B. "Men" (last chapter of Head Thus), VOKS, III, Nos. 3–4 (1932), 87–99.
Mikhailov, N. "The Fight for the Metal," VOKS, II, No. 4 (1931), 31–34.
Pavlenko, P. "Notes on the Spring" (from A Journey to Turkmenistan), VOKS, III, Nos. 3–4 (1932), 47–53.

Polonski, Vyacheslav. **Magnitostroi.** Moscow, Izdatelstvo "Federatsiya," 1931.
Sannikov, G. "The Struggle for Cotton Independence," *VOKS*, III, Nos. 3–4 (1932), 57–62.
Shaginyan, Marietta. "Soviet Transcaucasus: 1. Armenia. 2. Azerbaidjan. 3. Georgia," *VOKS*, III, Nos. 3–4 (1932), 140–84.

INDEX

"Abkhazia," see Shock workers of the pen
Afinogenov, Alexander N., 107-8, 130; see also Fear
Akhmatova, Anna, 156
Alekseyev, Gleb V., 62; see also Deeds and People of Competition
Alexandrovich, Andrew, 212; see also "Leninist Song," "Whistles Shrill . . ."
All-Russian Association of Peasant Writers, see VOKP
All-Russian Association of Proletarian-Kolkhoz Writers, see VOPKP
All-Russian Association of Proletarian Writers, see VAPP
All-Russian Central Council of Trade Unions, 45, 56-57
All-Russian Congress (1920), 11
All-Russian Union of Worker-Writers, 4
All-Ukrainian Union of Proletarian Writers, see VUSPP
All-Union Association of Proletarian Writers, see VOAPP
All-Union (or Pan-Soviet) Conference of Proletarian Writers, First, see VAPP
All-Union Congress of Proletarian Writers, First, see VAPP
All-Union Congress of Soviets, Fifth (1929), 22
"Ally or Enemy," 34, 135-37, 143, 219
"Amo" (Berman), 60
And Then the Harvest (Panfyorov), see Bruski
APPs (associations of proletarian writers), 16, 125, 135

Aristocrats (Pogodin), 201-2
Aseyev, Nikolai N., 41; see also "Dnieprostroi"
At-Lit-Post group, definition of, 119, 129; dictatorial censorship, 119; three praiseworthy campaigns, 120; monopolistic position of, 131-33; kolkhoz literature ignored, 134; fame of Fadeyev and Libedinski due to support of, 147; Party imitated, 154; see also At-the-Post, Averbakh, Litfront, Na literaturnom postu, RAPP
At the Edge of the World (Exler), 46
At-the-Post group, formation and platform, 9-11; 1923-25 fight, 13, 175; split in, 16; hegemony attained, 31; political realism of poetry, 112; stubbornness of, 126-27; Party hopes unfulfilled by, 153; most fanatical members, 173; see also At-Lit-Post, Averbakh, Na postu, RAPP
"At the Top of My Voice" (Mayakovsky), 121-22
Avdeyenko, Alexander, see I Love
Averbakh, Leopold L., 8, 16, 18, 125, 154, 155, 173, 175, 176, 214, 215, 216, 217; on proletarian literature, 12, 177; attacks on Voronski, 14, 215; Five-Year Plan of Art proposed, 22; on cultural revolution, 23-24; on social command, 31-32; journalistic approach to writing advocated, 35-36; prolet-writer characterized, 37, 39, 177; People of the Stalingrad Tractor Plant evaluated, 70-71; on role of literature, 75; on new liter-

INDEX

Averbakh, Leopold L. (*cont.*)
ary forms, 76; on Mayakovsky's fall, 122; his criticism characterized, 126; put on Orgcommittee, 126, 148, 151; speech at First Plenum, 129, 147, 148-52; bickering of RAPP's critics admitted, 130; on dualism of At-Lit-Post's position, 131; on overtaking and surpassing classics, 141; on creative method of dialectical materialism, 142, 144, 152; RAPP's inadequacy admitted, 153; on VAPP's work, 177; quoted by Mirsky, 200; on Oblomov type, 206; Trotskyite, 220, 224; inadequate understanding of theory, 223; *see also* At-Lit-Post, *Creative Paths, From RAPP's Diary, History of the Construction of the White Sea–Baltic Canal, History of Factories and Works,* RAPP

Babel, Isaak E., 121
Bagritski, Eduard G., 121
Bakhmetyev, Vladimir M., 128, 147, 176, 197
Bath, The (Mayakovsky), 121, 214-15
Bedbug, The (Mayakovsky), 121
Bedny, Demyan, 120, 175, 184-85, 199; Mayakovsky on verses of, 28; listed for suggested reading, 165
Belinski, Vissarion G., 2
Belomor (Averbakh, ed.), *see History of the Construction of the White Sea–Baltic Canal*
Berezovski, Feoktist A., 128, 149, 222
Berliner Tageblatt, 22
Berman, I., *see* "Amo"
Bezymenski, Alexander I., 8, 16, 25, 32-33, 112-13, 119, 139, 175, 197; on proletarian art, 12; report to Sixteenth Party Congress, 29-30; poet laureate, 121, 221; Mayakovsky reprimanded, 122; victim of RAPP's factionalism, 140; verses written as propaganda, 166-67; Trotsky on, 211-12; *see also Night of the Head of the Political Section, Shot,* "Stoker's Song," *Tragic Night*
Bill-Belotserkovski, Vladimir N., 140
Birth of a Hero, The (Libedinski), 139-40, 203, 221
Bogdanov, Alexander A., 3, 10, 173
Bread (Kirshon), 97, 103-7, 195, 197, 210; popularity of, 165-66
Brigade, First, 44-45; of Moscow Writers No. 1, 192
Brik, Osip M., 8, 30
"Brother Writers" (Mayakovsky), 40
Bruski (Panfyorov), 44, 97, 101-3, 195; noticed by At-Lit-Post critics, 134-35; example of socialist realism, 159; correct political viewpoint of, 164; listed for suggested reading, 165
Buachidze, B., 149-50
Bukharin, Nikolai I., 175, 177, 178, 223; on proletarian culture, 4; attitude towards At-the-Postists, 13; leader of Right Deviation, 19, 224; in *Bruski,* 102
Bulgakov, Mikhail A., 121

Catherine II of Russia, 1
Cement (Gladkov), 40, 78, 165
Central Committee of Communist party, 178; May (1924) Conference and Resolution of Press Department, 13-14, 30, 34-35, 54, 213; 1925 Resolution, 14-15, 16, 124, 159; resolution on literary themes, 33-34; decision on worker and peasant correspondents, 57-58; mobilization of workers for countryside, 63, 97, 98; 1932 Decree, 124-25, 153, 156, 159; plenum of January 7 (1933), 161; Department of Propaganda and Agitation, 180; newspaper editorial staffs appointed by, 194
Central Committee of Metalworkers, 45
Central Editorial Board, *see History of Factories and Works*
Challenge, The (Tretyakov), 52

INDEX

Chamberlin, William H., 20, 103
Chapayev (Furmanov), see Furmanov
Chariyev, 149
Chase, Stuart, 20
Cheka, see G.P.U.
Chernyshevski, Nikolai G., 2, 223
Chumandrin, Mikhail F., 39, 139; in praise of RAPP, 130-31; on RAPP's literary criticism, 137; on reports versus systematic work, 138; model job of self-criticism, 147, 149
Collective writing, 39, 67-74, 169, 177, 188, 198, 199; see also *History of Factories and Works*, *History of the Civil War*, Literary circles
Communist Academy, 119-20, 193
Communist Lighthouse, The (Tretyakov), 52
Communist party, line in literature, 2, 154, 155-56; struggle for control of, 17, 18-19, 155, 162; support given to Averbakh clique, 22, 119, 123, 131, 153, 157; Gladkov on resolutions of, 41; *rabkor* agents, 54, 58; instructions to RAPP disregarded, 123, 132, 153; line towards intelligentsia, 136-37, 155, 219; "wisdom and heroism" of, 158; party of revolution, 160; declared invincible by Stalin, 162; role shown in *History of the Civil War*, 198; see also Central Committee of Communist party, Conferences of Communist party, Congresses of Communist party
Conferences of Communist party, Thirteenth (1924), 14; Sixteenth (1929), 19, 22
Congresses of Communist party, Fifteenth (1927), 23; Sixteenth (1930), 29-30, 34-35, 39, 97; Fourteenth (1925), 77; Ninth (1920), 118
"Conquerors, The" (I. Katayev), 63-64
Constructivists, Literary Center of, 12-13, 18, 25, 120, 174-75; see also Selvinski, Zelinski

"Cotton" (Sannikov), 63
Council of Syndicates, Publishing Office's appeal, 58
Creative Paths (Averbakh), 151-52
Cultural revolution, 23-24, 31, 54, 84, 176, 177, 180-81, 226; *History of Factories and Works* manifestation of, 68; crusade against non-proletarian literary schools required by, 119; cultural *pyatiletka* overfulfilled, 162; great demand for books, 165; helped by literary *udarniks*, 169, 195; Lenin's description of, 179; Trotsky on mission of, 179-80; Soviet press "a lever of," 194

Days of the Turbins (Bulgakov), see Bulgakov
Deborin, Abram M., 223
"Decree to the Army of Art" (Mayakovsky), 6
Deeds and People of Competition (Alekseyev), 197
Desert, The (Pavlenko), 45
Diary of a Rabkor, The (Zhiga), 196
Dinamov, Sergei S., 16, 31, 217
"Direct (spontaneous) impressions," slogan of, 11, 142, 148, 174, 222
"Dnieprostroi" (Aseyev), 114, 212
Dobrolyubov, Nikolai A., 223
Driving Axle (Ilyenkov), 47, 90-92, 97, 208

Ehrenburg, Ilya G., 12; see also *Second Day*
"Electrofactory Newspaper, The" (Selvinski), 42-43, 50, 192
Energy (Gladkov), 78-79, 92; as political handbook, 163
Engels, Friedrich, 38, 116, 187, 212
Exler, I., see *At the Edge of the World*

Fadeyev, Alexander A., 16, 41, 125, 130, 139, 199; on RAPP's two periods, 129, 131, 132; on dialectical materialism in art, 144-45; speech at First Plenum, 147; unworthiness of At-the-Postists confessed, 153;

Fadeyev, Alexander A. (*cont.*)
  on beat-over-the-head criticism, 220;
  see also Last of the Udegs
Fear (Afinogenov), 108-9; popularity of, 165-66
Fedin, Konstantin A., 30, 199
Fellow-travelers (*poputchiki*), defined, 8; as regarded by At-the-Postists, 10; attacked by *Na postu*, 11-12; Party's 1924-25 attitude towards, 13-15, 124, 159; in VAPP, 18, 177; *pyatiletka* attitude towards, 34-35, 56, 120-21, 146, 155; fewer books by, 59, 62, 123, 126; between old and new, 77, 79; handling of intelligentsia theme, 107; Party's 1932 attitude towards, 126, 128, 155-56, 157; literary activity after 1932 Decree, 126; RAPP's loss of contact with, 127, 131-32; with RAPP against Litfront, 129; Voronski's attitude towards, 173; repudiated by VOKP, 177; in Union of Soviet Writers, 219-20; *see also* "Ally or Enemy," Intelligentsia, RAPP
Fifteenth Party Congress, *see* Congresses of Communist party
First Cavalry Army, The (Vishnevski), 53
First Cruise, The, *see* Shock workers of the pen
First Five-Year Plan (1928-32), 1, 20-23, 119, 167-68; intolerance demanded by, 17; optimal variant of, 19, 24, 162; fundamental task, 21; Five-Year Plan in four, 22, 75, 161; concentration on heavy industry, 22, 77; collectivization, 22, 96-97, 103, 208-9; purpose of, 22, 178-79; attitudes towards, 24-26, 33, 67, 68, 86-87, 117; period of war psychology, 24-25, 29-30, 80, 117-18, 170, 181-82; socialist competition, 53, 57-58, 94, 167, 169, 193; economic goal, 65; shortage of skilled labor, 72; American engineers, 86; emphasis on quantity, 117, 169; results of, 124, 156, 161-62, 169, 208; psychology of planning, 180; Party's motives for industrialization, 204
Fischer, Louis, 218; on RAPP's encouragement of worker-writers, 130; on RAPP's literary criticism, 146; on RAPP's dissolution, 155-56
Five-year plan (*pyatiletka*), *see* First Five-Year Plan, Fourth Five-Year Plan, Second Five-Year Plan
Five-Year Plan of Art, 22-23, 34; objectives, 1, 38-39; poor results achieved, 157, 169
Formalism, 123, 216
FOSP (union of *kolkhoz* proletarian writers), 125
Fourteenth Party Congress, *see* Congresses of Communist party
Fourth Five-Year Plan (1946–50), 156-57
From RAPP's Diary (Averbakh), 136
Furmanov, Dmitri A., 16, 121
Futurists, 6-7; reorganized as LEF, 8

Gabrilovich, Evgeni, 71, 175; *see also Year 1930*
Gastev, Alexei K., 6
Gladkov, Fyodor V., 46, 79, 129, 197; opposed to social command, 30; on participation in socialist construction, 40-41; judgment of Averbakh, 150; on socialist realism, 159; definition of art, 171; *see also Cement, Energy*
Glavlit (Central Department of Literary Affairs), 1, 3, 68
Goncharov, Ivan A., *see* Oblomov
"Good and Bad" (Mayakovsky), 27
Gorbachyov, Georgi E., 30, 121, 123, 175, 216; leader of Leningrad Lefts, 16
Gorky, Maxim, 53-54, 72, 120, 157, 183, 217, 224; on serving revolution, 26; on writer as class voice, 32; requirements of proletarian writer, 36-37; on need for writer's participation in construction, 48; on literary *udarniks*, 56, 195; on *udarnik* books, 59; on importance

of sketch-writing, 62-63; collective writing advocated, 68; definition of Soviet factory, 70; on role of literature, 75; on labor as hero, 117; on prematurity of demands for masterpieces, 117-18; on strife and confusion among critics, 124, 130, 144, 145-46; on RAPP's first period, 129-30; on being realists, 159; *Bruski* condemned, 164; on task of young writers, 186; on *History of the Civil War*, 198; appeal to participants in Civil War, 199; on Leonov, 205; *see also History of the Civil War, History of Factories and Works*
Gosizdatelstvo (State Publishing House), 36, 175
Gosplan (State Planning Commission), 20, 28
Gosplan literatura, 175; *see also* Constructivists
G.P.U. (Cheka), 26, 55, 72, 73, 201-2; *see also* Yagoda
Great Conveyer, The (Ilin), 71, 92
Groman, S., 45
Gromov, Boris, 46
Gronski, I. M., 148; definition of RAPP, 123, 130; program of Org-committee outlined, 128; speeches of RAPP's leaders judged, 147; on RAPP's inability to change, 154-55; demand for literary works of art, 158; criticism of Pereval, 215-16
Gublit (Provincial Department of Literary Affairs), 68

"Happy New Year!" (Inber), 114-15
Harper, Samuel N., 165
Head Thus (Lavrenyov), 193-94
"Hero of our times," 32, 76, 116-17, 203
Hero of Our Times, A (Lermontov), *see* Pechorin
Herzen House, 18
History of the Civil War, 68, 169, 198-99
History of the Construction of the White Sea–Baltic Canal (Averbakh, ed.), 55, 70, 71-74, 196-97, 198; quoted on collective, 39; *see also History of Factories and Works*
History of Factories and Works, 68-70, 167, 169, 199-200
History of the Izhorsk Plant, 70, 200-1; *see also History of Factories and Works*
Hydrocentral (Shaginyan), 35, 49, 191

Ilf, Ilya, *see Little Golden Calf*
Ilin, Yakov, 75; *see also Great Conveyer, People of the Stalingrad Tractor Plant*
Illesh, Bela, 129
I Love (Avdeyenko), 92-94
Ilyenkov, V. P., 140; *see also Driving Axle*
Inber, Vera M., 71, 175, 197; example given of RAPP's literary criticism, 139; on Averbakh's oratorical ability, 150; *see also* "Happy New Year!"
"Industrial 1931" (Semyakin), 60-61
Industrial Party trial, 26, 90
Institute of Literature and Art, 129
Intelligentsia, 31, 35, 223; "reorganization" of, 26, 107, 124, 135, 153, 155; constructivism reflection of mood of, 175, 192; *see also* "Ally or Enemy," Fellow-travelers
International, Communist (Third), 21-22, 28, 177
International Union of Revolutionary Writers (I.U.R.W.), *see* MORP
In the Fight for Metal (Mikhailov), 60
Ivanov, Vsevolod V., 32-33, 45, 71, 128, 199; publication forbidden by RAPP, 121; on necessity for literary tendentiousness, 159
Izvestiya, 46, 57, 202

Journey to Turkmenistan, A (Pavlenko), *see* "Notes on Spring"

Kalinin, Mikhail I., 124, 216
Kamenev, Leo B., 18-19, 177

INDEX

Katayev, Ivan I., 197; *see also* "Conquerors"
Katayev, Valentin P., 71, 208; writing of contemporary history urged, 68; *see also Time, Forward!*
Katsumoto, 129
Kaverin, Venyamin A., 30, 197; *see also* "Return of the Kirghiz"
Kazin, Vasily, 45
Kerzhentzev, Platon M., 214; *see also* Communist Academy
Kharkov Congress (1930), 142
Kirillov, Vladimir, *see* "We"
Kirpotin, Vladimir Ya., 128; on leading role of proletarian literature, 122-23; on *The Birth of a Hero*, 139-40; on dialectical materialistic creative method, 142-43; on importance of artistic form, 143; on socialist realism, 147; criticism of Averbakh's speech, 151-52; on future literary fights, 156; on success of First Plenum, 157-58; on Gorky's influence, 183; on Litfront theory, 214; on Bezymenski, 221
Kirsanov, Semyon O., *see* "Pyatiletka"
Kirshon, Vladimir M., 16, 25, 119, 125, 130, 139, 188, 199, 216; on RAPP's literary demands, 34-35; on proletarian writer, 39; appraisal of *udarnik* writings, 61-62; speech at First Plenum, 129, 147; on contradiction in At-Lit-Post's dual position, 131-32; explanation of defections from literary circles, 133; Stalin quoted, 158; *see also* Bread
Klychkov, Sergei A., 26, 126, 128; condemnation of Averbakh, 150
Kogan, Pyotr S., 30, 175
Komsomol (Young Communist League), Third All-Russian Congress (1920), 4; House of, 27, 183
Kon, Felix, 2
Kor, B., 136
Kotomin, 43
Kozakov, Mikhail E., 132-33
Krasnaya nov (Red Virgin Soil), 7, 11

Kuibyshev, Valerian V., 219
Kushner, Boris A., on proletarian writer, 39; criticism of writers' unpreparedness for trips, 46-47; on literary shock work, 57; on lag of proletarian literature, 141-42; on "direct impressions," 174; on journalism in literature, 202; on psychological realism, 220-21; on "living man," 222

Lapin, Yu., 62
LAPP (Leningrad Association of Proletarian Writers), 16, 39
Last Decisive, The (Vishnevski), 53, 76, 106, 193
Last of the Udegs, The (Fadeyev), 139
Lavrenyov, Boris A., *see Head Thus*
Lavrukhin, Dmitri I., *see On the Hero's Trail*
Lebedeva, 43
Lebedev-Polyanski, Pavel I., 3, 175
LEF (Left Front of Art), 8, 12-13, 18, 172, 174, 121; errors continued by Litfront, 214
Left Deviation (or Opposition), 17, 18-19, 177
Left Front of Art, *see* LEF
"Left, March!" (Mayakovsky), 26, 187
Lelevich, G., 9, 16, 171, 173, 175; on purpose of art, 1; At-the-Post's point of view given, 10-11
Lenin, Vladimir I., 7, 39, 177, 198, 221, 223; on literature, 2, 118; on proletarian culture, 3, 4; freedom for artist advocated, 30; on peasant salvation, 98; in *Skutarevsky*, 110; comment on Leo Tolstoy, 139; cultural revolution described, 179; on bureaucracy, 208
Leningrad Lefts, 16; *see also* At-the-Post, RAPP
"Leninist Song, A" (Alexandrovich), 182
Leonov, Leonid M., 18, 32-33, 41, 45, 107-8, 199, 227; "tourist to the pro-

letariat," 49; on stereotyped literature, 116; criticized for irony and lack of enthusiasm, 164; praised by Gorky, 205; *see also Skutarevsky, Sot*

Lermontov, Mikhail Yu., *see* Pechorin

Libedinski, Yuri N., 8, 9, 16, 121, 139, 175, 214, 216; on proletarian literature, 9; "ideological snipers," 16; on subjects of proletarian literature, 33-34, 202-3; concern for literary quality, 36; on proletarian writer, 37; novel criticized by factory workers, 42; on inadequate handling of rural themes, 44; on necessity for working within RAPP, 120; on how Mayakovsky joined RAPP, 121; speech at First Plenum, 129, 147; on task of proletarian literature, 139; criticism of Averbakh and his speech, 149, 151; *Bruski* commended as ideological tool, 164; on Proletcult, 171; against stereotyped literature, 221-22; *see also Birth of a Hero*

Lidin, Vladimir G., 33, 115, 117; *see also Spawning Time*

Literary circles (or clubs), 129, 188-89; Bezymenski on, 29; readings and talks to, 41-43, 67, 187-88; appeal to members of, 58; survived Party's 1932 Decree, 125, 128; unsatisfactory condition of, 133-34; propaganda tasks of, 164-65, 226; ridiculed by Ilf and Petrov, 218; discussion of *Soil Upturned*, 226; *see also* Collective writing, *Rabkor*, Shock workers of the pen

Literary Five-Year Plan, *see* Five-Year Plan of Art

"Literary Magna Carta," *see* Central Committee of Communist party (1925 Resolution)

Literary themes of First Five-Year Plan, 33-37, 43, 76-78, 115, 117, 120, 168, 186, 188, 198, 202-3, 219; collectivization, 52, 63-64, 97-103, 113, 209; socialist competition, 60, 73, 78, 87-88, 93-94, 96, 112, 197; wrecking, 63, 80-81, 82, 87, 90-91, 100, 102, 104-5, 109, 111, 170; fight for tempos, 65-67, 71, 86-90, 197; optimism about future, 73-74, 77, 79, 85, 89-90, 92, 93-94, 113-15, 203-4; intelligentsia, 78-79, 107-111; conflict of old and new, 79-86, 108-9, 111-12; self-criticism, 91, 94-96, 109, 121, 166-67, 213, 214-15, 218; deviations on agricultural front, 99, 103-4; relationship of members to Party, 105-6, 193, 210; antagonism between country and city, 106, 210

Literary Union of the Red Army and Fleet, *see* LOKAF

Literaturnaya gazeta (Literary Gazette), 18; on place of Soviet writer, 31; attempt to distort 1932 Decree, 127; resolution of RAPP's Fourth Plenum, 136; Fadeyev's article on dialectical materialism in art, 144-45; *see also* Dinamov

Litfront group, 8, 141, 174, 214; fight with RAPP, 120, 123, 129, 139-40; *Na literaturnom postu's* errors in struggle with, 217, 223; *see also* At-Lit-Post, RAPP

Little Golden Calf, The (Ilf and Petrov), 44, 94-96, 213, 218

"Living man," slogan of, 32, 142, 221-22

LOKAF (Literary Union of the Red Army and Fleet), 125, 129, 150, 193

Lugovskoi, Vladimir A., 45, 121; *see also Spring, To the Bolsheviks of the Desert*

Lunacharski, Anatol V., 175, 214; on proletarian culture, 4; futurism attacked, 7; Bukharin's policy supported, 13-14; on *The Little Golden Calf*, 95, 96

Luzgin, Mikhail, 136

Lyasho, 197

Magnitostroi (Polonski), 46, 65-67, 75, 181-82, 198, 206-7

INDEX

Magnitostroi of art (or literature), 24, 32-33, 115, 169
Mahogany (Pilnyak), *see* Pilnyak, *Volga Falls to the Caspian*
Maiakovsky, *see* Mayakovsky
Makarov, Ivan I., 125, 126, 147
Malyshkin, Alexander G., 46
MAPP (Moscow Association of Proletarian Writers), 8, 11-12, 13, 16, 121, 129, 135, 173; theses of First Conference, 10-11; unsatisfactory state of literary circles, 133-34
Marx, Karl, 38, 187, 212-13
Mayakovsky, Vladimir V., as Futurist, 6-7; reorganization as LEF, 8; on social command, 26-29, 40, 122; last public appearance, 27-28, 183-84; on requisites for poetic work, 28; creed of, 28; influence on Komsomol poets, 29, 112, 122; contact with masses, 40, 41; criticism of factory visits, 47-48; on up-to-the-minute material, 76; on speed, 88; suicide of, 121, 122; enrollment in RAPP, 121, 129, 172; attacked by RAPP, 122; on revolutionary poetry, 183-84; "Lost in Conference," 215; *see also* "At the Top of My Voice," *Bath, Bedbug,* "Brother Writers," "Decree to the Army of Art," "Good and Bad," "Left, March!" "Miracles"
May (1924) Conference, *see* Central Committee of Communist party
Men of the First and Second Five-Year Plans, 169
Metropolitan-Vickers trial, 111
Meyerhold, Vsevolod E., 32-33, 166
Mikhailov, N., *see In the Fight for Metal*
Mikhailovski, Nikolai K., 222
Mikitenko, Ivan, 141, 150; *see also Point of Honor*
Military correspondent, *see* Voenkor
Minayev, K., 45
"Miracles" (Mayakovsky), 41
Mirsky, Dmitri S., 71; on *Hydrocentral,* 49; on Soviet novel, 77; on value of *Soil Upturned,* 163; on *History of Factories,* 200
Month in the Village, A (Tretyakov), 52
MORP (International Union of Revolutionary Writers), 129, 131
Moscow Association of Proletarian Writers, *see* MAPP
Muravia Land (Tvardovski), 103, 209
My Friend (Pogodin), 210

Na literaturnom postu (At the Literary Post), reincarnation of *Na postu,* 16; inquisitorial campaign of, 17; final number of, 125, 219-20; resistance to 1932 Decree, 127; "Ally or Enemy," 136; Averbakh editor, 148, 176; Pereverzev's theoretical errors exposed, 214; mistakes in Litfront struggle, 217; *see also* At-Lit-Post, RAPP
Napoleon Bonaparte, 1-2, 123-24, 174
Na postu (At the Post), literary manifesto, 9-10; campaign against fellow-travelers, 11-13; censured, 14; reorganized as *Na literaturnom postu,* 16; Averbakh on board of, 176; *see also* At-the-Post, RAPP
NEP (New Economic Policy), period of, 7-15, 20, 27, 107, 203; attitude towards fellow-travelers, 34-35; attitude of "changing-landmarks" group towards, 173
Night of the Head of the Political Section, The (Bezymenski), 113
Ninth Party Congress, *see* Congresses of Communist party
"Notes on Spring," A *Journey to Turkmenistan* (Pavlenko), 45
Novikova, 129
Novy LEF (New Left Front), 172; *see also* LEF
Novy mir (New World), 30

Oblomov, 87, 206
October group, 8, 11-12, 13; platform of, 9-11; *see also Oktyabr*
OGPU, *see* G.P.U.

Oktyabr (October), 8; see also October
Olyosha, Yuri K., 128
On the Hero's Trail (Lavrukhin), 203
Optimistic Tragedy, An (Vishnevski), 193
Orgcommittee (Organizing Bureau of Union of Soviet Writers), 125; tool of Party, 127; First Plenum of, 127-29, 157-58
"Our Biography" (Selvinski), 192
Out of Chaos (Ehrenburg), see Second Day

Panfyorov, Fyodor I., 16, 39, 41, 125, 139, 199; victim of RAPP's factionalism, 135, 140; description of Five-Year Plan enthusiasm, 161-62; see also Bruski
Pantiyeleva, 129
Pao-Pao (Selvinski), 114, 212
Pasternak, Boris L., 54
Patronage societies, 189
Pavlenko, Pyotr A., 32-33, 45, 62; see also Desert, "Notes on Spring"
Peasant correspondent, see Selkor
Pechat i revolyutsiya (Press and Revolution), 8, 30
Pechorin, 85, 206, 211
People of the Stalingrad Tractor Plant (Ilin, ed.), 70-71, 166-67; see also History of Factories and Works
Pereval group, 11, 18, 120, 123; "not dissolved and not overcome," 215-16; see also Voronski
Pereverzev, Valerian F., 30, 214, 223; smashed by At-Lit-Post, 120, 123
Petrov, Evgeni, 208; see also Little Golden Calf
Pilnyak, Boris A., 30, 45, 79, 128; persecuted over Mahogany, 12, 120-21; belief in man's two lives, 205; see also Volga Falls to the Caspian
Plekhanov, Georgi V., 148, 223
Pletnev, Valerian F., 175, 176
Poems That Make Steel (Bezymenski), see "Stoker's Song"

INDEX 251

"Poet of the Revolution," see Mayakovsky
Poetry, proletarian, 112-15, 174, 184; lyric, 141
Poetry Helps to Produce Coal (Zharov), 113
"Poet's Declaration of Rights, A" (Selvinski), 192
Pogodin, Nikolai F., 67; see also Aristocrats, My Friend, Tempo
Point of Honor (Mikitenko), 203
Politburo, 14, 16, 19, 29, 155, 178
Polonski, Vyacheslav P., 123, 146, 172, 175, 214; fellow-travelers characterized, 8; on At-the-Postists, 10; on Pereval, 11; on methods of Na literaturnom postu, 16; opposed to social command, 30; brigade visit to Magnitogorsk, 46; on literary udarniks, 59; authors classified by heroes, 76-77; on new Soviet hero, 203; see also Magnitostroi
Poshekhonov, 189
Pravda, 13, 52, 70, 86, 103; Kushner article in, 46, 141, 174, 222; rabkor brigades of, 57; Literaturnaya gazeta exposed, 127; "Ally or Enemy" slogan denounced, 136-37
Press, Soviet, 168, 177-78, 181, 194-95; wall newspaper, 24, 25, 134, 180, 188, 195; see also Izvestiya, Pravda, Rabkor, Voenkor
Press Department of Central Committee, see Central Committee of Communist party
Professional writer, to become writing worker, 1, 38, 67-68; Averbakh on, 39; readings and talks to circles, 41-43, 168-69; observation trips and visits, 43-48, 62, 126, 168, 189; participation as member of enterprise, 48-53, 184, 190, 191; attributes usually lacking, 59-60; assigned reports of, 115; see also Fellow-travelers, Intelligentsia, RAPP
Proletcult (movement for proletarian culture), 3-5, 8, 10, 154, 171; Len-

Proletcult (*cont.*)
ingrad groups of poets, 4; heritage of, 12
Prologue, The (Kaverin), *see* "Return of the Kirghiz"
Propaganda, 180-81, 185; literature as, 1, 30, 75, 115-16, 157, 163-64, 168, 169-70; carried on by *rabkors*, 55, 58; anti-religious, 82, 84, 95, 105; tendentious drama, 103, 165-66, 226-27; Komsomol poets, 112-13, 166-67; mission of literary clubs, 164-65, 226; work on collective histories, 167, 169; *see also* Bedny, Mayakovsky, Press
Pushtorg (Selvinski), 192
"Pyatiletka" (Kirsanov), 113

Quality of First Five-Year Plan literature, 115-18
Quiet Don (Sholokhov), 44

Rabkor (worker correspondent), 49, 54-58, 62, 188, 194-95; factory raids, 196; best book by, 196; *see also* Collective writing, Literary circles, Shock workers of the pen
Radek, Karl B., 175, 202; quoted, xii; on proletarian culture, 4; on proletariat's attitude towards literature, 75; on subjugation of writer to Party, 159-60; on Sholokhov as interpreter of collectivization, 163; on *Bruski* as inspiration, 164
Ramzin, Professor, *see* Industrial Party trial
RAPM (Russian Association of Proletarian Musicians), 124
RAPP (Russian Association of Proletarian Writers), 6, 13, 173; organization of, 15-16; 1925 split, 16; reasons for survival, 17, 18; membership, 17; literary dictatorship begun, 22, 31; characterized by Bezymenski, 29-30; aesthetic code, 34; censor's demands, 37; First Brigade sent out, 44-45; literary challenges and shock tasks, 53, 169; *udarnik* writers promoted, 59, 218; "tearing away of masks," 79, 119-22, 146; propaganda value as literary criterion, 115; Party's support justified, 122-23; defined by Gronski, 123; reasons for liquidation of, 123, 132, 138, 153-55, 157; liquidated by Party's 1932 Decree, 124-25; resistance to 1932 Decree, 126-27; contact lost with fellow-travelers and allies, 127, 131-32, 218-19; necessity for criticism of mistakes, 127; first period of activity, 129-31; second period, 131-32, 137, 154; administrative mistakes, 132-37; Fourth Plenum (Sept., 1931), 135, 136, 219; errors in criticism, 137-46, 222; factions within, 139-40, 220, 221-22; orthodox theory of art, 139, 224; Averbakh general secretary of, 154, 176; worst methods continued by Dinamov, 217; headed by Trotskyites, 220, 224; *see also* At-Lit-Post, Averbakh, Litfront, Shock workers of the pen
Raznochintsy, 143, 223
R.C.P.(b) (Russian Communist Party [bolshevik]), *see* Communist party
REF (Revolutionary Front of Art), 172; *see also* LEF
Reizin, Avrom, 150
"Return of the Kirghiz, The," *The Prologue* (Kaverin), 63
Right Deviation (or Opposition), 17, 19, 164, 177-78
Rodov, Semyon A., 9, 16, 173, 175
Romanov, Panteleimon S., 126
Rosta (Russian Telegraph Agency) Windows, 27
Run, The (Stavski), 39
Russian Association of Proletarian Writers. *see* RAPP
Rykov, Alexei I., 19, 177-78, 224

Sailors (Vishnevski), 53
Saltykov-Shchedrin, Mikhail E., 116

INDEX 253

Sannikov, Grigori A., 45; see also "Cotton"
Schmidt, Professor Otto Yu., see "Sedov" arctic expeditions
Second Day, The (Ehrenburg), 47, 79, 84-86, 96, 187-88, 206, 210
Second Five-Year Plan (1933–37), 117, 169
"Sedov" arctic expeditions, 46
Seeds of Tomorrow (Sholokhov), see Soil Upturned
Seifullina, Lidiya N., 26
Selivanovski, A., 15-16
Selkor (peasant correspondent), see Rabkor
Selvinski, Ilya L., 30, 175, 191-92; report on Kamchatka trip, 45-46; work at Electrofactory, 49-51; see also "Electrofactory Newspaper," "Our Biography," Pao-Pao, "Poet's Declaration of Rights," Pushtorg
Semyakin, Vassili, see "Industrial 1931"
Serafimovich, Alexander S., 148
Serapion Brothers, 30, 159, 185
Sergeyev-Tsenski, Sergei N., 26, 126
Shaginyan, Marietta S., 32-33, 49, 64-65, 176, 191; on contact with masses, 40; on mission of Soviet writers, 75; on inadequacies of RAPP's criticism, 140-41; see also Hydrocentral, Soviet Transcaucasus
Shakhty counter-revolutionary plot, 18, 87
Shklovski, Viktor B., 71-72, 128
Shock workers of the pen (literary udarniks), 56-62, 117, 189, 196-97; Smithy poets, 6; called by RAPP, 17, 38, 56-57, 130, 131, 133; "Abkhazia" cruise, 67; artistic failure of, 115, 123; dropping out of cadres, 133; agitational value of creations, 167; literary brigades disbanded, 169; Gorky on, 195; literary consultation bureaus for, 197; in Union of Soviet Writers, 219-20; see also Collective writing, Literary circles, Rabkor

Sholokhov, Mikhail A., 121, 182; see also Quiet Don, Soil Upturned
Shostakovich, Dmitri D., 32-33
Shot, The (Bezymenski), 113, 140, 221; propaganda value of, 166
Sixteenth Party Conference, see Conferences of Communist party
Sixteenth Party Congress, see Congresses of Communist party
Sketch-writing, 38-39, 43, 62-65, 115, 170, 194, 197; Writers to the Shock Brigades, 197
Skutarevsky (Leonov), 43-44, 109-12, 170, 172, 211; "doubtful work," 164
Slonimski, Antoni, 36, 186
Slonimski, Mikhail L., 128
Smenovekhovstvo, 11, 173
Smithy group, 5-6, 112, 113, 130, 175, 215; dismay at NEP, 7, 173; decline and merger of, 8, 13
Social command, 22, 43, 115, 169; Mayakovsky, 26-29, 122; Bedny, 28, 184-85; Bezymenski, 29-30; 1929 controversy, 30-32, 214; Pilnyak, 79; books produced by, 170
"Socialism in One Country," 18, 19, 157
Socialist realism, 128, 159; Kirpotin on, 147, 152, 159
Soil Upturned (Sholokhov), 97-100, 209, 210; noticed by At-Lit-Post critics, 134-35; example of socialist realism, 159; weapon in social struggle, 163; discussed at "Serp i Molot," 226
Sokolov-Mikitov, Ivan S., 46
Solovyov, Vladimir S., 80
Sot (Leonov), 79, 81-84, 112; reflection of contemporary reality, 35, 44, 49, 205
Soviet River (Leonov), see Sot
Soviet Transcaucasus (Shaginyan), 64-65
Soviet Writers' Congress, First (1934), 159-60
Spawning Time (Lidin), 49

INDEX

Special Construction Bureau (O.K.B.); see G.P.U.
Spring (Lugovskoi), 45
Stalin, Joseph V., struggle for control of Party, 18-19, 155, 162, 177-78, 198; on fundamental task of Five-Year Plan, 20-21; on significance of Five-Year Plan, 22; supplements to Plan initiated, 22; on tractor industry, 71; construction of Canal entrusted to G.P.U., 72; on tempos, 87; 1930 declared year of great change, 97; "Dizzy with Success," 97, 99; on peasant mentality, 99-100; in *Bruski*, 102; disgusted by results of RAPP's régime, 124, 155, 157, 216; speech to industrial administrators, 135; on writers as engineers of human souls, 158; socialist realism dictated by, 159; on successes of First Five-Year Plan, 161, 162; "country must know its heroes," 181; on socialization of agriculture, 208-9; *see also* Communist party
State Publishing House, *see* Gosizdatelstvo
Station (Stavski), 39
Stavski, Vladimir P., 16; *see also Run, Station*
Stetski, A., 163
"Stoker's Song, The," *Poems That Make Steel* (Bezymenski), 113
Subbotnik, 48, 190-91
Subotski, L. M., 126, 128; RAPP an obstacle to Party line, 154
Sutyrin, 139
Svarog, Vasili S., 46

Tairov, Alexander Ya., 32-33
Tarasov-Rodionov, Alexander I., 150
TASS (Telegraph Agency of the Soviet Union), 46
Tempo (Pogodin), 86-87; propaganda value of, 165
Theatre, Soviet, 165-66, 168, 170, 188, 193, 218, 226-27
Third International, *see* International

Thirteenth Party Conference, *see* Conferences of Communist party
Tikhonov, Nikolai S., 45, 54, 62
Time, Forward! (V. Katayev), 47, 48-49, 55-56, 76, 87-90, 98, 195, 206-7, 227; example of socialist realism, 159; refrain in *The Bath*, 215
"To All Men of Letters and Art" (appeal), *see* Magnitostroi of art
Tolstoy, Alexei N., 72, 173, 182; on First Five-Year Plan, 25; on quality of First Five-Year Plan literature, 116, 117; on black and white literary criticism, 138-39; RAPP accused of breaking ties with past, 141
Tolstoy, Leo N., 8, 36, 173
Tomski, Mikhail P., 19, 178
To the Bolsheviks of the Desert (Lugovskoi), 45
Tragic Night (Bezymenski), 113
Tretyakov, Sergei M., quoted, 8; on identification of author with Five-Year Plan, 25; novel praised by *kolkhozniks*, 42; on writer's ignorance of country, 44; work at *kolkhoz* "Lighthouse," 51-52; book production lines foreseen, 67-68; on words and deeds, 118; *see also Challenge, Communist Lighthouse, Month in the Village, We Will Feed the Globe*
Trotsky, Leon D., 130, 175, 176, 177, 202; on proletarian culture, 4-5; fellow-travelers defined, 8; leader of Left Deviation, 18-19; Party commands to art opposed, 30; on mission of cultural revolution, 179-80; on Bedny, 184-85; on Bezymenski, 211-12; on policy in field of art, 225
Tvardovski, Alexander T., *see Muravia Land*

Udarnik (shock worker), *see* Shock workers of the pen
Union of Peasant Writers, 11, 12, 57
Union of Soviet Writers (S.S.P.), 158, 159; created by Party's 1932 Decree, 124-25, 155; resolution on

Zoshchenko and Akhmatova, 156; future fights within, 156; *Na literaturnom postu* on, 219-20
Utkin, Iosif P., 137-38, 197

VAPP (All-Russian Association of Proletarian Writers), 9, 14, 125, 218-19; First All-Union (or Pan-Soviet) Conference of Proletarian Writers, 10; point of view given, 10-11; foundation of, 11, 176; attack against fellow-travelers, 11-12; First All-Union Congress of Proletarian Writers, 15-16; opposition within, 16; led by Leonov, 18; resignations of Pilnyak and Zamyatin, 121; Averbakh on work of, 177; on literary themes, 202; *see also* RAPP
Vardin, I. V., 10, 16
Veresayev, Vikenti V., 197
Villon, François, 40
Vishnevski, Vsevolod V., 32-33, 52-53, 140, 193; criticism of Averbakh's speech, 150; *see also* First Cavalry Army, Last Decisive, Optimistic Tragedy, Sailors
Vishnya, Ostap, 218-19
VOAPP (All-Union Association of Proletarian Writers), 39, 141, 176; federation of RAPP, VOPKP, and VAPP, 18; resolution acclaiming OGPU, 26; liquidated by Party's 1932 Decree, 124-25; creation of, 175; criticism of *The Last Decisive*, 193
Voenkor (military correspondent), 193-94, 195; *see also* Rabkor
VOKP (All-Russian Association of Peasant Writers), became VOPKP, 18, 177
Volga Falls to the Caspian, The (Pilnyak), 79-81, 83, 182, 195, 205
VOPKP (All-Russian Association of Proletarian-*Kolkhoz* Writers), developed from VOKP, 18
Voronski, Alexander K., 173-74, 175, 176; on Party role in literature, 9; on art, 11, 174; errors exposed by

At-Lit-Post, 11, 120, 123, 130, 148-49, 172; policy towards fellow-travelers approved, 14; Averbakh's attacks on, 14, 215, 223; *see also* Pereval
VUSPP (All-Ukrainian Union of Proletarian Writers), 218-19
Vydveezhentsy, 108, 211

War Communism, period of, 3-7, 80
"We" (Kirillov), 5
We (Zamyatin), *see* Zamyatin
We Will Feed the Globe (Tretyakov), 52
"Whistles Shrill . . . , The" (Alexandrovich), 113-14
Wolf, Friedrich, 129
Worker correspondent, *see* Rabkor

Yagoda, Genrikh G., 72, 223-24
Yasenski, Bruno, on First Plenum of Orgcommittee, 128; on MORP's clannishness, 129; attack on Dinamov, 217
Year 1930, The (Gabrilovich), 64, 180
Yermilov, Vladimir V., 16, 126, 222; on RAPP's literary criticism, 115; speech at First Plenum, 129, 147; on Libedinski, 139; criticism of *raznochintsy* recalled, 143; RAPP's methods outdated, 153
Young Guard group, 11-12, 174
Yunkor (correspondent of youth organization), *see* Rabkor

Zamoiski, Pyotr I., 18
Zamyatin, Evgeni I., 140, 185, 221; persecuted for *We*, 120-21; on real literature, 206
Zelinski, Kornely L., 72; on spirit of Five-Year Plan, 25; examples of proletarian authors given, 39; description of Shaginyan, 49; on Sholokhov, 98; on literary class war, 119; on Mayakovsky's death, 122; on continuation of struggle,

Zelinski, Kornely L. (cont.) 156; constructivism defined, 175; on Litfront ideas, 214; on Pereverzev's theoretical errors, 214; on *Na literaturnom postu's* mistakes, 217; on opposition within RAPP, 220

Zharov, Alexander A., 113, 139; see also *Poetry Helps to Produce Coal*

Zhdanov, Andrei A., on engineer of human souls, 158-59; slogan of socialist realism advanced, 159; on optimism of Soviet literature, 203-4

Zhiga, Ivan F., 197; see also *Diary of a Rabkor*

Zinoviev, Grigori E., 18-19, 177

Zoshchenko, Mikhail M., 72, 156, 187